# *A TIME TO SPEAK OUT*

## The Leipzig Citizen Protests and the Fall of East Germany

WAYNE C. BARTEE

*Foreword by Uwe Schwabe*

PRAEGER

Westport, Connecticut
London

**Library of Congress Cataloging-in-Publication Data**

Bartee, Wayne C., 1936–
   A time to speak out : the Leipzig citizen protests and the fall of East Germany /
Wayne C. Bartee.
     p.  cm.
   Includes bibliographical references and index.
   ISBN 0–275–96982–7 (alk. paper)
   1. Protest movements—Germany (East)—Leipzig.  2. Leipzig (Germany)—Politics and
government.  3. Leipzig (Germany)—Church history—20th century.  4. Protestant
churches—Germany—Leipzig—History—20th century.  I. Title.
DD901.L58 B37  2000
943'.21220878—dc21      00–038560

British Library Cataloguing in Publication Data is available.

Library of Congress Catalog Card Number: 00–038560
ISBN: 0–275–96982–7

First published in 2000

Praeger Publishers, 88 Post Road West, Westport, CT 06881
An imprint of Greenwood Publishing Group, Inc.
www.praeger.com

Printed in the United States of America

The paper used in this book complies with the
Permanent Paper Standard issued by the National
Information Standards Organization (Z39.48–1984).

10 9 8 7 6 5 4 3 2 1

# Contents

*Photo essay follows page 101.*

# Foreword

Although a long tradition of overt opposition and quiet resistance in the German Democratic Republic (GDR) can be traced since its founding, no comprehensive study of this subject exists. In Leipzig one has only to recall the popular rising of 17 June 1953, the "Beat" demonstration of 1965, and the unrest at the time of the demolition of the university church in 1968. According to Leipzig police reports, youth groups such as "Capitolbande" and the "Lindenfelsmeute" promoted a "terrible state of affairs" in Leipzig. Their "offense" consisted solely in the introduction of "western dances such as Rock and Roll." By the end of the 1970s former *Bausoldaten* who had refused active military service organized groups.

In the early 1980s an independent, youthful counterculture developed, ranging from punks to squatters in unoccupied buildings. The "Open Youthwork" group organized with its "open cellars." A lively cultural scene blossomed with the "Eigenart" Gallery, and there were independent literary publications like "Second Person." By the mid-1980s youth-oriented alternative cafés and pubs opened in vacant buildings that had been occupied. A significant launching point for events which developed later in the 1980s were the peace prayer meetings.

For many the peace prayers are connected inseparably with the events of the fall of 1989. It is not generally recognized that they had a long history. Prayer meetings for peace were already being held in Leipzig in the fall of 1981. The idea "we should pray for peace" went back to an admonition from Pastor Christoph Wonneberger. In response to the decision about missile emplacement, he sought as early as 1980 to launch an initiative that had two components: to preserve peace; and to allow contacts among like-minded people. When a chain letter with signatures of 5,000 parishioners calling for a social peace service alternative to military service was stopped and a planned meeting was not allowed, Wonneberger sought to accomplish his purpose another way. At the beginning of 1981 he had proposed in Dresden to begin peace prayers, "where people can gather to discuss essential things." Many people in various cities responded, including Leipzig, Rostock, and Magdeburg. In Leipzig the theology students and church workers took up the idea. The Working Group in the Service of Peace, which had formed in the mid-1970s out of a group of former *Bausoldaten*, began the Monday peace services on 13 September 1981. They held the opinion that it was not sufficient to pray just once a year for peace, but it should be done at least weekly. At first only a small group gathered.

In September 1987 Wonneberger, who had been a pastor in Leipzig since 1985, took over the coordination of the peace prayers. After this, a new orientation and purpose appeared. Wonneberger wanted to make more people aware of the services, and he motivated the existing groups to participate in programming them. Also, the changing situation (perestroika in the Soviet Union) led to more communication and closer networking among groups all over the GDR. The Environmental Library in Berlin became the center for this.

The official party, the Socialist Unity Party (SED), reacted angrily to this breach in its monopoly on news and information. In September 1987, when the GDR sponsored the Olof Palme Peace March, many group members joined in with their own banners. In spite of efforts of the *Freie Deutsche Jugend* (FDJ) (Communist) youth groups to push them out, the experience of this event was of great significance for Leipzig. The official party had opened a door and the groups had immediately stuck a foot in it.

Thereafter the groups sought, without discontinuing the peace prayer meetings, to reach a wider audience outside the tight walls of the church. The environmental problems of Leipzig, above all the pollution of the Pleisse River, led to marches. Public protest actions in this period grew out of the peace prayer services. For example, during the Documentary and Short Film Week in 1988, members of the Initiative for Life Group made remarks after the service on 28 November about the intolerable censorship policies of the GDR. The occasion was the prohibition of the Soviet magazine *Sputnik* as well as various Soviet films which were concerned with the subject of Stalinism. Members of this group also wrote the titles of forbidden films and the word *Sputnik* on balloons, went to the Capitol Theatre, headquarters for the film festival, and released them. Then began a wild chase after the balloons by Stasi spies with lighted cigarettes and umbrellas to destroy these "unlicensed flying objects."

When tensions arose between the church leadership, the St. Nicholas parish council, and the groups, Pastor Christian Führer played the role of mediator. Thanks to him, the relationships between them were never completely disrupted. St. Nicholas Church and the square surrounding it thus became a gathering place where people could express their discontent with state authorities. This was due to the long tradition of the peace prayers and to the reporting of these events on television in the West.

The ninth of October 1989 became the deciding day for the future of the country. Despite the eerie sense of angst that pervaded Leipzig, some 70,000 people came into the inner city and through peaceful demonstration brought the State Security cartel down to its knees. Much has been written and speculated about the events of this day. Documents indicate that guns and ammunition were prepared for use. The State Security cartel had planned to strike down the "counterrevolution," but when faced with the masses on the streets and the clear intentions of the Soviet Union, they could not carry it through.

Demonstrations, informational meetings, strikes, and prayer vigils spread out from Leipzig like a fast-moving fire across the entire GDR. From August 1989 to April 1990, 3,115 such events were organized and carried out. The revolution succeeded only because of these widespread protests throughout the entire country.

Uwe Schwabe

# *Preface*

Johann Wolfgang von Goethe has something new to see and meditate upon—if statutes could see and meditate. The famous Goethe statute in downtown Leipzig which has looked for many years across the Katherinenstrasse to Auerbach's Keller now also views the adjoining "House for German History" under construction. A historical exhibition will soon open to celebrate the tenth anniversary of the famous Leipzig demonstration of 9 October 1989, which contributed so much to the downfall of the East German regime.

Leipzig and Germany have experienced many constructions and reconstructions of history since Goethe enjoyed his student days at Auerbach's. The city has changed much since those years and indeed much since the epic events of 1989. The impending tenth anniversary of the great demonstrations, the dissolution of the German Democratic Republic, and Germany's sudden reunification in 1989–1990 inevitably calls to mind Goethe's opening words in *Faust*, Part One: "Ihr naht euch wieder, schwankende Gestalten," "You reappear, flickering shadows (of the past)." Leipzig's epic events of the 1980s will again be remembered. They have produced their share of heroes, martyrs, and legends and left many questions for historians. If it is already too late to prevent legends, it may be still be too early to attempt the historian's task of searching for truth in past events. Miles and miles of official document files remain to be organized and reviewed, memoirs are yet to be written, and present bitterness may fade, allowing more objectivity. Yet if "contemporary history" is to exist, historians should not leave it to others; they must attempt to write it. Moreover, broad general histories need to be tested and modified by studies focusing on localities. If the chasm between languages and cultures is to be bridged, historians must put forth the effort—hence this book.

Chapter 1 offers an overview of the protest movement in Leipzig and its antecedents in the context of East Germany. Discontent took many forms over many years, but it found a focus, inspiration, and unifying structure in the Monday night prayer meetings. Mounting discontent led to demonstrations, culminating in the mass crowd scenes of October and November 1989; which became a model for the rest of the country as the regime imploded.

Chapter 2 reviews the history and problems of the GDR generally and then turns to Leipzig and considers the repressive policies of the state and why they failed to destroy the opposition there.

Chapter 3 describes the policies of the Lutheran Church especially in Saxony in relation to the state and to the oppositional groups. The activist role of a minority of clergy and laity offered leadership, shelter, legitimacy, and hope to the discontents, despite the reluctance and ambivalence of the higher church leadership.

Chapter 4 takes a rather detailed look at the alternative groups, their various activities, their networking, and growing cooperation in programming the Monday prayer services in a unique environment in Leipzig.

Chapter 5 uses the author's survey data and compares other data to analyze the characteristics and motives of the prayer meeting attendees and reasons for the growing popularity and political significance of these Monday services. The cooperation of the various discontented elements in addition to the structures developed in Leipzig made possible the city's emergence as the national center of oppositional activity.

Chapter 6 also uses the author's and other data to investigate the characteristics, motives, and agenda of the demonstrators. It deals with the complex questions of the relationship between prayer meetings, demonstrations, and official policy and the changing agenda and composition of the November–December demonstrations. It ends with the formation and growth of the secular political movements that emerge from the churches and with the push for reunification.

Chapter 7 concludes by reviewing the situation in Leipzig and the interaction of state, church, and oppositional groups, especially in regard to the prayer meetings and demonstrations. It offers an interpretation of their significance.

The author wishes to thank the many colleagues and friends who provided assistance and information. Herr Uwe Schwabe generously guided me into the resources of Leipzig's Archive of the Citizens Movement (*Archiv Bürgerbewegung*), compiled names for the survey, and interviews and freely shared his own experiences as one of the opposition ringleaders. Pastor Rolf-Michael Turek and many other Leipzig citizens kindly shared their memories and perspectives. Katherina Führer generously shared her thesis on the prayer meetings the moment it was finished. In this country Professor Carol Miller of the Sociology Department of Arizona State University initiated me into the mysteries of proper survey questioning and data usage, as did my colleagues in my own university (Southwest Missouri State), W. R. Miller and Joel Paddock. Brian Kirby assisted in translating the documents in the Appendix. Shirley Murphree drew the map of Leipzig. Librarians Francis Wolff and Willa Garrett provided invaluable assistance on many occasions. Margie von der Heide has given yeoman services in typing and editing the manuscript. Last and most important, I am indebted to my wife, Alice Fleetwood Bartee, for sustaining inspiration and support.

Finally, I wish to express my profound regard for those individuals who so boldly and consistently put themselves at risk to participate in the Monday prayer meetings in St. Nicholas Church and other churches and to march in public demonstrations. From an American perspective it is indeed heartening to recall such courage in behalf of human rights, democracy, and social justice. There is no need to glorify or romanticize the individuals who engaged in these activities; the truth is enough. To them this book is dedicated.

Leipzig
June 1999

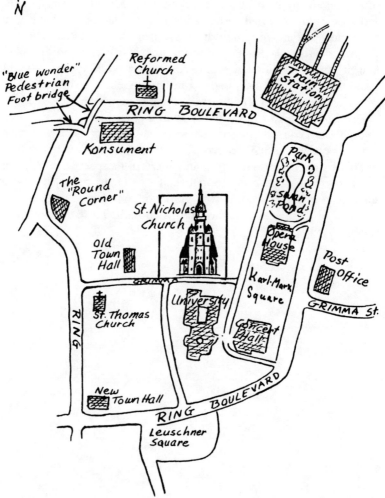

"Blue Wonder"
Pedestrian
Foot bridge

Reformed
Church

Train
Station

RING BOULEVARD

Konsument

Park
asean Pond

The
"Round
Corner"

St. Nicholas
Church

Opera
House

Old
Town
Hall

Post
Office

GRIMMA

Karl-Marx
Square

GRIMMA St.

RING

St. Thomas
Church

University

Concert
Hall

New
Town Hall

RING BOULEVARD

Leuschner
Square

LEIPZIG, INNER CITY, 1989

ONE KILOMETER

ONE MILE

# 1

## We Are the People!

The first Monday in September 1989 was Fair Monday in Leipzig, traditional host city for international trade fairs since medieval times. Reporters and cameramen from the western media would be in town to cover the fair. The first Monday also meant resumption of the weekly peace prayer meetings in the downtown St. Nicholas Church at 5:00 P.M. It was possible a demonstration might occur afterward, perhaps even a march by demonstrators into the nearby city center. Local party and government officials had labored all summer to prevail on church leaders to cancel the meetings, but they had failed. The meetings had become a Monday evening ritual with attendance swelling to more than 1,000 in May and June, in contrast to the handful in past years.[1]

Church leaders had anxieties of their own; their efforts to keep the prayer meetings from becoming too political and upsetting the delicate relationship between church and state had only partially succeeded. The local church superintendent would speak, but who could be sure who else might attempt to speak or unfurl a protest banner in the church? The question producing even more angst was "What would happen outside in the streets afterward?"[2]

Most members of the twenty-some opposition groups in Leipzig looked forward to Fair Monday with hopeful anticipation. With representatives of the western media in town, this Monday would offer a golden opportunity for publicized protest in front of the cameras, while the police would be much less likely to intervene. The image-conscious leaders of the German Democratic Republic were eager to avoid any photographed instances of police roughness. Such scenes might damage improving relations with West Germany, on which the GDR was economically dependent, and erode its newly achieved status of international respectability. A good image was vital in this summer of 1989 when the elaborate celebration of the republic's 40th anniversary was only a month away.

St. Nicholas Church filled up quickly that Monday, and the service concluded without incident. Afterward, however, a crowd gathered in front of the church and marched through the city center as far as the train station. The marchers were much the same as those in the spring, mostly young people wanting to leave the country but unable to obtain exit visas. Many of them hoped making a little trouble would lead to their expulsion. The predominant chant from this crowd was by now a familiar one: "We want out! We want out!" However, one observer, himself a veteran activist, recalled his surprise at hearing another chant:

I was astonished to hear the slogan: "We're staying here! We're staying here!" because this slogan seemed so friendly. . . . No one could say anything against this slogan. Nevertheless, this slogan implied a warning to the system.[3]

This chant resonated more and more loudly on following Mondays as the crowd grew. By 2 October it and its companion, "We are the people!" rose above all others.[4] This new chant indicated a major shift in the public mood. Those who wanted to stay, not just those wanting to leave, had decided to act openly, knowing full well they were risking their reputations, jobs, perhaps even their lives. The demonstrations escalated rapidly, despite official opposition, until in October the massive demonstrations first in Leipzig, then in Berlin, Dresden, and many cities and towns, destroyed the credibility of the regime, forced the resignation of the longtime head of party and state, Erich Honecker, and ushered in the *Wende*, the "Big Turn." Within weeks the notorious Berlin Wall would be opened, and within months the German Democratic Republic would dissolve, with its component pieces merging into West Germany's Federal Republic.

These events and the incredible speed with which they occurred astonished the world and raised many questions. How could a well-armed police state collapse when challenged only by demonstrators marching peacefully with candles? Did all this occur spontaneously or was it orchestrated by some leader or group inside the GDR—or did outside conspirators or events compel the collapse? What roused the Germans, long stereotyped as patiently obedient to all higher authorities, to risk everything and take to the streets? Why did the citizens of Leipzig lead out? In Saxony, Martin Luther's home, the cradle of Protestantism, were there significant connections between the church-sponsored prayer meetings and the massive, nonviolent demonstrations of 1989?[5]

## ORIGINS OF THE PROTESTS

Protests and prayer meetings did not suddenly begin in East Germany in 1988 and 1989; they grew and diversified through many and various forms during the forty-year lifetime of the GDR. An overview of earlier events and the context in which they occurred is essential to obtaining plausible answers to the questions surrounding 1989. Since Leipzig, the unofficial capital of the GDR, emerged as clearly the leading protest center, it deserves to be the focal point of this study.[6] Only in Leipzig did prayer meetings and protests intertwine so regularly and continuously with such catalytic impact on each other and on the political climate of the country.

The Marxist regime calling itself the German Democratic Republic came into existence in 1949 in the aftermath of World War II and the dispute among the victorious powers about Germany's future. Responding to the western powers' creation of the Federal Republic in their three zones, the Soviets established their own republic in their zone, modeled on the U.S.S.R. "Anti-fascist" political parties were forced to merge into the Communist-dominated Socialist Unity Party (SED) or disband. Election ballots offered to voters only the candidates of the SED "bloc parties." The regime entrenched itself with Soviet backing and eventually won the tolerance if not the hearts of the 17 million Germans it controlled.[7] Despite the heavy burdens imposed by Soviet "reparations" and continuing occupation, East Germany gradually recovered economically. It attained the highest standard of living in the Soviet bloc, but its leaders' hopes of catching up to and surpassing the Federal Republic never reached fulfillment.[8]

Discontent with the SED regime existed from the beginning and manifested itself to the world in the 1953 uprising, which extended well beyond East Berlin.[9] The harsh repression by Soviet tanks made it obvious that the only viable alternative for those actively opposing the regime was to flee. Thousands did, until the "escape hatch" in Berlin was closed by the Wall in 1961. Whatever its human cost, the Wall ended the mass exodus, stabilizing the regime and allowing considerable progress for its centrally planned economy, at least into the late 1970s.[10]

The GDR leaders, Walter Ulbricht and (after 1971) Erich Honecker, labored methodically to socialize business and industry, collectivize agriculture, and centralize all political and public life in the SED and its affiliated organizations. They encountered the greatest obstacle in the churches.

In 1949 the Evangelical and Lutheran churches claimed nearly 15 million of the GDR's 17 millions as members. Over the years membership declined steadily and substantially to less than 7 million by the late 1980s, and only a fraction of the members, perhaps one-tenth, attended regularly. Nevertheless, these churches constituted an autonomous force in society outside the direct control of the party apparatus and from time to time spoke out openly against official policy. The 1.2 million Roman Catholics and the

100,000 or so members of the free churches rarely joined in the protests, being inclined to stay out of public affairs.[11]

Relations between the State and the churches ranged from belligerent confrontations to cautious rapprochement after 1949. The Ulbricht regime at first launched a militant campaign against religion. Religious instruction in the schools virtually ended, church publications were curtailed and censored, and financial support was cut off, while a barrage of atheistic propaganda poured forth, targeted especially on the youth. All party members and government office holders had to renounce their church membership. Church members found professional opportunities for themselves and educational opportunities for their children deliberately limited. Party organizations and rituals were set up to rival and replace those of the churches.

By the late 1960s the decline in church membership and attendance and the breakaway of the eastern churches from the West German church federation lessened the party's perception of the churches as any "threat" to the new order; indeed the State discovered the churches could be manipulated for its own purposes. Church ties to international church groups could be utilized to build the respectability and international recognition which the GDR regime desperately sought. Church-operated charitable institutions helped care for the ill and aged. Then, when opposition groups grew more active in the late 1970s and 1980s, state officials sought to recruit the churches to restrain and monitor these groups.[12]

On their part, the church leaders gradually shifted from general opposition to reserved acceptance of the new socialist order and the state that guarded it. This acceptance they defined as "the church within socialism," not against it, not apart from it, but also not merged into it.[13] Church leaders reached an agreement with party chief Honecker at the well-publicized "summit meeting" in 1978 which guaranteed the churches a recognized status and certain limited privileges. They could publish periodicals "for church use only," sponsor youth groups, and hold meetings inside their buildings without special permits. Church kindergartens, theological schools, and charitable institutions could operate with minimal state interference.

Tensions of course remained, and innumerable discussions in the years that followed centered on the line between the State's control and the churches' privileges, but the essence of the agreement endured until 1989. Indeed, most church leaders settled rather comfortably, in Bishop Albrecht Schönherr's words, into "this given society, not separated from it, nor in opposition to it."[14] However, some clergy and laity resisted this stance. They wanted the churches to act as strong advocates for society's needy and for its victims, including persecuted political oppositionists. They argued that the churches should function actively as the conscience of society, speaking out freely on social and political issues. A few even encouraged the organization of church-related groups to advocate peace, human rights, protection of the environment, freedom to travel, and other issues.[15] Church leaders reacted rather ambivalently to such initiatives. They usually tolerated the groups and allowed them to use church facilities as long as they kept a religious dimension in their activities and refrained from overt political attacks on the regime. Church leaders themselves contested the secular youth dedication ceremony introduced to replace church confirmation and spoke out against the introduction of universal military conscription in 1962 and military studies in the high schools after 1978. Their protests did have a limited effect. They apparently pushed the State to create an alternative service program, the "construction soldiers" (*Bausoldaten*) in 1964, the only such in the East Bloc. Leaders' protests usually took the form of official resolutions or letters from church assemblies or quiet behind-the-scenes diplomacy.

Already in the 1970s a few individuals acted on their own initiative. Pastor Oskar Brüsewitz sealed his personal protest with a fiery public suicide in 1976. A former *Bausoldat* hoisted an unauthorized poster in a 1977 May Day parade calling for the "Realization of Human Rights." Gatherings for other purposes sometimes metamorphosed into political protests, as for example the youth rock concert the same year in Berlin, which turned into an all-night riot with unconfirmed reports of casualties.[16] In Leipzig on a November Saturday in 1983, a group of some 50 young people gathered in the main market square to light candles, stand silently, and pray as their protest contribution to the "Luther Year," the 500th anniversary of the reformer's birth. Police quickly took them away, but on the next Monday participants in the prayer service for peace at nearby St. Nicholas Church walked over toward the same spot carrying lighted candles. Again the police intervened, and officials called in church leaders to demand that they not allow prayer services to motivate public demonstrations.[17]

## THE NEW GENERATION OF PROTESTERS

By the early 1980s groups were indeed proliferating all over the GDR in and around the churches and the "Church from Below" began to speak out. They gathered in apartments, parish halls, and churches to discuss controversial issues; they composed leaflets, printed them on old mimeograph machines, and distributed them clandestinely; they circulated petitions, went to prayer meetings, and finally they marched. They discovered inside the churches "a little bit of freedom to hear about and talk about subjects one dared not mention elsewhere."[18] In the second-largest city of the GDR, Leipzig, the best-known, most regularly frequented place was the downtown St. Nicholas Church on Monday at 5:00 P.M., for the weekly peace prayer meeting.

Why did Leipzig assume such a leading role? East Berlin, Dresden, Jena, indeed nearly every town and village eventually witnessed prayer meetings and marches.[19] Yet from early 1988, if not before, Leipzig's activities set the tone and the pace, both in regularity, attitude, and numbers. As Leipzig's 530,000 inhabitants looked about them at the shabby, neglected buildings and generally deteriorating infrastructure, they felt a special sense of being neglected, as compared to East Berlin.[20] They worried about the gross air pollution produced by use of the cheap lignite coal which was strip-mined up to the very edge of the city. They were less and less amused by the joke that in Leipzig one could see what one was breathing. Water pollution was equally alarming, as the Pleisse River and other streams periodically turned red and yellow with chemical wastes.[21]

Perhaps other factors contributed to Leipzig's discontent: some of the oppositional spirit of the old Social Democracy may have lingered; the daring and creativity of the opposition groups flourishing there deserves mention. Leipzig served as one of the very few places where discontented emigrant applicants (*Ausreiswillige*) and stay-at-home reformers (*Hierbleiber*) overcame much of their rivalry and mistrust and learned to cooperate.[22]

More significant than any one of these factors are the regular Monday night peace prayers and programs held in Leipzig from 1981 onward. Prayer meetings in other cities and towns also functioned to sustain and nourish dissent, but they typically met less regularly, moved in time and place, and enjoyed sympathetic support from fewer local clergy and laity. Moreover, the prominent downtown location of Leipzig's St. Nicholas Church offered a very convenient and accessible locus between the Market Square and the huge Karl-Marx Square and was near to the Ring Boulevard which encircled the inner city.[23] It also proved an excellent departure point for demonstrations.

The need to pray for peace certainly appeared greater than ever with the intensification of the Cold War in the late 1970s and early 1980s. The 1979 NATO decision to place intermediate-range missiles in the Federal Republic and the Soviet invasion of Afghanistan reinvigorated peace movements in both Germanies. Also, the GDR's introduction of military studies into the school for 14- to 16-year-olds "to protect peace" that same year aroused concerns. Evangelical church leaders publicly objected to this new curriculum and responded with a peace studies program for its youth groups and an annual ten-day "decade" of prayers and programs across the country. The first of these, held in November 1980, drew substantial crowds that included many young people. Both Germanies used the clever theme "Frieden schaffen ohne Waffen" (Wage peace without weapons), which was often quoted during the 1980s.[24] Peace weeks or decades became an annual November event thereafter. The theme for the second year was "Swords to Ploughshares," and bookmarks displaying a drawing of the famous statue at the United Nations were distributed, with the Bible reference from Micah 4:3. The emblem caught on as a protest symbol and began appearing on clothing, especially jackets. Even through the statue had been a gift to the

UN from the Soviet Union, the regime was not at all pleased and banned the wearing of it in public.[25]

Peace "decades" were of course held in Leipzig and in St. Nicholas Church, which also welcomed a new pastor in 1980, Christian Führer. The historic old church already held a certain fame for having shared the services of Johann Sebastian Bach with nearby St. Thomas Church and for its lovely baroque interior. Pastor Führer recalls standing inside the church after the conclusion of the last service of the 1981 "decade" and noticing over a hundred young people lingering in the church, engaging in serious, informal discussions.[26] He knew that since September several students, members of the church youth group, had been meeting for prayer, calling themselves the Working Group in the Service of Peace (*Arbeitsgruppe Friedensdienst*). The pastor and this group decided to extend the peace prayers indefinitely, scheduling them for Monday evenings at 5:00 P.M.[27] The attendance remained small, sometimes only five or ten, meeting in a side room in the church, but gradually some nonchurchgoers joined them, mostly young, and often members of the grassroots opposition groups (*Basisgruppen*) which were proliferating. The various groups began to share in arranging the programs.[28] The pastor encouraged "outsiders" to come and placed a sign "Open for Everyone" outside the church door, which became a sort of landmark.

The transfer of Pastor Christoph Wonneberger from Dresden to St. Luke's in Leipzig brought new energy and a broad perspective to the peace prayer meetings in 1985. Wonneberger had developed contacts with opposition groups in Czechoslovakia and Poland and had himself witnessed the entry of Soviet tanks into Prague in 1968. He had previously pastored in Leipzig, and so was familiar with the city.[29] While in Dresden Wonneberger had become greatly concerned about the militarization of society and also the numbing isolation of individuals who acted or felt in any serious way oppositional to the State. He had organized an appeal for a community work peace service (*Sozialer Friedendienst*, or Sofd) as a more satisfactory alternative to military service than the semimilitary *Bausoldaten*, an appeal sharply rejected by the State.[30] Wonneberger, again pastoring in Leipzig, looked for ways to draw people out of their isolation and into church-protected groups. He involved himself in the Monday evening peace prayers and in 1987 became the official church coordinator for them. Under his leadership the number of groups and individuals participating grew and the topics discussed became more varied and on occasion more political. Representatives of participating groups formed a district coordinating committee to be responsible for programming the prayer meetings.[31] They also continued to network with groups in other areas through the "Concrete for Peace," the loose national association which since 1983 held annual meetings for information sharing and mutual encouragement.[32]

Intellectuals, artists, and entertainers also expressed their discontent but rarely belonged to these oppositional church groups; they formed a sub-culture, often a counterculture, of their own, loosely linked to the groups by shared concerns. Whenever the discussions or work of the intellectuals extended beyond their small private circles into public manifestations such as unauthorized publications, they experienced censorship, arrests, and often expatriation. A brief period of cultural liberalization in the early Honecker years ended abruptly in 1976 with the expulsion of the songwriter Wolf Biermann. A protest note signed by many of the literary elite such as Christa Wolf, Stefan Heym, and others led only to more arrests and expulsions.

Intellectual critics within the SED remained few and were silenced one way or another. Robert Havemann had to live under house arrest after he wrote to Soviet premier Leonid Brezhnev in 1981 to urge demilitarization of both Germanies; Rudolf Bahro suffered imprisonment as a "revisionist" for daring to suggest that "real existing socialism," GDR-style, needed re-forming. The regime's policy zigzagged, expelling offenders who wanted to stay and refusing exit visas to many who sought to leave.[33]

In addition to the church-related groups and the intellectuals, others re-sisted the regime's pressures and opposed its policies. This third element consisted of unorganized groups who protested the collectivization of ag-riculture, the building of the Berlin Wall, and the crushing of the "Prague Spring." Among the youth a subculture developed which admired Western trends in clothing and rock music; sometimes their gatherings turned into political protests.[34]

It seems ironic that among the factors producing what Stefan Heym called the "groundswell" of interest in peace activities must be counted the re-gime's own massive propaganda efforts which along with anti-NATO dia-tribes repeatedly mentioned the danger of nuclear war. Actions such as more frequent civil-defense drills, conscription of women, and military courses in the high schools alarmed GDR citizens and apparently increased interest and participation in opposition groups and in the public protests they began to organize by the late 1980s.[35]

Focal points for the activities of the new generation of protesters in the 1980s were first Jena and East Berlin, and later Leipzig, Dresden, and other towns.[36] The old university town of Jena had long harbored a restive youth subculture. As early as November 1982 at the time of the peace prayer "decade," 20 members of the Jena Peace Society staged a brief protest in the main square by forming a circle and unrolling a banner with only one word, "peace," on it. When they attempted a second protest in December, the police were ready and quickly dispersed them. Using expulsions and harassment, the authorities eventually destroyed the "Jena peace scene," but not before the western media discovered it and publicized it in both Ger-manies.[37]

The first large peace mobilization occurred in February 1982 in Dresden during the annual commemoration of the allied bombing raid in 1945. Excitement over the NATO missile deployment and opposition to it in West Germany ran high and some 5,000 people, mainly young, some conspicuous with long hair, responded to a nationwide appeal to come to Dresden. The local bishop persuaded them to attend a church-sponsored peace forum instead of an unauthorized rally. The forum, which became an annual event, gave opportunity for freer discussions of concerns than could be found anywhere else than the church. After the forum ended, a thousand people walked with candles in hand to the ruined *Liebfrauenkirche* (Church of Our Lady), providing a model for future marches. In the year that followed, the Free German Youth (FDJ), the SED youth auxiliary, tried to preempt the occasion with its own ceremonies, but unauthorized candlelight marches continued. Dresden would continue to play a significant role in protests,    . from the church festival that drew nearly a half million in July 1983 to the train depot riot in October 1989.[38] Dissidents in Dresden, however, lacked a regular weekly time and place as a focus for their activities.

East Berlin, capital of the GDR, of course contributed much to the protest movement. Its Prenzlauer Berg district served as a gathering place for all sorts of dissidents and intellectuals. Pastor Rainer Eppelmann, encouraged by his Marxist philosopher friend, Robert Havemann, issued his daring "Berlin Appeal" early in 1982 calling for withdrawal of *all* occupation forces from Germany and all nuclear weapons from Europe. The appeal earned him a jail sentence but failed to stop his activities, including sponsoring politically tinged rock concerts in his church which drew large crowds.[39] Berlin served as home base for opposition groups who were learning how to attract the western media and to network and establish branches across the GDR.[40] Workshops, programs, and prayer meetings kept a continuing drumfire of criticism and dialogue alive despite unrelenting efforts of the regime to repress such goings-on. The Ecology Library (*Umweltbibliothek*) in Berlin's Zion Church, begun by the Peace and Ecology Group in 1986, became the unofficial headquarters for publication and distribution of leaflets and newsletters, a sort of nerve center for the groups. Books and pamphlets smuggled into this library from West Berlin attracted a growing number of visitors, also.[41] Berlin, however, served also as headquarters for the Stasi and locus for the regime's most strenuous efforts to show the "best face" of the GDR and to repress dissent. Police acted in 1987 to raid the Ecology Library and rounded up more than 100 dissident leaders, expelling most of them. Berliners would share in, but could not really lead, the protest movements until November 1989.

Appeals from individuals and groups for reforms, or at least for dialogue, with GDR leaders continued to fall on deaf ears. It proved more difficult to ignore the reform policies of Mikhail Gorbachev after 1985. The well-worn slogans about learning from the Soviet Union, "our great model," continued *pro forma*, but Honecker and company viewed with suspicion and increasing alarm the advance of *glasnost* and *perestroika* in the U.S.S.R.

and across eastern Europe. By 1986 and 1987 dissidents in the GDR saw new hope in "Gorbi" and began to turn the slogans about learning from the Soviets into demands for change.

## EXPRESSIONS OF DISCONTENT MULTIPLY

At about the same time, certainly by 1986–1987, GDR leaders faced mounting economic difficulties. In contrast to the stagnating economies of its neighbors, the GDR had maintained some modest economic growth during the 1970s. Many factors apparently contributed to the economic stagnation and decline that clearly set in: changing world economy, gasoline shortages, decline in foreign trade, mistakes and delays in investment in new technologies, problems inherent in the system of bureaucratic central planning, lack of incentives for innovation, etc.[42] The regime used various expedients in response, such as limiting production and imports of consumer goods, using cheap domestic coal, putting off purchase of new equipment, neglecting environmental concerns, allowing the foreign debt to mushroom, even "selling" political prisoners to West Germany. None of these resolved basic problems; indeed, often they only fueled the growing dissent, especially in neglected cities and towns such as Leipzig.

Expressions of discontent multiplied and became more public in 1987 and 1988. Four events in particular aroused interest all over the GDR, including Leipzig, and indeed shifted the center of oppositional activity to that city: the Olof Palme March for Peace in September 1987; the police raid on the Ecology Library in Berlin in November; the Luxemburg-Liebknecht demonstration in Berlin in January 1988; and the annual Dresden memorial service and events surrounding it in February 1988.

The regime's official peace council organized the "Olof Palme March for a Nuclear-free Zone in Europe" and invited church groups to join in it. And join they did, some wearing the banned "Swords to Ploughshares" emblem, some with homemade banners with slogans like "Peace minus Freedom equals zero." This march served as a significant first for many pastors and church people to go out into the streets in public protest.[43] Dissidents were learning how to join an officially approved activity and add their own dimension of protest to it. Many Leipzig groups joined the march, which stretched from the Baltic to the GDR's southern border. The unusual official tolerance of the groups and their independent banners raised hopes in the minds of some for the dawning of *glasnost*, while others cynically viewed it as an expedient gesture tied to Honecker's concurrent state visit to West Germany.[44]

The latter view proved correct when official policy quickly stiffened after Honecker's return and the raid on the Ecology Library occurred on 24–25 November 1987.[45] The "Battle at Zion," as some dubbed it,[46] had just begun with the arrests at the Zion Church and roundup of Berlin opposition leaders. Within hours the news spread and a memorial prayer watch (*Mahn-wache*) was underway in downtown East Berlin with individuals standing silently, holding lighted candles. They were joined in the days and weeks which followed by members of 200 groups all over the GDR who had ties to the library. Church leaders were appalled that police should raid a church building and opened their church doors for prayer meetings for the imprisoned. The western media took up the cause, which meant nearly all GDR citizens could hear about it. Faced with mounting foreign and domestic indignation, the regime caved in and released or expelled their prisoners. They had discovered that the soft-line policy for the Olof Palme March had only encouraged the dissidents, while the hard-line move at Zion Church only made martyrs of them and rallied the church leadership and the potent western media to their defense. Attempts to keep news of Soviet *glasnost* out by banning the Soviet magazine *Sputnik* provoked still more protests.[47] In Leipzig these events evoked intense interest and sympathy and became the subject of the Monday prayers. The Stasi learned that Pastor Wonneberger and members of several groups were meeting to draw up plans for Leipzig's own ecology library.[48]

More trouble came very soon. In 1988 a Berlin group of emigrant applicants decided to appear uninvited at the traditional January parade in honor of party martyrs, Rosa Luxemburg and Karl Liebknecht, *and* to invite the opposition groups to join them. Until this time there had been little cooperation and in truth little love lost between them. The minds of most applicants had turned totally against the GDR and migrated westward; all that remained was to find some means to move their bodies also. They tended to suspect the opposition groups as being too compromising toward the system and dismissed their reform-of-socialism approach as weak and useless. For their part, the opposition groups had generally excluded applicants from membership or at least from leadership, thinking their desire to stir up trouble opportunistic and selfish.

It has also been argued that a certain class difference worked as a factor here, since most of the applicants came from mainstream, middle-class society while the oppositionists were often from society's fringes and associated with the "subculture."[49] In Leipzig the two had already begun to draw together at St. Nicholas and in Berlin some of them decided to march together.

So the two dissident elements laid their plans and cleverly selected a quotation from Rosa Luxemburg: "Freedom means always the freedom of those who disagree."[50] The omnipresent Stasi spy network learned of their plans and launched "preemptive strikes" against applicants and oppositionists as they left their homes on the morning of the parade, January 17. Some got through and marched, but over 120 were arrested and detained, including nearly all prominent members of the Berlin dissident scene.[51]

These arrests evoked a nationwide outburst of protest, even greater than in the preceding November. In 40 cities "solidarity" (with the prisoners) committees were formed and unprecedented networking and cooperation among groups developed. Memorial watches and prayer services blossomed all over the country in packed churches. In Leipzig a new coordinating committee formed to oversee daily prayers for those imprisoned in Berlin, headquartered in the district church youth office. They utilized the church telephone with its long-distance capability (normally lacking in residential telephones) to share information with other groups and even obtain news from the west. They also posted the names of the prisoners in the windows of St. Nicholas for everyone to see.[52]

Berlin events brought greater notoriety and networking, but not unity, to the protest movement. Facing the harsh option of imprisonment or emigration, most of the Berlin prisoners chose to leave, creating a vacuum of leadership in the capital and leaving a residue of ill feeling on the part of some, who regarded emigration as a selfish betrayal of the movement.[53] Suspicions lingered between the groups and the applicants—who made up most of the crowds at services and protests but were frequently excluded from any part in programming them.

Although leadership from Berlin was for the moment lacking, protests in other cities, such as Dresden, continued with growing support. Some 300 protesters there joined the 3,000 attending the annual February bombing memorial service and rallied afterward, armed with protest banners.[54] Authorities seemed unsure how to react to the united efforts of the two protest elements. They arrested hundreds, but this time they refused to expel them. High-level pressure on the churches from state officials sought to rein in the protests.[55] The SED Politburo member responsible for church affairs, Werner Jarowinsky, summoned Bishop Werner Leich, chair of the Evangelical Leadership Council, to reprimand the churches for allowing politicizing of their activities and abuse of their hospitality. Honecker himself met with church leaders in March on the tenth anniversary of the 1978 agreement. Church leaders did attempt to restrain the heightening exit fever and overtly political activities of the groups they sheltered, but they also presented the state with their agenda of pressing problems needing to be addressed.

Protests in Leipzig escalated during 1988, stimulated by news of protests in other cities. In March during the Spring Fair week, 200 emigrant applicants staged a silent march into the city center after Monday prayers at St. Nicholas. As they anticipated, the authorities did not intervene, fearing western media representatives would film embarrassing police activity. Large attendance at the special prayers for the Berlin prisoners encouraged the planning of more events. Ties between the stay-in-the-GDR oppositionists and the would-be émigrés had already strengthened; indeed, activist pastors had befriended some of the latter and held special services and programs in St. Nicholas just for them.

Tensions mounted as citizens of the GDR began to sense that change might be in the air—but what sort? During the remainder of 1988 the political weathervanes veered uncertainly. The regime relented and allowed Bärbel Bohley and a few expelled dissidents to return after pressure from church leaders, the west, and even SED party moderates.[56] In December the regime relaxed emigration restrictions slightly, but only after it had banned *Sputnik*, the Soviet magazine, in November. The regime appeared to be temporizing out of expediency, not from any sudden conversion to *glasnost*.

In Leipzig oppositionists organized a march along the polluted Pleisse River in June. The police did not intervene, even though no permit had been issued.[57] The underground press reported on activities in other cities and reprinted Pastor Friedrich Schorlemmer's "Twenty Theses for Societal Renewal" from Wittenberg.[58] The groups programming the Monday prayers grew bolder and the militant would-be émigrés joined the regular attendees in increasing numbers until some of the church authorities became alarmed. In August church superintendent Friedrich Magirius stepped in and took programming away from the groups. Considerable argument and confrontations in the church followed until a compromise eventually allowed the groups to resume participation with pastoral guidance the next April.[59] During the fall and winter months while they were excluded, oppositionists stood around outside the church in the square and as soon as the service adjourned held informal discussions and set up "speakers' corners," intermingling with the departing churchgoers to make it more difficult for the Stasi and police to ferret them out and stop them.

According to the Stasi spy reports, 500 people in Leipzig comprised the grand total of participants in all the groups in late 1988, and they remained disparate and their cooperation spasmodic. Could they truly work together or would the Stasi apparatus be able to divide and ultimately repress them? Stasi officialdom busied itself with contingency plans and with creating a special computer database listing all known participants in the Monday peace prayers.[60]

Nevertheless, the pot continued to boil in public. In October oppositionists joined would-be émigrés as 100 people gathered around the Bach Memorial at St. Thomas Church in silent protest. Then on 31 October, Reformation Day, the subject of a new alternative peace service was again raised at the service in Pastor Wonnesberger's St. Luke's Church. The annual peace "decade" in November drew very good crowds. Oppositional leaflets appeared in mailboxes and around town despite increased police efforts to catch publishers and distributors and a crackdown by censors on the "inner-church" publications.[61] At the time this seemed only an unending cat-and-mouse game between the authorities and a few hundred dissidents, with an indefinite string of warnings, prayers, protests, arrests, detentions, and expulsions. Then came the events of 1989.

## 1989: THE "YEAR OF DECISION"

The beginning of 1989 witnessed what seemed at first to be only a continuation of the climate of 1988, but soon the pace accelerated. The number of emigrant applicants and the number actually leaving, legally and illegally, increased relentlessly with the Leipzig and Dresden districts providing the highest numbers.[62] Leipzig activists staged a series of events which attracted larger crowds than ever.

Yet official intransigence and repression continued. In Berlin the circle around Honecker seemed myopically focused on the international scene and preparations for a triumphant 40th anniversary celebration in October. Assurances from the central planners that minor adjustments would ameliorate economic problems won their easy acceptance. Reassuring reports from the Ministry for State Security that dissent was being closely monitored and generally under control met few doubts.[63] Honecker's advancing age and fragile health drew the interest of his top lieutenants to the succession question, rather than to such matters as obscure prayer meetings and petty marches out in provincial cities like Leipzig.

And in Leipzig the praying, marching, and other activities continued despite rather sharp differences among the church leaders, opposition groups, and emigrant applicants. All agreed, however, with the bishop's statement to hostile officials that "the Monday service in St. Nicholas exists, as we see it, as a consequence of the fact that those who are coming can find no other place for discussion," and therefore must by all means continue.[64] And continue they did, with the groups adding new activities.[65] On 15 January over 500 responded to the appeal of leaflets, (clandestinely stuck in mailboxes) and gathered for the Luxemburg-Liebknecht anniversary. The police hastily dispersed them with arrests.[66] They attempted a public gathering again on May Day. When May elections for local offices approached, they tried to nominate independent candidates, and failing that, placed observers at the polling stations. Elections in the GDR were ceremonial affairs, with only one official list of candidates. The voters might vote "no," but if they entered the voting booth to do so instead of immediately dropping in a "yes," or if they failed to vote, they risked being labeled "enemies of the state" and suffering discrimination. Results of such elections had invariably shown incredibly high voter turnout and unanimity.

Opposition groups appointed observers at the May 1989 elections in Leipzig and all over the GDR. They documented many instances of fraud and manipulation, stirring unprecedented protests. Many looked doubtfully at the triumphant banner headlines of the party newspaper, *Neues Deutschland*, reporting 98.78 percent of eligible voters cast ballots, with 98.85 percent of them voting "yes."[67] They also questioned the bland assurances of the National Elections Commission chair, Egon Krenz, that all was properly done.[68] Church leaders demanded an official investigation and in Leipzig hundreds of protesters appeared in the streets around St. Nicholas after prayers the following Monday.

In April the groups had been allowed to resume participation in programming the prayer meetings and they renewed efforts to network with other church groups. Representatives traveled to Dresden for the third national meeting of the Ecumenical Assembly for Justice, Peace and Protection of the Creation. The assembly issued a strongly worded statement on these subjects included in its name which fueled still more oppositional activity over the summer and at the fall synod of the East German Church Federation in September.[69]

As spring faded into summer in Leipzig, some recall a foreboding, a sense that a giant storm was brewing and also uncertainty about what the outcome would be. Would it produce "showers of blessings" in reforms or a flood of destructive repression?[70] The attitude of the regime seemed, if anything, to have hardened even more toward any public sign of protest. When environmental groups attempted to repeat their march along the Pleisse River in early June, the police did not stand by this time but quickly dispersed and arrested would-be marchers. They did not interfere with the opening and closing church services associated with the march and attended by some 500 people.[71]

On 10 June group members organized a street music festival, attracting around 2,000 mostly young people from many parts of the GDR, despite official refusal to grant a permit. A large police presence and various warnings failed to keep the musicians and audience from filling the old Market Square and nearby streets with music during the sunny Saturday morning. Early in the afternoon the police intervened, swinging their rubber nightsticks freely and arresting about 150. Some fled, but others regrouped, singing and playing around nearby St. Thomas Church into the evening of this tumultuous day.[72]

Reports of police treatment of these "heroes" circulated swiftly into the western media and through the underground press, further undermining the standing of the regime.[73] In July hundreds boldly signed a letter to the *Volkskammer*, the GDR parliament, protesting police brutality against the street musicians.[74]

After the May elections, every Monday evening included increasingly political statements in the church, and confrontations occurred just outside after service. Sharp words by two speakers to the 700 present on 8 May accused high church officials of clinging to neutrality and called for aggressive public actions on the model of Martin Luther King, Jr.[75] Afterward, some 500 lingered outside in the square in continuing discussion, while a small group of emigrant applicants attempted to stage a demonstration. Police quickly intervened making 16 arrests, but it was the first time so many nonapplicants had also lingered in the church square.[76] Attendance at the prayers continued to grow, averaging around 1,000 and reaching 1,250 on 6 June when the bishop spoke.

The usual summer recess of the peace prayers in June and July brought little respite in the tense situation in Leipzig. During 6–9 July the church held its long-planned *Kirchentag* (Church Day Rally), attracting nearly 90,000 to Leipzig. Some of the groups sponsored protest gatherings and an alternative rally in St. Luke's Church.[77] Late in August three theology students attracted media attention by launching a protest fast in St. Thomas Church.[78]

Events outside the GDR impinged more and more on the situation in Leipzig during the summer. The Chinese government's brutal suppression of unarmed students in Peking's Tiananmen Square, 3–4 June, evoked congratulations from high Berlin officials but only stirred up new activity among the groups. Special memorial prayer services for the victims continued for weeks at St. Mark's.

News that Hungary was dismantling its armed frontier with Austria, followed by rumors of relaxed border control, struck many in Leipzig and elsewhere like a bolt of lightening. Here a window of opportunity seemed to open—but for how long? Hungary was a favored vacation spot, and some East Germans already there on vacation just headed for the border. Others headed for Hungary or climbed fences into West German embassies in Eastern Europe as western television cameras recorded the scenes. The mass exodus focused attention as never before on the seriousness of the situation. The emigrant applicants grew bolder than ever, while those intending to stay felt "shattered, sad, and disconcerted" and spent sleepless nights wondering why so many, mostly young people, were happily exiting and what they themselves should do next.[79] One response was: get organized to demand change. Gunter Weissgerber, a cofounder of the new Social Democratic Party, remembers the opening of the Hungarian border was for him "*the* decisive event of the summer!"[80] A near-frenzy of organizing all over the GDR would produce by the end of September "New Forum," "Democracy Now," "Democratic Awakening," and the new Social Democrats and others. They busied themselves drafting reform programs with a zeal that one underground newsletter labeled "program fever."[81]

Honecker, meanwhile, was ailing and underwent surgery in July, which kept him out of action until late August. Most of the top Politburo leaders went on vacation, postponing decisions until the boss returned. In Leipzig the district first secretary, Horst Schumann, was also ill, adding to the paralysis of policymaking.

As events unfolded, tensions increased in Leipzig and local chapters of the new organizations began to form. And more and more attention focused on one date: 4 September, the Monday of Fair Week, when the peace prayers in St. Nicholas were scheduled to resume. Since oppositionists in

Berlin and Jena had been scattered and those in Dresden were less well organized, Leipzig with its well-known prayer meeting began to assume a nationwide importance, at least in opposition circles. The prayer programs had served effectively as a forum for inspiration and information and a launching pad for protests for the few hundred members of the groups, but circumstances were changing rapidly. What should their role be when 4 September came?

At least four views on this question can be delineated. One came from the regime, which had long wanted the prayer meetings terminated, postponed until the western media left town after Fair Week, or at the very least strictly "theologized," that is, depoliticized.[82]

Another view was that of the higher church leadership, especially Bishop Johannes Hempel and his associates in the church headquarters in Dresden and Superintendent Magirius in Leipzig. When repeatedly subjected to the state demands, they continued to defend the church's right to hold the meetings and refused to delay them. They insisted that they were doing what they could to influence the programming, which was primarily in the hands of a committee, and distanced themselves from any encouragement of public protest after the meetings.[83] State officials considered the Dresden church headquarters weak and ineffective[84] and Magirius "unreliable"; they suspected they were being put off with promises and excuses.[85]

A third view came from the activist pastors and the twenty-some oppositional church-related groups. Stasi reports of 1988 and 1989 frequently— and correctly—named pastors such as Christoph Wonneberger at St. Lukes'; Rolf-Michael Turek at St. Mark's; Klaus Kaden, the district youth pastor; Michael Bartels, the student chaplain; and Dr. Berger.[86] The inclusion of Berger was *pro forma* to protect his cover, since he was a Stasi informer.[87] There were other activist pastors, about a dozen out of the 80 serving in the Leipzig district.[88] They and the groups differed as to just how far in a political direction the programs ought to go and which area of interest should be uppermost, but all agreed the prayer meetings should go forward and open up matters of public concern to free discussion. And by September some had decided to go out on the streets to demonstrate.

The emigrant applicants held a fourth view.[89] They saw the prayer meetings as a convenient gathering place to launch public protests. If the results were either relaxation of emigration restrictions, or their own expulsion, they would be pleased either way. They would help fill up St. Nicholas and be first on the streets afterward. In an odd sort of way they unwittingly provided cover for the other dissidents, since the authorities focused mainly on them and tended to blame them for all street protests.

Caught amongst these four were the pastor of St. Nicholas and the parish council, with which he shared authority. The state authorities listed Pastor Führer with the activists, considered his attitude toward them "arrogant," and kept him under close surveillance.[90] His church superiors worried about his initiatives and his friendship with dissidents. During the 1988 clash between church authorities and some of the groups, some group members accused him of betraying them.[91] The applicants, however, consistently regarded him as one of their few truly sympathetic friends.[92] An activist's comment which credits him for serving as a bridge between the various parties probably comes nearest to a fair evaluation of his key role in Leipzig.[93] He helped mediate the compromise that allowed the groups to resume participation in programming Monday services in April 1989. He pulled the disparate groups together and persuaded them to be less hostile toward the applicants. As chair of the parish council of his church, he led their steadfast resistance to terminating or postponing the services or to bringing in the "Open to All" sign when the mayor and state officials tried to pressure him. And his council backed him when church officials accused him of becoming too political.[94]

So St. Nicholas again opened its doors to everyone for peace prayers on Monday, 4 September. This opening coincided with Fair Monday, which meant representatives of the western media were in town. Stasi spies warned it would be a "hot Monday evening."[95]

While party and state officials anticipated the day with anxiety and church leaders with nervousness, militant activist groups viewed it as a special opportunity and made a bold decision: they would attempt a public demonstration with banners outside the church after 6:00 P.M. They rightly expected that emigrant applicants would also demonstrate and hoped the presence of western media would give them publicity and would restrain the police.[96] Such action by anyone intending to stay would have been almost unimaginable just a year before, even at the height of the indignation over the banning of *Sputnik*.[97]

A congregation over 1,000 strong filled the church to hear Superintendent Magirius speak at the 5:00 prayer service. He commemorated the fiftieth anniversary of the opening of World War II with a plea for reconciliation and bridge-building. The mood outside immediately afterward, however, grew less pacific as hundreds of emigrant applicants began shouting. "We want out!" At that point a new chapter in the history of these Monday evenings opened as the opposition group members quickly unfurled their banners with their own chant: "We're staying here!" Few followed their effort to begin a march, however, and the Stasi and police pulled down their banners and quickly dispersed the crowd, but not before western television cameramen had caught the images and sounds. Only a few had screwed up enough courage to make their public statement before the eyes of the world, but they had gotten away with it. Police made no arrests.[98]

The next Monday, 11 September, did not pass so peacefully. The fair days were past, the reporters were gone, and the authorities were determined to make their own statement, with force if necessary. Pastor Führer spoke to a packed church with a reassuring message for the emigrant applicants: Just as God was with Jacob during his flight into the wilderness and opened for him a door to heaven, so flight and hope still traveled together and St. Nicholas Church, open to everyone, stood firmly as a "House of Hope."[99] Police had cordoned off St. Nicholas Square and were waiting with loudspeakers to demand immediate dispersal as soon as the churchgoers poured out and began to mix with some 1,000 people milling around in the square. When the crowd hesitated and boos and whistles responded to the loudspeakers, the police moved in, pushing, shoving, and arresting at random more than 100 persons. It was the severest police action in St. Nicholes Square to that date.[100]

Most detainees were released the next day but faced heavy fines; nine remained behind bars. The response to this police heavyhandedness was a proliferation of special prayer vigils in churches in many DDR cities, usually held daily, to pray for the release of the prisoners. Lists of the prisoners were posted in church windows with candles and flowers accumulating outside beneath them.[101] A new citywide coordinating committee formed, meeting in St. Mark's parish hall, and mimeographed weekly newsletters.[102] The parish telephone with long-distance connections allowed the committee to receive and share news such as the Berlin New Forum group's plan for organizing chapters to petition for sweeping reforms.[103]

That same week the Federation of Evangelical Churches in the GDR held its annual synod in Eisenach, not far from Leipzig. In their boldest declaration yet, the church leaders called for reforms including the right to demonstrate publicly, freedom to travel, and a multiparty political system.[104] On 11 September another momentous event occurred. The Hungarian government announced that citizens of the GDR could cross the Austro-Hungarian border freely and in the days following thousands did just that.[105]

Black was the favored color in St. Nicholas the next Monday, 18 September, but hope was the subject of the evening. Black commemorated those arrested and imprisoned the week before. So many wanted in that the pastor opened the little-used second balcony. A Catholic priest, Father Bernhard Ventzke, out of the Leipzig-Grünau Peace Circle, took Joshua 6:1–21 as his text: the falling of Jericho's walls. Walls hem in everyone, he said, but with hope, love, and trust one can bring them down.[106] Some 1,500 had gathered in the church square by 6:00 P.M. when the service ended. The crowd dispersed peaceably, but zealous police nonetheless arrested 31 persons, some apparently preselected as known opposition leaders. Church officials complained formally and vigorously to city officials that such police actions were improper.[107] Indeed, people all over the GDR were adding their protests as Leipzig Monday evenings attracted nationwide attention. In the small town of Forst on the Polish border, free-church Baptists listened intently to an eyewitness account of the 18 September arrests and joined local Lutherans, not only to pray for the prisoners but to put 85 signatures on a letter written boldly to the Leipzig district government to demand their release![108]

Leipzig witnessed its first truly large demonstration the next Monday, 25 September. Two thousand people jammed St. Nicholas, sitting in the aisles and front right up to the altar, while another thousand or more stood outside.[109] Pastor Führer read the church protest letter about the police action the previous Monday, then Pastor Wonneberger spoke on the use of force. He translated the biblical "They who take the sword shall perish by the sword" into the contemporary, "Whoever wields a rubber nightstick had better wear a protective helmet," which received prolonged applause. Christ's statement "all power is given to me" can apply to Christians as they act responsibly and, "against such 'all power' the Stasi apparatus, the militia units and dog teams are mere paper tigers." His outspoken words called for inner strength and for avoidance of physical violence: "one injured policeman will lead unavoidably to escalation." At the conclusion of this rousing sermon, the crown poured out into the uncertainty of the evening singing "We Shall Overcome."[110]

How did the remarkable demonstration that followed, the first mass march through downtown Leipzig, really begin? "Spontaneous cooperation," not clever leadership or systematic planning seems to be the best explanation of why thousands came and then marched.[111]

During the warm, sunny afternoon the police had been busy cordoning off the area around the church. They hoped a massive police presence would deter would-be demonstrators and also the crowds of curious onlookers who had become another feature of Monday evenings. As the large crowd poured out of the church, the police provided only one exit opening in their cordon. This forced everyone to go out into the street which led toward Karl-Marx Square, just one short block away. Others, especially emigrant applicants, joined the existing throng which moved on toward the square, becoming a procession. Some 4,000 people marched on across the large square to the Ring Boulevard on its eastern side, then northward as far as the train station. Shouts and chants punctuated the air; for the first time "We're staying here!" echoed more frequently and loudly than "We want out!" Other chants: "Allow New Forum!" "We are the People!" resonated also. Police did nothing to stop the march and made very few arrests for reasons still unclear. Perhaps the size of the crowd and the unexpected, sudden transformation of home-going church attendees into chanting demonstrators surprised them? Perhaps orders to avoid mass arrests or overt force on the eve of the GDR's fortieth anniversary celebrations left them little choice?[112]

In any case, the district party and government officials were angry the next day and determined not to allow such a provocative event to reoccur. At the district party meeting on 27 September they laid plans for employing water cannons, rubber nightsticks, and other riot gear the next Monday. They would mobilize the party's own armed militia, the *Kampfgruppen*, to occupy and control the downtown area. As a second initiative, they exerted renewed pressure on the bishop to "theologize" the prayer meetings and remove activist pastors like Wonneberger. Pliant members of the "Christian Democrats," the SED partner party, would be sent to talk with parish councils. A third initiative would be a renewed press campaign attacking the demonstrators as punks, rowdies, and skinheads. Meanwhile party officials would call meetings and preach loyalty throughout the vast network of party organizations. Detention of a few key leaders and a close watch, especially of theology students, they believed, should obviate any need for mass arrests.[113] In other words, the party could think of no new approaches, no creative remedies, and certainly never considered dialogue with any dissidents. The pen of propaganda and the sword of repression which so far had utterly failed in Leipzig would simply be wielded more energetically!

The attempt to pressure the church encountered stiffer resistance than usual. The highest-ranking official responsible for church affairs, State Secretary Kurt Löffler, traveled to Dresden to tell Bishop Hempel to stop or restrain the prayer meetings and discipline the activist clergy, but the bishop refused. He warned the state to address the deeper problems of society, not the symptoms.[114] In Leipzig, Superintendent Magirius replied to the new pressure with the comment "It concerns me very deeply that neither Party nor State has responded to the question I have put forward again and again, 'What must we do so that people will gladly live and remain in our land?' " He pointedly declined invitations to participate in Fortieth Anniversary events.[115]

No one seemed to be listening to such remarks in Leipzig, or in Berlin where the smoothing over or postponement of all domestic problems was the order of the day as Honecker and his associates prepared for the grand anniversary. The regime disparaged the emigrants overflowing the West German embassies in Eastern Europe as deserters, but it agreed to allow those at the Prague embassy to go west if their trains came through the GDR so they could be technically expelled while in the GDR. Leipzig's troubles were left to local authorities to handle.[116]

## THE OCTOBER CRISIS: LEIPZIG BECOMES THE "HERO CITY"

Monday, 2 October, dawned in Leipzig with many sensing an impending showdown. Fears of police action mingled with hopes that change might actually be possible and that public demonstration might help bring it about. Before 5:00 P.M. some 10,000 people flooded downtown Leipzig, quickly filling St. Nicholas Church and also the nearby Reformed Church, which had opened for a second prayer meeting.[117] The police mobilized in riot gear while a host of Stasi agents infiltrated the crowds standing around the churches.

Pastor Klaus Kaden, district youth pastor, spoke at St. Nicholas and chided the congregation for avoiding in times past the slightest involvement in public life. He quoted the Bible: "If you don't do what you know is right, you have sinned." A police report claimed he incited the crowd and that his call for resignation of the Politburo and Council of State drew "frenetic applause."[118]

At 6:00 P.M. those leaving the churches mingled with the waiting thousands and marched along the Ring "with a mixture of determination, courage and doubts," as one recalled. He remembered his initial angst quickly turning to jubilation as he saw the vast throng, filling the Ring as far as he could see, chanting "Liberty, Equality, Fraternity" and singing the "Internationale." The faces of the lines of police and young militia, revealed to him their doubts and uncertainty. One responded to the crowd's invitation to break ranks and join them with "I have only a few more days and then I'll be in there, too!"[119] However, nearly all the members of the security forces moved into action when ordered. One bystander recalled her 17-year-old daughter receiving a firsthand history lesson of a special sort when "naked force was in action there, with night sticks, fierce dogs, shouts on loudspeakers, and we were shocked at how fast the security units could form lines and chase down people."[120] Water cannons helped scatter some of the protesters who tried to regroup at St. Thomas Church. This night witnessed the largest demonstration *and* the most extensive use of force Leipzig had yet experienced.

If 2 October represented an enormous escalation in both crowd size and police response, the outcome remained indecisive. The massive show of strength indicated that the authorities meant business, but they had vacillated before and might again. Higher authorities in Berlin had sent conflicting signals on 2 October. One party militia commander understood that at first the instructions for local authorities were to do whatever they deemed best, but later in the afternoon an order came to use all necessary means against the demonstrators.[121] Given the risks now so clear, would people venture downtown again the next Monday?

The week between the first two Mondays in October deserves the name "Week of Decisions" for Leipzig, and indeed for all East Germany. A series of events pushed the situation rapidly toward an unexpected and dramatic climax. For Berlin officials it was the week for the long-planned Fortieth Anniversary; for Leipzig officials it offered all too short a time period to manage the local celebrations and to figure out how to prevent another Monday demonstration. For Leipzig church leaders there was the challenge to sustain the prayer meetings while discouraging demonstrations, at least violent ones, afterward. Activists looked forward hopefully to another "hot Monday" that could force the regime to enter into dialogue about reform, but they too worried about crowd violence provoking the security forces. Participants had risked discrimination in schools and workplaces, but they now were seriously worried about being clubbed, drenched by water cannons, arrested, or perhaps shot if they returned downtown. Many wondered about the large majority of Leipzig's citizens who had so far not involved themselves but who had read, seen, or heard about last Monday—what if anything would they do? Yet this tense situation seemed far from any revolutionary threat to the regime. Thus far the streets had always cleared by 9:00 P.M. and the demonstrators had gone home to get a decent night's sleep so they could be at work punctually the next morning.[122]

Events outside Leipzig only added to the supercharged atmosphere in the city. At Berlin's famous Gethsemane Church and in churches all over the GDR, special prayer vigils remembered the Leipzigers imprisoned on 2 October.[123] The Tuesday announcement that the regime had ended visa-free travel to Czechoslovakia appeared to begin to close the "window of opportunity" for emigration via East Bloc countries and fueled mob scenes in Dresden on Wednesday and Thursday. The requirement that trains bearing the East German refugees out of Western Germany's embassy in Prague pass through the GDR backfired. Thousands of East Germans, desperate to emigrate, attempted to storm and board the trains en route to the west at the Dresden station, despite police lines. Rocks flew, a police car burned, and several were injured in the tumult. Even Leipzig had not experienced such a bloody confrontation—but would it be next?[124]

The national holiday and the regime's triumphant celebrations fell on Saturday, 7 October. Eighty foreign delegations joined Honecker and GDR dignitaries in the reviewing stand in Berlin for a carefully orchestrated parade, followed by dinners and receptions. Around the fringes of the official ceremonies uninvited protesters waved placards, chanted slogans, and scuffled with police, especially in Berlin's working-class district, Prenzlauer Berg, where some 10,000 gathered and police arrested nearly a thousand. Similar protests occurred in other cities including, of course, Leipzig.[125]

Zealous police in Leipzig quickly broke up Saturday gatherings and roughly rounded up people in the vicinity of St. Nicholas Church, including some uninvolved passersby. They trucked them off to spend an anxious, chill, unpleasant night in a horse barn outside the city.[126]

News of a more hopeful event came out of Dresden on Sunday, 8 October. Thousands marched and then filled the cathedral and three other churches and sent Bishop Hempel and church officials to city hall to seek an appointment with the mayor to express their concerns. While some marchers encountered police roughness and were arrested, the mayor agreed to see a delegation the next day. Could this be a step toward real dialogue?[127]

Leipzigers wanted to be encouraged, but they worried about what was happening in Berlin. They suspected, and rightly so, that the regime might consider a "Chinese solution" to squelch the Leipzig protesters. And indeed the party hierarchy seemed divided. Mikhail Gorbachev had met with the

Politburo while in Berlin and given his now-famous warning: "Life itself punishes those who heed too late." He may also have indicated privately that no Soviet tanks would come out to protect the regime this time; Honecker and company were on their own.[128] Egon Krenz, the heir apparent, had just returned from congratulating China on the Tiananmen Square repression, but he claimed later that back in Berlin he was urging restraint and dialogue, while Honecker and Mielke favored the hard line.[129]

The National Defense Council, chaired by Honecker, ordered forces to be sent into Leipzig and prepared to declare a "state of emergency." The Party and State would be ready to suppress violence and keep order, but exactly what they intended to do if the crowds remained nonviolent but swelled to many thousands still is not clear.[130]

On Monday, 9 October, Leipzigers opening their morning paper, the *Leipzige Volkszeitung*, read that "young rowdies" influenced by the western media had disturbed the peace of the inner city on Saturday and that upset citizens were demanding decisive action to prevent further disturbances.[131] Readers likely recalled an even more threatening piece that had appeared the preceding Friday over the signature of the commander of a local party militia unit: The prayer meetings at St. Nicholas Church could no longer be allowed to turn into counterrevolutionary provocations; his unit was ready to put a stop to demonstrations, "and if it must be, with weapon in hand!"[132] In the GDR's controlled press, such statements never actually expressed individuals' opinions but were well known to be official policy statements no matter which official signed them.

All morning preparations moved relentlessly forward to preclude last Monday's situation when embarrassed officials had to report that "due to the aggressiveness and large numbers present the planned clearing of the church square and control of [crowd] movement could not be accomplished."[133] Police, armed forces, and party militia mobilized a massive presence around the expected trouble centers: St. Nicholas, St. Thomas, and the Reformed Church. First aid stations were set up, hospitals were notified to increase supplies of blood, and doctors were called in who were trained to deal with gunshot wounds.[134]

The authorities employed other strategies also. A large number of party members including even university professors were ordered to come early and fill up St. Nicholas Church, which they did by 2:00 P.M. Schools and factories closed at noon after stern warnings from party unit leaders to go home and avoid the downtown, where suppression of the "rowdies" might well become violent. Honecker, it was rumored, had issued shoot-to-kill orders.[135]

Among those who heard this rumor was Professor Walter Friedrich, founder and longtime director of the Central Institute for Youth Research, headquartered in Leipzig.[136] GDR leaders tolerated this institute, perhaps because Friedrich was a personal acquaintance of Krenz, although they had abolished other polling agencies after regularly receiving unwelcome statistics from their opinion polls. Friedrich had long attended the prayer meetings and closely observed the mounting tensions. He had witnessed the police roughness on Saturday and decided to try to communicate the seriousness of the situation directly to Krenz. Securing a Monday morning appointment, he had spent the weekend writing a 20-page paper in which he analyzed the situation and appealed for police restraint and dialogue with dissidents. In a separate addendum he argued for the removal of Honecker. On Monday Friedrich left early and arrived at Krenz's office for his 10:00 appointment. He found Krenz receptive to his information and worried about imminent bloodshed. Krenz later stated that he had spent much of the day talking with officials in Berlin and Leipzig about how to avoid a bloody confrontation.[137]

While party and government leaders talked and implemented their plans, anxious church leaders looked for ways to calm the tense situation. Bishop Hempel, who had slept little during this week of intense official pressure, supported the decision to continue the prayer meetings and decided to come to Leipzig himself.[138] Leipzig clergy remained divided as to the best course to take concerning the demonstrations, but they did agree that four churches instead of two would open for Monday night prayers.[139] The bishop would visit all of them. During the day he sought an appointment with Dr. Reitmann, the Leipzig official charged with church affairs, and urged him to meet with dissident representatives and see that prisoners were released. The choice was simple: dialogue or violence. In Dresden they prepared for dialogue. Reitmann for the first time agreed to meet with dissident representatives and to do so on Tuesday.[140] Meanwhile at 10:00 A.M. more than 200 people, primarily theology teachers and students, met in the Reformed Church for a communion service and to pray earnestly for a peaceful course of events that evening.[141]

Opposition leaders also worried about the potential for disaster confronting them. In view of the violence in Berlin, Dresden, and Leipzig, itself in recent days how could officials be expected to react except with massive force? The only hope lay in the totally pacific, nonviolent mood and actions of the crowd. But could the mood of the nucleus of prayer service attendees sustain itself and permeate the expected crowds, or would some tossed rock or random blow or sound transform the situation into a bloody riot? New Forum distributed a leaflet calling for strict observance of the principle of nonviolence. Marchers should never force any police line, should quietly hold onto any drunks, provocateurs, or overzealous fellow marchers. Other groups issued similar appeals.[142]

The appeal credited with the most impact became known as the "Appeal of the Six." A series of hasty telephone calls led to an afternoon gathering in the home of Leipzig's world-renowned symphony conductor, Kurt Masur. Three district party officials, a theology professor, and a well-known

cabaret entertainer put their heads together with Masur to draft an appeal
for calm and dialogue.[143] It was the first time ranking party officials had ever
joined in such an initiative on their own. The highest-ranking official, Dr.
Roland Wötzel, remembered not feeling particularly heroic, but forced to
agree with Masur and the others that the threat of violence loomed so om-
inously that an extraordinary step had to be taken.[144]

Around town and in the suburbs people nervously discussed whether to
come downtown that evening. Anxiety and tension hung heavy in the minds
of many as the fateful hour of 5:00 P.M. drew nearer. Those who determined
to go packed food and drink, sent small children to relatives, and asked
neighbors to look after their pets in the event they did not come home that
night. One remembered his neighbor, a medical doctor, coming out to
plead with him not to go, telling him about the hospital alert and the call
for blood supplies. He went anyway.[145] An elderly lady recalled hearing
gratefully that St. Thomas Church would open for prayers, because it was
on the Ring and she could escape more easily than from St. Nicholas if
shooting began. She worked downtown and packed extra food that morning, fearing that if she first went home after work, police lines would prevent
her return for the prayer meeting.[146] A girl remembered that as an eight-
year-old child, she sensed something very scary was about to happen when
her parents gave her strict, detailed instructions on what to do if they were
very, very late coming home.[147]

Lines of military vehicles and some 8,000 to 10,000 armed men transformed the inner city into what might have appeared to be an armed camp,
had not so many thousands of citizens arrived to throng the streets. Many
attempted to talk with the uniformed militia, soldiers, and police, urging
them to break ranks and join them, handing them bouquets of flowers. One
participant recalls finding no soldier willing to accept her bouquet, so she
threw it up over the side of an open truck, only to be shocked by the snarls
and barking of police dogs there![148] Streetcars stopped, ringing their bells
in vain to clear a path while members of the crowd tapped on the windows
urging the driver and passengers to step out and join them, which they often
did.[149]

As 5:00 P.M. neared, the hundreds of party faithful at St. Nicholas Church
shifted nervously on the hard wooden benches. The pastor had come out
to greet them about 2:30, remarking gently, but with irony, that most working people did not get off work until 4:00, so the balconies would be reserved until after that time in order that some Christians and members of
the proletariat could also attend the prayer meeting.[150]

Crowds overflowed all four churches at 5:00 while thousands of people
gathered outside to wait for an hour until the opening of the church doors
would be the signal to begin to march. Inside St. Nicholas, the program
moved forward in the usual way with singing, prayers, information, and a
sermon, but in moments of quiet the murmuring of innumerable human

voices outside filtered in. Were they murmurs of fear? distress? Were the security forces moving in? In spite of this distraction, the service continued. Bishop Hempel appeared, urging calm, and read the Appeal of the Six, which seemed to open the way at last to "dialogue," the magic word. Other appeals were also read.

The defining moment of the evening for the pastor and others of the 2,400 crammed into the church came at the conclusion of the service, when the church doors opened, revealing the huge crowd massed outside, some holding candles. The pastor asked the crowd to step back so that the church-goers could exit. The crowd good-humoredly backed away. While anxious and tense, they remained peaceful and grew increasingly confident in the safety and success their vast number seemed to offer. The security forces made no move. Seeing the scene and remembering that it takes two hands to keep a candle burning, leaving none to hold a rock or club, Führer began to feel "a bit of hope."[151]

Professor Friedrich also felt some easing of his anxieties. He had hurried back to Leipzig and before 6:00 P.M. was moving through the crowd and noticing the "very peaceful mood." They were chanting "We are the people," "Allow New Forum," and "Gorby help us," as they patiently waited for the prayers to conclude. The crowds overflowed to fill all the side streets for blocks around so there was no way the security forces could "cordon them off" or control them short of using their weapons.[152]

A few blocks away at St. Thomas Church the defining moment for the elderly lady came just after 5:00 when the bishop made his first appearance to read the Appeal of the Six. She remarked with relief to her friend that this was a historic moment, a new turn of events.[153]

For others, the defining moment came during the march that began at 6:00. Slowly and tensely, in an orderly fashion, the crowds moved along the usual route from the church toward Karl-Marx Square and thence northward along the Ring toward the cavernous train station. Police had stopped marchers at that point, if not before, on previous Mondays. On the radio and over loudspeakers the Appeal of the Six was being broadcast. Some, hearing the loudspeakers, but too far away to understand them, feared it was the usual police command to disperse that preceded the application of force, but they quickly learned otherwise. One marcher recalled scanning intensely the entryway of each building and each side street he passed, pre-pared to spring for cover at the first alarm, and how greatly relieved he became when he realized his precautions were unnecessary.[154]

The crowd surged on past the train station but hesitated at the "Blue Wonder," the prominent pedestrian bridge a little further on the Ring. The police had stretched their human cordon across the wide boulevard at that place. Confronted, however, by such an overwhelming mass of peaceful, increasingly confident marchers, the police fell back and the crowd marched on without opposition.[155] One final challenge remained, and especially for

those in the vanguard of the crowd, their defining moment: Stasi headquarters. This building, nicknamed the "Round Corner," because of its
shape, also stood on the Ring, but no marchers had ever gotten so far
before. For many Leipzigers the Round Corner epitomized more than any
other spot in the city the repressive, secretive policies they hated and feared.
And it could just be the place where police, military, and Stasi would take
action to break up the march forcibly, or where the remarkable patience of
the crowd might falter and they might turn to storm the building.

The Round Corner lay dark with only a few police units nearby as the
marchers arrived and they passed on by, confining themselves to derisive
whistles and catcalls; no one moved to stop them. Some had expected this
to be the boiling point, but no explosion occurred.[156] The crowd's anxieties,
already fading, now virtually disappeared as they cheerfully reveled in their
success and numbers and marched on around and around again. By 10:30
P.M. the crowds dispersed, to go home or to friends' homes to listen and
watch news accounts of the evening. They heard that crowds estimated at
between 50,000 and 70,000 had marched without violence and without
hindrance from security forces. Key officials such as the SED acting first
secretary, the police chief, and the militia commanders, lacking specific orders, had cautiously let events unfold as long as no violence erupted. Krenz
in Berlin had belatedly confirmed their course and he and various others
hastened to claim credit for the peaceful outcome. In the usual GDR bureaucratic party fashion, they even attempted to portray the evening as a
success for official policy![157] The Leipzig newspaper, the *Leipzige Volkszeitung*, in its 10 October edition, abandoned the usual diatribes against "rowdies" and instead praised the peacefulness of the crowds. During the next
few days it published calls for dialogue and even an appeal from New Forum![158]

The cloud of explanations, excuses, and self-congratulations thrown up
by Party and State could not hide the fact that a major change had occurred
in Leipzig, a turn, or as the Germans said, a *Wende*. Unable or unwilling
to repress the discontent manifested in such a monster demonstration, the
authorities had agreed at last to dialogue. Rumors flew that Honecker's days
were numbered, and in fact they were. As the next Monday approached, the
National Defense Council issued an order clearly prohibiting the use of force
against unauthorized demonstrations unless they turned violent. According
to Krenz, the council acted over Honecker's objection and plans to remove
him moved forward rapidly in the highest party circles. The "Miracle of
Leipzig" consisted not only in the successful use of people power to force
an authoritarian regime to amend its ways, but in the astonishing fact that
the great change came off nonviolently![159]

Between Mondays Leipzig authorities took several conciliatory steps: 20
prisoners held from previous demonstrations were released; the mayor invited church leaders to meet with him; Dr. Reitmann received representa-

tives of the oppositional church groups to begin conversations. Still, much remained unclear with no major concessions, and tension remained high.

Monday evening, 16 October, witnessed another, even larger gathering of people in downtown Leipzig. In five churches they prayed "for us personally, for our friends, for the cities Leipzig, Berlin and Dresden, for all who now want reforms in our land to become reality."[160] Nearly 150,000 people, almost double the previous week's crowd, filled the inner city. They had concluded that the danger had passed and packed no lunches, nor did they seem worried about the rather small number of security forces present. The crowds listened cheerfully to chants, unfolded banners, hoisted posters, and marched triumphantly around the Ring after the prayer services adjourned at 6:00 P.M. Thousands were meeting and marching also in Dresden and all over the GDR as the world watched in amazement.[161]

## ENDING AN ERA: NAPOLEON, HONECKER, KRENZ, AND KOHL

On Tuesday in Berlin the Politburo demanded, and on Wednesday, 18 October, the Central Committee received, Chairman Honecker's resignation. It was the anniversary of Napoleon's great defeat at Leipzig in 1814.[162] The new Krenz government belatedly offered a series of concessions to the new spirit. Rallies, rock concerts, and of course prayer meetings and marches continued pressure for serious dialogue and more than cosmetic personnel changes.

Leipzig continued to lead the nation in the size of its demonstrations and in the opening of public discussions about the future. On 23 October and 30 October crowds approaching 300,000 jammed churches, squares, and downtown streets for prayer services and to hear speakers in Karl-Marx Square despite cold, wet weather.[163] Serious dialogue began when the "Leipzig Six" held an open forum in the *Gewandhaus* Concert Hall on 22 October, and soon dialogue meetings sprang up everywhere. Resignations of unpopular officials multiplied, with one of the early ones being Leipzig's mayor, who quit on 3 November. The same day Stasi chief Erich Mielke and other high officials resigned in Berlin and the government granted a permit for a huge demonstration there.

The Berlin demonstration on the Alexanderplatz on 4 November became the largest ever in the GDR with some 500,000 peacefully appearing. Instead of Stasi spy cameras, state television covered the event live, including speeches from leading dissidents. One of them, Christoph Hein, paid tribute to Leipzigers:

I think that our memories are not so dull, but that we know who began to break up the power structure, who ended the sleep of reason. It was reason seen in the street demonstrations of the people. . . . And here Leipzig is to be named in first place. I think the mayor of our city, on behalf of the citizens of Berlin all here assembled, should propose to the Council of State and Parliament that they designate Leipzig the "Hero City of the GDR." This title would announce our gratitude.[164]

News of resignations was followed by growing revelations of functionaries' privileged lifestyle and abuse of power. This fueled bolder demands from angry demonstrators as the prayer services and mass demonstrations continued through November. Vague reform promises and shuffling of personnel in high office would not suffice. "The SED must go!" "The Wall must go!" "Travel restrictions must go!" joined "We are the people," and "Legalize New Forum!" as frequently heard chants on 6 November. The stream of concessions that followed came too late to save the regime: recognition of New Forum, Krenz's open criticism of his predecessor, even the opening of the Berlin Wall on 9 November.

Those events affected Leipzig in various ways. Many took their first look at the west and came home more dissatisfied than ever. Attacks on officials still holding onto office increased. The number of participants declined, but the cold and rainy November Mondays still saw many thousands turning out to overflow seven churches, march around the Ring, and listen to speakers in the big square. Even when so much smog blanketed the city that the alarms sounded on Monday, 13 November, they came. In St. Nicholas Church the speaker noted that after seven days of marching by Joshua and the Israelites, the walls of Jericho fell, and now after seven Mondays of Leipzigers marching the Berlin Wall had also fallen![165]

Changes in the composition of the crowds and in their mood and demands could be noted in late November. Groups with special causes appeared: women's rights, disabled persons' needs, student demands. Rightwing groups pushed forward. The first banners calling for unification floated among the crowds at least by 20 November, and the chant "We are one people!" began to rise.[166] The once-feared Round Corner of the Stasi needed the locked arms of demonstrator "guards" to protect it from the crowds. For a few weeks they contented themselves with bedecking its front window sills and steps with candles. On 4 December opposition leaders arranged a peaceful occupation of the building to protect its records from destruction and preclude a violent storming by the passing marchers. It was "closed for inventory," as one sign aptly noted.[167]

Leipzigers had remained unmoved by Krenz's visit to the city on 25 November and his compliment that Leipzig had "sent out a signal across our land."[168] As the speaker of the 27 November prayers noted, the citizens of the GDR had, like Israel of old, wandered forty years in a dry wilderness and hence were very thirsty,[169] but were they thirsting for reformed socialism? Outside the church afterward, banners called for "No more experiments—reunification now!" and fiercely, even crudely, attacked the SED, caricaturing Krenz as a wolf in sheep's clothing.[170]

The *Wende* accelerated with dizzying speed in early December: Krenz resigned on 6 December; arrests of prominent, recently resigned officials began, including Mielke and Willi Stoph, chair of the Council of Ministers; the central Roundtable began meeting, with church oppositional and newly installed government leaders attending. In Leipzig a citizens' committee planned for free elections and launched investigations into party and government actions in the recent past.

Leipzig prayed and marched again on 11 December, 150,000 strong despite deepening winter. Posters with "We're weatherproof" and "Better 40 below than 40 more years" summed up the demonstrators' determination. Numerous banners called for reunification.[171] In St. Nicholas Church speakers reminded the congregation that the new freedom offered hope but meant taking responsibility and a willingness to listen to differing opinions.[172]

During the week that followed, the SED held an extraordinary party congress and transformed itself into the Party of Democratic Socialism. The Interior Ministry redefined the role of the police to harmonize with the new freedom. The party *Kampfgruppen* militia dissolved, and Wandlitz ceased to be the secluded settlement for the party elite. It would become a health resort for sick children and the disabled. In Leipzig church and group leaders published a pamphlet inviting demonstrators to make the last Monday before the Christmas break a memorial time for victims of recent police brutality and all Stalinist oppression by marching silently with candles.

Although the huge demonstrations had overshadowed their prayer meeting origins, the Leipzig churches again succeeded in setting the agenda on 18 December. In St. Nicholas Monsignor Hanisch took as his text Ecclesiastes 3:7, "There is a time to keep silence and a time to speak." He urged his listeners to pause to reflect on all that had been said and done in recent weeks, all the slogans and demands. He expressed unease at the changing mood in recent weeks, at slogans some marchers directed now against fellow marchers, at extremist banners showing a reunited great Germany with the 1937 borders. In the other churches prayers of thanksgiving were offered that "forty years of angst lie behind us" and for those who had resisted and suffered for their actions.[173]

When services ended at 6:00 P.M., the congregation quickly and quietly moved out to merge with the 200,000 awaiting them all around the Ring Boulevard. When the church bells rang at 6:15, everyone lit a candle, voices were hushed, and for one-half hour the huge crowd honored its heroes with deep silence and the glow of innumerable candles. Church bells rang again at 6:45 to signal the end of the 1989 Monday prayer services and demonstrations. Leipzigers looked back on 1989 that Monday; when next they would gather in January they would be looking forward into 1990, a year of even more change. Few imagined that the bells that December Monday were in effect ringing out the German Democratic Republic.

The very next day thousands would greet Chancellor Helmut Kohl in Dresden with a sea of black-red-gold banners and reunification posters. During 1990 the focus would shift somewhat away from Leipzig to Berlin and elsewhere, and from prayers and marches to election rallies and unification of currency, then country.

"People power" all over the country had challenged, undermined, and ultimately toppled an inflexible, authoritarian, well-armed regime, and had done so with almost no violence. Leipzig had led, and its prayer meetings and demonstrations had played a prominent role. As Pastor Führer in an October sermon had aptly quoted one of the GDR's top leaders: "We were prepared for anything, only not for candles and prayers!"[174] The task that remained was for scholars to attempt to interpret this remarkable series of events.

## NOTES

1. Excerpts from selected prayer meeting programs can be found in Günter Hanisch et al., eds., *Dona Nobis Pacem: Fürbitten und Friedensgebete Herbst '89 in Leipzig* (Berlin: Evangelische Verlagsanstalt, 1990); and police reports and related documents in Christian Dietrich und Uwe Schwabe, eds., *Freunde und Feinde: Dokumente zu den Friedensgebeten in Leipzig zwischen 1981 und dem 9. Oktober 1989* (Leipzig: Evangelische Verlagsanstalt, 1994).

2. For a detailed description of this and other prayer meetings, see Katharina Führer, "Vom Friedensgebet zur Montagsdemonstration. Zur Geschichte der Friedensgebete in der Leipziger Nikolaikirche vom November 1980 bis zum 9. Oktober 1989" (Berlin: Humboldt University of Berlin, *Diplomarbeit*, 1995). Führer is the daughter of St. Nicholas pastor Christian Führer.

3. Interview with Detlef Pollack. Roland Mai and Marianne Ramson also heard it that evening. Ramson thought she might have heard it during the Spring Fair. Interviews in Leipzig, June 1995.

4. Bernd Lindner recalls hearing it more loudly than "We Want Out" already on 18 September. See his "Soziologie der Losungen" in Wolfgang Schneider, ed., *Leipziger Demontagebuch* (Leipzig and Weimar: Gustav Kiepenheuer Verlag, 1992), 169. Reinert Tetzner heard it as the "main shout" by 2 October. See his *Leipziger Ring: Aufzeichnungen eines Montagsdemonstranten, Oktober 1989 bis 1. Mai 1990* (Frankfurt/Main: Luchterhand Literaturverlag, 1990), 7. Neither this chant nor the phenonemon of demonstrating began on 25 September, as some sources suggest. See Mary Fulbrook, *Anatomy of a Dictatorship* (New York: Oxford University Press, 1995), 250.

5. Karl-Dieter Opp, a prominent Leipzig sociologist, has concluded after extensive study that the demonstrations, at least in Leipzig, developed spontaneously. See Karl-Dieter Opp, Peter Voss, and Christiane Gern, *Origins of a Spontaneous Revolution: East Germany, 1989* (Ann Arbor: University of Michigan Press, 1995), 28–29.

6. Leipzig was the largest city in the GDR next to divided Berlin and sometimes received this title. Hartmut Zwahr, *Ende einer Selbstzerstörung: Leipzig und die Revolution in der DDR* (Göttingen: Vandenhoek and Ruprecht, 2d ed., 1993), 9. For a comprehensive account of oppositional activity in other parts of the GDR, see Ehrhart Neubert, *Geschichte der Opposition in der DDR 1949–1989* (Berlin: Christoph Links Verlag, 1957) especially chapters 5, 6, 7.

7. For a sympathetic account of the beginnings and progress of the GDR, see Hans Heitzer, *GDR: An Historical Outline* (Dresden: Verlag ZeitimBild, 1981).

8. Mike Dennis, *Social and Economic Modernization in Eastern Germany from Honecker to Kohl* (New York: St. Martin's Press, 1993), chapter 1.

9. See Armin Mitter and Stefan Wolle,: eds., *Unbekannte Kapital der Untergang auf Raten DDR Geschichte* (Munich: C. Bertelsmann Verlag, 1993), 8–10, 96–110, 154–62. They see the 1953 rising as beginning an ongoing process of demonstrations on through 1989. Some interpret the 1953 episode as a burden the GDR regime never overcame on its steady downward path. In Leipzig some 8,000 workers from six factories are estimated to have participated. Arnulf Baring, *Der 17. Juni 1953* (Bonn: Deutscher Bundes-Verlag, 1957), 37–50.

10. Dennis, 8–16.

11. For an analysis of membership and attendance trends, see Robert Goeckel, *The Lutheran Church and the East German State: Political Conflict and Change under Ulbricht and Honecker* (Ithaca, N.Y.: Cornell University Press, 1990), 9–10, 20ff.

12. Goeckel, 148–58.

13. See Heino Falcke, "Kirche in Sozialismus," in Günther Heydemann and Lothar Kettenacker, eds., *Kirchen in der Diktatur: Drittes Reich und SED-Staat* (Göttingen: Vandenhoek & Ruprecht, 1993), 259–81.

14. Quoted in Goeckel, 173–74. See Albrecht Schönherr, *... aber die Zeit war nicht verloren* (Berlin: Aufbau, 1993).

15. Interview with Pastor Klaus Kaden, June 1995. See also his and other comments in Dirk Philipsen, *We Were the People: Voices from Germany's Revolutionary Autumn of 1989* (Durham, N.C., and London: Duke University Press, 1993), 140–60.

16. John Sandford, *The Sword and the Ploughshare: Autonomous Peace Initiatives in East Germany* (London: Merlin Press, 1983), 23.

17. See the official report in Dietrich and Schwabe, eds., 67–68, and minutes of the meeting of state and church officials in Christoph Kaufmann, Doris Mundus, and Kurt Nowak, eds., *Sorget nicht, was ihr reden werdet: Kirche und Staat in Leipzig im Spiegel kirchlicher Gesprachsprotokolle, 1977–1989. Dokumentation.* (Leipzig: Evangelische Verlagsanstalt, 1993) 203–11.

18. An entry in the guest register of St. Nicholas Church dated 7 May 1989 (Dietrich and Schwabe, eds., 312).

19. This is documented in detail for 511 towns and districts by Uwe Schwabe, "Wir waren doch das Volk? Oder? Warum schon wieder eine Chronik?" (unpublished research paper, 1996), 3.

20. Zwahr, 9.

21. Peter Unterberg, "Vorgeschichte, Entstehung und Wirkung des Neuen Forum in Leipzig" (Bochum: unpublished *Diplomarbeit*, 1991), quoted in Christian

Joppke, *East German Dissidents and the Revolution of 1989: Social Movement in a Leninist Regime* (London: Macmillan, 1995), 144.

22. Joppke, 145–48.

23. See map of Leipzig. The distance from the church through Karl-Marx Square (now renamed Augustusplatz) and around the Ring Boulevard was only about one mile.

24. Führer, 6. Interview with Thomas Seliger, June 1995.

25. Sandford, 50, 68. See Figure 2 in Photo Essay for illustration of this emblem.

26. Interview with Pastor Führer, June 1993. See Goeckel, 262–63.

27. Uwe Schwabe, "Friedensgebete in Leipzig" (unpublished paper, 1995). An invitation to attend is printed in Dietrich and Schwabe, eds., 42.

28. Führer, 7–8.

29. Christian Dietrich, "Der Protest Formiert sich. . . . Zur Entwicklung der Opposition am Ende der DDR in den 80er Jahren," in Berndt Lindner, ed., *Zum Herbst '89: Demokratische Bewegung in der DDR* (Leipzig: Forum Verlag, 1994), 40. See also Christoph Wonneberger, "Ich habe immer tun müssen, was ich für richtig hielt," in ibid., 192–99.

30. Sandford, 32–33.

31. Report of the organizational meeting of the committee (the *Bezirkssynodalausschuss*, known as the BSA) is in Dietrich and Schwabe, eds., 94. District church superintendent Friedrich Magirius sponsored this organization.

32. Wolfgang Rüddenklau, ed., *Störenfried: DDR Opposition 1986–1989, mit Texten aus den Umweltblättern* (Berlin: BasisDruck, 1992), 34.

33. Joppke, chapter 2. See also the interviews with artists and writers from Leipzig's alternative culture in Uta Grundmann, Klaus Michael, and Susanne Seufert, eds., *Die Einübung der Aussenspur. Die andere Kultur in Leipzig, 1971–1990* (Leipzig: Thom Verlag, 1996).

34. Hubertus Knabe, "Kirche, Intellektuelle, unorganisierter Protest," in Lindner, ed., 22–23.

35. See chapter 4 herein for discussion of the various groups.

36. Rüddenklau, 32.

37. Joppke, 92–93.

38. Klaus Ehring and Martin Dallwitz, *Schwerter zu Pflugscharen: Friedensbewegungen in der DDR* (Reinbeck: Rowohlt, 1982), 70–87.

39. Joppke, 93–94.

40. A good example of this is "Women for Peace." See Chapter 4 herein.

41. Rüddenklau, 68–72. Rüddenklau was one of the founders of the Ecology Library.

42. See Philip J. Bryson, *The End of the East German Economy* (New York: St. Martin's Press, 1991), 22–25.

43. Friedrich Schorlemmer, *Bis alle Mauern fallen: Texte aus einem verschwundeten Land* (Berlin: Verlag der Nation, 1991), 28.

44. Dietrich article in Lindner, 48; Rüddenklau, 109–11.

45. The Stasi had planned to catch members of the group, Initiative for Peace and Human Rights, in the very act of printing their illegal newsletter, *Grenzfall*, but found only the legal *Umweltblätter* in production. Nevertheless, they made arrests on the spot and rounded up several known Berlin group leaders. The director of the library had in fact agreed to let the group publish *Grenzfall*, if they brought their

own printing equipment. Police found the antiquated equipment, but not yet in working order. Rüddenklau, 114–22.

46. Dietrich article in Lindner, 48; See report in *Umweltblätter*, Nr. 16 (15 December 1987), in Rüddenklau, 151–54.

47. A series of articles in *Sputnik* on the Soviet Union during World War II which referred to the close ties between Stalin and Honecker and other German communists in exile apparently led Honecker personally to order the ban. The offending articles were picked up and published by the underground press. Rüddenklau, 196–97.

48. Stasi report dated 15 December 1987 in Dietrich and Schwabe, eds., 108.

49. Joppke, 127–32.

50. Rosa Luxemburg, *The Russian Revolution and Leninism or Marxism?* (Ann Arbor: University of Michigan Press, 1961), 69.

51. See the report in the *Umweltblätter*, Nr. 2 (12 February 1988), in Rüddenklau, 203–8.

52. They called themselves Coordinating Group for Prayers for the Prisoners (*Kontaktgruppe Friedensgebet für die Inhaftierten*). Führer, 17–18. News of these Berlin happenings circulated throughout the GDR, including Leipzig, by word of mouth and by means of the underground press. See, for example, *Fussnote 3—Eine Dokumentation* published by members of IFM (Initiative for Freedom and Human Rights), 3 July 1988, in Das Archiv Bürgerbewegung (hereafter, ABL).

53. *Umweltblätter*, Nr. 2 (12 February 1988), in Rüddenklau, 203–23.

54. Joppke, 136–37.

55. The local Stasi report and a memoir of a participant is in Dietrich and Schwabe, eds., 136–39, 142–43. See also Erich Mielke's report given in a session with the Stasi leadership on 3 March 1988 in Gerhard Besier and Stephan Wolf, eds., *Pfarrer, Christen and Katholiken: Das Ministerium für Staatssicherheit der ehemaligen DDR und die Kirchen* 2d ed. (Neukirchen/Vluyn: Neukirchener, 1991), 550–59.

56. Egon Krenz later claimed credit, but he admitted that Berlin's Bishop Gottfried Forck had interceded for her. Egon Krenz, *Wenn Mauern fallen: Die friedliche Revolution: Vorgeschichte-Ablauf-Auswirkungen* (Vienna: Paul Neff Verlag, 1990), 124–25.

57. Dietrich article in Lindner, ed., 51.

58. *Streiflichter*, 23 August 1988. ABL. See Appendix.

59. Dietrich and Schwabe, eds., 178, 181, 216–18, 248–51.

60. Ibid., 526.

61. See *Umweltblätter*, Nr. 11 and 12 (December 1988) in Rüddenklau, 249–52).

62. Joppke, 138–39, 145.

63. A typical example is the Stasi report on the demonstrations of 8 May 1989, which conceded that 300 people marched from St. Nicholas Church, but added comfortingly that they were promptly dispersed with minimal effort, no banners were displayed, no chants were heard, and no western media were present. Dietrich and Schwabe, eds., 322–23.

64. Letter of Bishop Johannes Hempel to the Leipzig district official responsible for church affairs, Dr. Hartmut Reitmann, 15 November 1988, in Dietrich and Schwabe, eds., 244–45.

65. Uwe Schwabe, "Friedensgebete," 21.

66. Ibid., 22–23. See Appendix for this leaflet and related documents.

67. Newspaper page reprinted in Gerhard Rein, ed., *Die Protestantische Revolution, 1987–1990: Ein deutsches Lesebuch* (Berlin: Wichern Verlag, 1990), 136.

68. Krenz, 126–27.

69. Excerpts of the assembly statement are in Rein, 131–35. For Schorlemmer's remarks, see ibid., 339–58.

70. Rein, 129.

71. See the account in *Umweltblätter*, Nr. 16 (May, 1989) p. 9, in Rüddenklau, 336–39.

72. Numerous eyewitness accounts are in Steffen Lieberwirth, *Wer eynen Spielmann zu Tode schlägt: Ein mittelalterliches Zeitdokument anno 1989* (Leipzig: Edition Peters, Militz Verlag, 1990).

73. See *Umweltblätter*, Nr. 17 (May 1989), 9ff. In Rüddenklau, 339–42.

74. Text in Lieberwirth, 169.

75. Statements of the two are in Dietrich and Schwabe, eds., 313–18. Stasi reports follow, 319–26.

76. Führer, 28.

77. The Stasi made elaborate plans for security and surveillance of the *Kirchentag*. Besier and Wolf, 618–25.

78. Dietrich and Schwabe, eds., 374–375.

79. The words of Christa Wolf, *Reden im Herbst* (Berlin: Aufbau Verlag, 1990), 77.

80. 1995 interviews with Herr Weissgerber. He was later elected to the *Bundestag* and discusses this in an unpublished memoir, "1989/1990: Die SED zwischen Massenausreise, Leipziger Montagdemonstrationen, Mauerfall und deutscher Einheit—Aus der Sicht eines Demonstranten," 2–3.

81. *Umweltblätter*, Nr. 25 (September 1989) in Rüddenklau, 355–57. See chapter 4 on these groups.

82. See for example, excerpts from the minutes of meetings in 1988 and 1989 between state and church officials in Dietrich and Schwabe, eds., 179, 215, 225, 272, 276; correspondence between Reitmann and Bishop Hempel, ibid., 231, 244; and the Leipzig mayor's letter to the bishop and St. Nicholas parish council dated 25 August, ibid., 376–77.

83. See Magirius's comments in a meeting with the mayor and the St. Nicholas parish council, 1 September 1989, ibid., 380–82.

84. Official report, ibid., 287–93.

85. The Stasi had thought this for some time. See report of 29 July 1988, ibid., 287–93. See also the city government's report of 1 August, ibid., 176.

86. Official report of 29 March 1988 in ibid., 148; minutes of meeting of Leipzig officials and church leaders, 28 October 1988, ibid., 215–16; official report of 27 February 1989, ibid., 287–93. Clergy outside the Lutheran Church, such as Pastor Hans-Jürgen Sievers of the Reformed Church and Monsignor Günter Hanisch of Holy Trinity Catholic Church counseled with and encouraged the groups also.

87. See examples of Berger's reports in ibid., 130, 174, 208–13.

88. Pastor Kaden's estimate. He believes about 100 pastors throughout the GDR could be classified as activist. This would mean the Leipzig district had more than the average (1995 interview). See also his comments in Philipsen, 353–56.

89. For a revealing letter from one emigrant applicant to Pastor Führer, see Appendix.

90. Stasi report on "Eagle" (Pastor Führer) dated 20 October 1989, in Besier and Wolf, eds., 671–72.

91. Open letter from the groups to Bishop Hempel, 5 September 1988, Dietrich and Schwabe, eds., 190–92.

92. Letter from applicants to church officials dated 13 September 1988, ibid., 206–8.

93. Schwabe, unpublished memoir, 19–21.

94. See correspondence between state and church officials in July and August and minutes of the meeting between Mayor Bernd Seidel and Pastor Führer and the parish council in ibid., 370–76, 380–82. See also Führer, 26–27, and extensive Stasi reports in Besier and Wolf, eds., 664–76.

95. Dietrich and Schwabe, eds., 379.

96. Schwabe, unpublished memoir, 25.

97. Paul Gleye, an American professor living in nearby Weimar, noticed "universal outrage" over the banning of *Sputnik*. When Gleye suggested a street demonstration, the protesters immediately vetoed it as not worth the penalties which the authorities would impose; they confined themselves to signing a petition. Paul Gleye, *Behind the Wall: An American in East Germany, 1988–89* (Carbondale: Southern Illinois University Press, 1991), 44–45.

98. Stasi report dated 5 September in Dietrich and Schwabe, eds., 384–85. See also Zwahr, 19, and Hans-Jürgen Sievers, *Stundenbuch einer deutschen Revolution* (Göttingen: Vandenhoek & Ruprecht, 1990), 30.

99. From Genesis 27: 44–28:19. Führer thesis, 32.

100. For an eyewitness account by Pastor Führer's daughter, see Dietrich and Schwabe, eds., 386–88.

101. Photographs of St. Nicholas windows with lists and flowers and of other dramatic scenes are in Schneider, ed., 21, *et passim*. The underground newsletter, *Forum für Kirche und Menschenrechte*, circulated a full report on these events and states that fines ranged from 1,000 to 5,000 marks. Nr. 11 (16 September 1989), ABL.

102. The newsletter for 23 September is printed in Dietrich and Schwabe 414–16.

103. See the 17 September protest letter composed by the new Leipzig chapter of New Forum, in Dietrich and Schwabe, ed., 397–98.

104. Rein, 204.

105. Gale Stokes, *The Walls Came Tumbling Down: The Collapse of Communism in Eastern Europe* (New York: Oxford University Press, 1993), 136.

106. Text in Hanisch et al., 21–25.

107. See the letter dated 20 September from the Leipzig superintendent's office and the St. Nicholas parish council, signed by pastors Manfred Wugk and Führer. Dietrich and Schwabe, eds., 404.

108. Diary entry of Regina Sensel in Jörg Swoboda, ed., *Die Revolution der Kerzen* (Wuppental and Kassel: Oncken Verlag, 1990). English abridged edition, *The Revolution of the Candles* (Macon, Ga.: Mercer University Press, 1996), 99. Text of the letter is in Dietrich and Schwabe, eds., 403.

109. The Stasi crowd estimate; their estimates tended to be low. Dietrich and Schwabe, eds., 422–23.

110. Excerpts from Wonneberger's sermon are in Dietrich and Schwabe, eds., 417–22, and in Hanisch et al., 26–32.

111. Leipzig sociologist Karl-Dieter Opp and his associates conclude that the "spontaneous cooperation model" best explains the whole GDR revolution. Opp, Voss, and Gern, chapter 12.

112. For recollections of participants, see Reinhard Bohse et al., eds., *Jetzt oder nie—Demokratie: Leipziger Herbst 1989* (Leipzig: Forum Verlag, 1989), 31–33; K. Führer, 33–34; Sievers, 42–45. Party officials estimated that 4,000 were "incited" to march, while the Stasi estimated 3,500. Dietrich and Schwabe, eds., 423.

113. Minutes of Leipzig district officials' meeting, 27 September, in Dietrich and Schwabe, eds., 425–29.

114. Ibid., 432–33.

115. Letter to the chairman of the Leipzig District Council dated 29 September 1989 in ibid., 430–31.

116. Joppke, 137–38.

117. Pastor Hans-Jürgen Sievers had doubted that anyone would come and was pleasantly surprised to see the church quickly packed. He too, joined the march afterward. Interview, June 1995. See also Sievers, 51–52.

118. James 4:17CEV. Excerpt from text in Hanisch et al., 34–36; Police report in Dietrich and Schwabe, eds., 442–43. Although Kaden warned of the risks of demonstrating, he himself joined in! Ibid.

119. Bohse et al., 46–47.

120. Ibid., 50–51.

121. Ibid., 47. See memoir of a party militia member in the Appendix.

122. Comment by Detlef Pollack, 1995 interview.

123. Swoboda, 37.

124. Joppke, 138.

125. Rein, 206–7.

126. See the account of Gabrielle Schmidt, a passerby who experienced this treatment, in Bohse, 66–69.

127. Hannes Bahrmann and Christoph Links, *Chronik der Wende: Die DDR zwischen 7. October und 18. Dezember 1989* (Berlin: Christoph Links Verlag, 1994), 11–13. Hans Modrow, Dresden district party boss, implies it was his willingness to enter into dialogue that led mayor Berghofer to agree. Hans Modrow, *Aufbruch und Ende* (Hamburg: Konkret Literatur Verlag, 1991), 16.

128. Günter Schabowski, *Das Politbüro: Ende eines Mythos* (Hamburg: Rowohlt, 1990), 74. The extent of the direct influence of Gorbachev and Soviet leaders on events in the GDR remains unclear. See one attempt to show it was very strong in Jeffrey Gedmin, *The Hidden Hand: Gorbachev and the Collapse of East Germany* (Washington: American Enterprise Institute Press, 1992), 92–109.

129. Krenz, 32. Honecker was receiving detailed reports from Leipzig via the Stasi. See the report on the 2 October events in Dietrich and Schwabe, eds., 437–40.

130. The prepared "state of emergency" declaration was never proclaimed by Leipzig officials.

131. Excerpt of newspaper article is in Bohse, 71.

132. Ibid., 63.

133. Report of Leipzig party secretary to Honecker, in Dietrich and Schwabe, eds., 439.

134. See recollections of these preparations and the events of the day by Pastor Führer, Kurt Masur, Egon Krenz, and others in Kuhn, 74–84 *et passim*. See Appendix for Führer's memoir.

135. Controversy continues about Order 8/89, which has never been found. Was it written or oral, explicit or permissive? See Fred S. Oldenburg, "The October Revolution in the GDR—System, History and Causes," *Eastern Europe Economics* 29/2 (Fall 1990), 62–63; Joppke, 152; Kuhn, 85. Contemporaries in Leipzig certainly believed it existed. See letter from Meyersdorfer Club to the district mayor dated 14 October 1989. ABL, Box 2. For the recollections of a party member sent to help fill up the church, see Appendix, Document 9.

136. The *Zentralinstitut für Jugendforschung* was founded by Dr. Friedrich, a psychologist, in 1966. For an example of his studies, see his "Mentalitätswandlungen der Jugend in der DDR" in *Aus Politik und Zeitgeschichte* (13 April 1990) 16/17 (1990): 25–37.

137. See Friedrich's paper in Kuhn, 84–111, and Krenz's version there and in Krenz, 135–36. For the view that Krenz for a time had actually favored the "Chinese Solution," see Wolfe, 110.

138. Minutes of the 5 October meeting between Hempel, the two church superintendents and state officials, in Dietrich and Schwabe, eds., 447–50.

139. Sievers, 49–51, 64–65.

140. Minutes of Hempel-Reitmann meeting, 9 October, in Dietrich and Schwabe, eds., 453–55.

141. Sievers, 68–69.

142. Texts of appeals are in Kuhn, 82–84. See Appendix.

143. The "Leipzig Six" were Masur; Dr. Roland Wötzel, first secretary of the SED city party organization and second secretary for the district; Kurt Meyer and Jochen Pommert, also district party secretaries; Dr. Peter Zimmermann, university theology professor (and later exposed as a Stasi informer); and Bernd-Lutz Lange, cabaret entertainer popular as a political satirist. (Kuhn, 112–23; Dietrich and Schwabe, eds., 459.) See text of appeal in Appendix.

144. Kuhn, 116–19.

145. Interview, June 1995, with Reinhard Bohse. See Appendix.

146. Kuhn, 125–26.

147. Interview with Reinhard Bohse and daughter, Tilia, June 1995.

148. Interview with Peter Knolle and Frau Knolle, June 1995.

149. Interview with Pastor Rolf-Michael Turek, an eyewitness, June 1995.

150. Interview with Pastor Führer, June 1993. See also Kuhn, 120–21.

151. Kuhn, 126–27.

152. Ibid., 128–30.

153. Ibid., 126.

154. Tetzner, 15–20.

155. Pastor Martin Kind's recollection in "Es war nicht umsonst" in Berndt Lindner and Ralph Grüneberger, eds., *Demonteure: Biographien des Leipziger Herbst* (Bielefeld: Aisthesis Verlag, 1992), 214–15. For a graphic account of a policeman at the train station, and his doubts, see Christian Weber, *Alltag einer friedlichen Revolution* (Stuttgart: Quell Verlag, 1990), 15–17.

156. Albrecht Döhnert and Paulus Rummel, "The Leipziger Montagsdemonstrationen," in Wolf-Jürgen Grabner, Christiane Heinze, and Detlef Pollack, eds., *Leipzig in Oktober: Kirchen und alternativen Gruppen im Umbruch der DDR* (Berlin: Wichern Verlag, 1990), 153.

157. See the local report of the SED, of government officials, and of the state secretary for church affairs to the Central Committee in Dietrich and Schwabe, eds., 458–62; Krenz, 135, 204; Bahrmann and Links, 136–37; K. Führer, 35–38.

158. See various articles reprinted in Bohse et al., eds., 94–101.

159. Krenz, 135–40; Hanisch et al., eds., 61.

160. Hanisch et al., eds., 72.

161. *New York Times*, 17 October 1989, p. 1.

162. Leipzigers also found new significance in the name of the Avenue of 18 October which led out to the battlefield, the site of Napoleon's defeat at the "Battle of Nations" on that date in 1814.

163. Schneider, ed., 59, 73.

164. Annegret Hahn, Gisela Pucher, Henning Schaller, and Lothar Scharsich, eds., *4 November '89: Der Protest, die Menschen, die Reden* (Berlin: Propyläen Verlag, 1990), 195–96.

165. Bohse et al., eds., 240–42.

166. Schneider, ed., 118. Eyewitnesses disagree on the first appearance of nationalist banners and chants. The slogan "We are one people" at first meant all citizens of the GDR should be united and aimed to discourage the security forces from using force on their fellow citizens in the demonstrations. See "Appeal of the Leipzig Groups" in Appendix.

167. Ibid., 125, 147–51. For an account of the takeover of the Round Corner, see *Stasi Intern: Macht und Banalität*, complied by the Leipzig Citizens committee (Leipzig: Forum Verlag, 1992), 20–48.

168. Bahrmann and Links, 140.

169. The text was Revelation 21:6: "To him who is athirst I will give of the water of life freely." Hanisch et al., eds., 157–58.

170. Schneider, ed., 127–28, 133. One of the cruder signs read: "End of you, SED, kiss our ass!" For a list of slogans, see ibid., 140.

171. Ibid., 152–54.

172. Hanisch et al., eds., 192–96; report in the *Leipzige Volkszeitung* excerpted in Schneider, 153.

173. Texts in Hanisch et al., eds., 210–19.

174. Horst Sindermann, Politburo member 1976–1989, president of the *Volkskammer*, the parliament, and vice chair of the State Council. Quoted by Führer in his sermon of 31 October. K. Führer, 37.

# 2

# The GDR: "A House without Doors and Windows" and Its Guardians

"The GDR seemed to its own inhabitants . . . a house without doors and windows." (Helmut Zwahr, Leipzig professor).[1]

"Our workers and farmers state is the guardian of the revolutionary traditions of the German working class and of the humanist heritage of the German people." (Erich Honecker, speech to the Central Committee of the Socialist Unity party during the celebration of the GDR's 30th anniversary in 1979)[2]

An air of expectancy hung thickly over the large room in which more than 200 members and candidate members of the Central Committee of the Socialist Unity party had assembled for a hastily called meeting at party headquarters in East Berlin. A *Blitztelegramm* the previous day had superseded the earlier call for the next regular meeting at a later date with its agenda to hear the Party's strategy for the 90s. It was 2:00 P.M., Wednesday, 18 October, 1989, just eleven days since the elaborate celebration of the GDR's 40th anniversary, nine days since 70,000 people had defied the authorities to march in Leipzig, two days since 150,000 had again marched there, and one day after the Politburo members had quietly forced Erich Honecker to agree to step down.

With the Politburo members seated in their usual prominent places, Honecker read his letter of resignation on grounds of ill health and nominated Egon Krenz to succeed him as Party general secretary and then walked out of the room. As he left, everyone dutifully rose to give standing applause to the 77-year-old party warhorse who so long had led the SED in its self-proclaimed role of guardianship of Germany's revolutionary socialist and humanist traditions.

Egon Krenz was among those present who recalled a similar scene in the very same hall on 3 May 1971 when Walter Ulbricht resigned and Honecker took over. Honecker's administration had achieved international recognition for the GDR and, at least in its first decade, political and social stability with substantial economic progress. Although now confronted by serious economic problems and unprecedented displays of public discontent, perhaps the Party, by a change of top leadership, could again manage to overcome its difficulties and lead the GDR upward toward its Marxist ideals? Or had change come too little, too late, and, as Gorbachev had warned the Politburo members a few days earlier, history would punish those who came too late?[3] The answers came almost immediately. Demonstrators responded to the Krenz appointment with posters showing Krenz as the wolf posing as Red Riding Hood's grandmother and bearing the caption, "Grandmother, what big teeth you have!"[4] They would continue to march until the Berlin Wall opened. In less than two months Krenz and the entire Politburo resigned, and in 1990 the voters opted in free elections to dissolve the GDR and merge with the Federal Republic.

Interpretations and evaluations of the GDR have ranged from the bitter Cold War attacks of its enemies to the self-congratulations of its friends and adherents. Historians are just beginning to sift through the mountains of documents it left behind to seek to reach a more objective evaluation. Some understanding of its structure, functioning, and complex history is certainly essential to the study of the Leipzig protest movement and its role in the dissolution of the GDR.

Created in 1949 as the Soviet Union's response to western sponsorship of a West German state, the German Democratic Republic struggled from the beginning to define its national identity, secure the allegiance of its citizens, and use the Marxist model for postwar economic recovery and sustained growth. The west viewed it as "a repressive little state built on public self-congratulation and pervasive policing," a view that continues to dominate western interpretations.[5] Yet even critics acknowledge that many believed in it in good conscience, and many more accepted it and tried to make it work.[6] If genuine popular enthusiasm remained weak and all the efforts at ideological indoctrination yielded little fruit, still the vast majority of its citizens found ways to achieve *Anpassung*, that is, accommodation to it, at least until the late 1980s, and appreciated the job security and "welfare state" benefits it provided.

Contemporary views of the GDR by its own citizens are of particular interest here. The sense of being "walled in" appears again and again.[7] Helmut Zwahr, professor of history at Leipzig's Karl-Marx University, described the GDR as increasingly "a house without doors and windows."[8] It was caricatured as a prison trying to convince its inmates it was a pleasurable resort. (See Figure 1 in Photo Essay.)

Discontinuities with Germany's past are easily noted, yet there were potent continuities also. Of course, the regime seemed to be light-years away from the Kaiser's Germany, the Weimar Republic, or Hitler's Third Reich, whose persecutions and prisons remained all too vivid a memory for Honecker and his peers. On the other hand, the regime's paternalism, its central control of the economy, censorship, and regimentation of its citizens had roots in Hohenzollern Prussia all the way back to the Great Elector in the seventeenth century.[9] The GDR was, after all, the legatee of the Prussian state centered in Brandenburg. Indeed, the only major areas included in the GDR that had not been in Prussia were Saxony and Thuringia, with Leipzig and Dresden their largest cities.

Like old Prussia, the GDR was a bureaucratic, centrally controlled state, but unlike its predecessor, it was first and foremost a party-state. Following the Soviet model, the GDR was from the beginning dominated by the Socialist Unity Party (SED), its only political party, whose task to lead the people upward toward more perfect socialism was prominently enshrined in the constitution of 1968.[10]

## THE EMERGENCE OF THE GUARDIANS

The Communists in Germany had endured severe persecution during the Nazi years. Some were killed, some sent to the camps, but many of the top leaders escaped to the Soviet Union, where they preserved their party organization. Thus, they were ready to return in 1945 and assert a claim to lead the "anti-fascist" forces of Germany. When they fared poorly in free elections in Berlin in 1946, they decided to "merge" with the Social Democratic Party of Germany (SPD) and form a bloc with the bourgeois parties in the Soviet zone. Backed by the Soviets' coercive persuasion, the Socialist Unity Party (SED) came into existence, led by Walter Ulbricht. The SPD members who joined were largely purged by the early 1950s and the Leninist tactic of "democratic centralism" dominated the organization. The Party constituted the revolutionary elite, whose prime task was to educate the workers and farmers about the benefits of socialism while repressing any counterrevolution. To western critics this simply meant the SED had organized a dictatorship aspiring to totalitarian control.[11]

The SED grew into a sort of a "state within a state," with over 2 million members, 90 percent of all newspapers, a monopoly on the sale of newsprint, its own party militia (*Kampfgruppen*), and its huge security arm, the State Security (Stasi), which included not only hosts of spies, but its own armory containing 3,500 tanks and more than 700 heavy machine guns. The Party bureaucracy, the security apparatus, the network of subordinate affiliated organizations, especially the unified trade union (FDGB), the party youth organization (FDJ), and bloc parties fused into one vast control mechanism. The organs of government, totally controlled by party members, merely legitimatized and implemented party decisions.[12]

The SED hoped to raise up a new generation of believers through the youth organization, which grew to over 2 million and embraced two-thirds of youth aged 14–25. Both Honecker and Krenz rose to the top party leadership by virtue of serving as party youth leaders.[13] Children from kindergarten onward were drawn into the Young Pioneers to begin their comprehensive socialist education. No rival organizations were allowed except the church youth groups, which served as havens for nonconformists and were objects of special surveillance by the Stasi.[14]

Although in theory the Party Congress elected the Central Committee, which elected the Politburo, in practice the Politburo ran the SED and thus the country. Memoirs of Egon Krenz, Günter Mittag, and Günter Schabowski, prominent members, offer some insights into its workings.[15] The 21 members and several candidate members met every Tuesday at 10:00 A.M. Everyone was careful to come early to be seated by 9:59, when Honecker entered and the meeting began. All subjects had to be cleared in advance with him. Schabowski describes a "classroom atmosphere" with the "teacher," Honecker, talking at length, members giving reports, and everyone taking notes. Business was "cut and dried," discussion was rare, votes nearly always unanimous. Decisions were announced, not formulated at meetings. Each member held substantial authority: Schabowski was first secretary for the Berlin District; Günter Mittag was economic czar; Erich Mielke ran the Stasi; and Krenz, the heir apparent, was responsible for security and other matters. The memoirs, even if discounted for the self-serving hindsight element, strongly suggest that Honecker made the big decisions outside formal meetings in consultation with whomever he chose, especially Mittag and Mielke.[16] There was more suspicion than socializing among the group. Honecker preferred that his colleagues remain isolated from each other so as to prevent factions. He did enjoy reminiscing about the "old days" with senior members during lunch, but he never invited any of them to social affairs at his house, except Mittag. Although they all were required to live for security reasons at Wandlitz, the secure sylvan village north of Berlin, they rarely visited or socialized even there. Mielke, described as having a "pathological desire" to know everything, was suspected by his colleagues of tapping their phones.[17] Whisked from Wandlitz to their offices by limousines, the Politburo members lived a comfortable, isolated life and held office indefinitely. Many, like Honecker, reached their late seventies or eighties with no thought of retirement.[18] According to Krenz, his efforts to introduce serious discussion of reform resonated but faintly among his colleagues. They enjoyed the perquisites of office, including special access to scarce luxuries and western-made items, and remained content to let Honecker make—or not make—decisions in the name of the Politburo.

Western political parties rely heavily on polling to help them know public opinion, but not so the SED leaders. In 1978 they closed the Institute for Opinion Research in Berlin, apparently because of the yawning gap between official propaganda and polling reports on public perceptions of the realities of the GDR. The rulers feared that the numbers, top secret of course, would leak out and prove embarrassing.[19] They preferred to rely on the voluminous reports of the Stasi. Occasional polls were conducted through the media but kept secret. The Central Institute for Youth Research in Leipzig barely survived efforts to close it too, and it was not allowed to research political questions. Its questionnaires required prior approval from Berlin, and "controversial" questions were struck out. It is worth noting that the head of this institute, Professor Walter Friedrich, is the person whom Krenz acknowledges as alerting him to the volatile situation in Leipzig on 9 October.

Each of the 15 governmental districts into which the country was divided possessed a party organization which mirrored the national one. A first secretary, assisted by various second secretaries, implemented orders coming down from the top. The first secretaries met occasionally in Berlin to hear long speeches from Honecker and other Party leaders. A district first secretary like Schabowski, who was also a Politburo member, apparently enjoyed somewhat more influence throughout the byzantine channels of party and government than did Leipzig's undistinguished and ailing first secretary, Horst Schumann, or Dresden's Hans Modrow, who was rather out of favor.

The SED thus dominated the political life of the GDR, and Party structure paralleled the state structure, with Party bosses responsible for areas of quasi-governmental responsibilities. Rarely did the Party elite except Honecker also hold government offices, although they might chair special commissions. Krenz chaired the electoral commission in 1989 when the SED claimed to have triumphed overwhelmingly at the polls in the May communal elections with 98.85 percent voting "yes" for its list.[20]

In the last resort, however, the regime depended not on elections, but on repression. The presence of 300,000 Soviet troops in the country and the growth of the National People's Army (NVA) undergirded the regime. Soviet tanks had stopped rebellion in 1953 and, it was assumed—before Gorbachev—remained ready to move out again. The rearmament program, ostensibly directed against NATO, built the army into a rather well-trained, well-armed force. In addition to the regular police (DVP), there were reserve and paramilitary police units, including some 400,000 men in the *Kampfgruppen*, the party's own armed militia organized within factories and workplaces, and the "voluntary helpers," police reservists, another 120,000.[21]

The function of the Party centered on making decisions, while the State's role was to implement them. The official duality of Party and State served as a facade for a highly centralized, combined party-state institution, which under Ulbricht and then Honecker operated as a *de facto* personal dictatorship. The organs of government created in the first constitution in 1949 resembled those of the Federal Republic: a president with very limited powers, a two-house parliament, and five "federal" states (*Länder*). During the 1950s and 1960s the regime tinkered with the organs and organization of the state in various ways. Fifteen administrative districts replaced the states, the upper house of parliament was abolished, and the office of president transformed into a collective presidency, the Council of State, whose chair functioned as head of state. A National Defense Council, chaired by Honecker, exercised overall control of army, police, and, at least theoretically, Stasi and all other security forces. The constitution later incorporated these changes, and the SED was officially written in as the nation's "leading force." Although Party and State remained inseparably intertwined until the end, differences in function can be distinguished. For example, state officials, not party officials, dealt with church leaders and pastors.[22]

## THE COMMUNIST PHOENIX

After initial hope that the GDR might prove a magnet to draw all Germany together as "one fatherland" faded, the regime shifted to a policy of "delimitation." This new German state, rising like a phoenix from the ashes of fascist folly and World War II, was defined as a progressive upward step in German history, a special socialist, that is, communist, Germany quite distinct from its retrograde, capitalist German-speaking neighbor. Every all-German organization, such as the Evangelical Lutheran Church, came under pressure to divide along the new political fault line, as the church finally did in 1969. Even the singing of the first verse of the new national anthem was no longer allowed because of its reference to "Germany, One Fatherland."[23] Tight control of any travel across the sealed frontiers and the building of the Berlin Wall in 1961 closed the "doors" if not quite all the windows to the vast majority of GDR citizens. By education and indoctrination designed to demonstrate the success of the social and economic merit of real-existing socialism, the regime attempted to mold its ideal of a GDR citizen: loyal to the State and Party, industrious, uncritical, satisfied with the GDR brand of welfarist socialism. Citizens did not need to think or accept personal responsibility: the pervasive organs of State and Party would do all that for them.[24] For many years and with many people this attempt appeared to succeed. Yet the forty-year effort to define and build support for the GDR's distinct national identity ultimately failed, as the strong vote for merger with the FRG in 1990 would show.[25]

This end result remained far from obvious. From 1949 to 1989, the GDR had gained the acceptance, if not love, of its citizens; it rose from the destruction of war to create the highest living standard in the Eastern Bloc and it had gained international recognition and respectability. Some historians view its history in retrospect as a depressing tale of civil strife and an ever-downward slide toward disaster. When the prop of Soviet bayonets fell away, they argue, it immediately collapsed.[26] Others seek to balance its achievements with its problems and see a "rise and fall" trend.[27] After the debacle of 1953, the regime tightened its grip, revised some policies, and achieved political stability with economic growth, which continued through the 1960s into the 1970s. Revolution in Hungary, continuing unrest in Poland, the "Prague Spring" scarcely resonated in the GDR. It seemed a quiet society with the great majority of its citizens outwardly in compliance with its demands. The malcontents retreated to their private niches with only a handful apparently unhappy enough to create public nuisance, and they could be easily expelled to the west. Upon his accession to power in 1971, Honecker increased consumer goods production, promoted education and science, and appointed technocrats to high positions. He followed the Soviet lead in agreeing to "normalize" relations with the FRG in various ways.[28] Better relations with the "other Germany" opened the way at last to general international recognition, admission to the United Nations in 1973, and participation in the Helsinki Accords in 1975. While Honecker never received the coveted invitation to the White House, he did finally make a state visit to the FRG in 1987.

Honecker also proved resourceful and perhaps more innovative than Ulbricht in dealing with internal opposition and the evangelical church federation. He had observed Ulbricht's policies, which enjoyed only a limited success: There had been an all-out propaganda war on the church, pressure on officeholders to renounce their church membership, and financial "warfare" with cancellation of state collection of the church tax and refusal or delay in paying rents and fees for church-owned properties the state had seized. Children in the schools no longer received religious instruction; instead they learned the Marxist approach to religion. In 1954 the State instituted the secular coming-of-age ritual, the *Jugendweihe*, for 14-year-olds as a substitute for confirmation into the church. Church requests for support to rebuild war-damaged buildings went to the bottom of the state's priority list. A special ministry for church affairs was created in 1956 and a Politburo member assigned to keep an eye on church-state relations.[29]

State pressure produced a massive exodus of nominal church members and reduced the churches to penury. By the early 1960s the churches seemed more an ongoing nuisance than a serious threat.[30] Nevertheless, even Ulbricht discovered that churches could be useful for peace propaganda, for sending delegations abroad to achieve quasi-official recognition for the GDR, and to help shoulder social burdens of the sick, poor, and elderly at home. Thus by 1961 the frontal assault on the churches faded as Ulbricht decided to receive a delegation of prominent church officials led by "progressive" Leipzig theologian Emil Fuchs.[31] Official policy shifted, as a later state secretary for church affairs put it, "to make the church feel at home in our republic and gradually win over its potential for the stable, internal development of our republic and our peace policy."[32] A velvet glove now covered the iron fist.

Honecker took the accommodationist approach further with the State-Church agreement of 1978. By granting the churches a recognized place in the socialist state, he intended to co-opt them. Of course, he never considered restoring the old throne-altar relationship or moving toward pluralism. The regime seemed to regard the Evangelical Church as an elderly, increasingly feeble dowager, too respectable to attack directly, holding too many assets to ignore completely. The best strategy seemed to be to treat her politely in public and channel her small and declining energy into harmless religious exercises, charitable work, and the chaperoning of marginal dissident cliques while awaiting the inevitable end.[33] Although some church leaders responded favorably to this policy, others did not,[34] yet the accommodationist strategy seemed to work fairly well for nearly ten years. Behind the polite facade the regime consistently worked to undermine Christianity as a belief system through education and to infiltrate and manipulate the church leadership. The regime sought to influence church policies through the Christian Democratic Union, the "partner party" in the Socialist Unity Front, the Pastors Alliance (*Pfarrerbund*), and the international Christian Peace Conference, but few clergy or lay members joined them.[35] On the other side of this facade, discontent clergy and laity sheltered and encouraged oppositional groups of all sorts and pushed the bishops to assert a "watchman" role over society. Yet both sides remained at pains to preserve the facade.

The State dealt more summarily with other dissident or potentially dissident elements. Intellectuals had to join Party-controlled organizations if they expected to receive permission to publish their writings or display their art. By censorship and by expulsions the regime prevented the intellectuals from reaching the general public. Nonconformity among the youth and the working class was more diffuse and more difficult to deal with. Activists who appeared to share stated goals of the regime such as peace and a more just society, who wanted to improve the socialist state and not abandon or overthrow it, proved difficult also. Forbidding their meetings drove them into the shelter of the churches and ironically often strengthened their efforts as they found clerical sponsors, like-minded nonconformists, and "safe space." State expectations that the high church leadership could and would "theologize" or somehow discipline and restrain these nonconformists were largely disappointed.

Explanations for the "rise" of the GDR as well as those for its "fall" are many and varied with little consensus. Further research and analysis is needed to find generally satisfactory answers. Clearly, the GDR faced an escalating financial and economic crisis by the late 1980s. The highly centralized command economy rested on the principle of the "unity of economic and social policy." This meant subsidizing prices for basic foodstuffs and rent plus funding the extensive social programs like health care and free daycare for children of working mothers. Ideology prevented Honecker and his economic czar, Günter Mittag, from modifying this system, even when monetary costs forced the regime to live beyond its means. Changes in the world economy, beginning especially with the oil shortage of 1973 and continuing with the growth of microelectronics and computers, affected the GDR deleteriously. The system motivated production managers to meet quantitative goals by traditional methods, rather than to innovate or take risks. In fairness to the GDR, it should also be noted that the country possessed few natural resources except for the brown coal (lignite) around Leipzig, which it exploited extensively without regard to environmental impact. Thus the Politburo decided in 1981 to increase mining of brown coal so that it could increase its use of domestic sources of energy from 60 percent to 63 percent while reducing imports of oil and natural gas.[36] Various other expedients—such as neglect of the infrastructure, limits on investments in new enterprises, sweeping relaxations of health and safety regulations in regard to air and water pollution—only stored up trouble for a future reckoning. Increasing reliance on the Federal Republic for loans, credits, and "sale" of political prisoners bought time but carried political consequences. It has been further argued that the party bosses and technocrats running the economy were not only too old and too long in power, but even in their youth in the 1950s and 1960s were typically mediocrities who had lacked the energy or initiative to flee the country while it was still possible. They had stayed, learned caution and conformity, and received promotions beyond their abilities. Confronted with growing problems and constrained by the "union of economic and social policy," they found it easier to try to maintain obsolete equipment, cut back on new investments, and rely on foreign credits and expedients than to risk their careers by pressing for change.[37]

Other problems increasingly beset the GDR regime. After 1975 human-rights groups gained courage from the regime's signature on the Helsinki Declaration of Human Rights and demanded compliance. The official peace organization, directed against NATO, lost control of the peace movement, which challenged the regime to explain why a Marxist "peace state" needed a large army and military indoctrination of schoolchildren. Official denials could not clear the increasingly polluted air and water, nor stop the growing environmentalist protest movement. Then, after 1985, Gorbachev's reforms in the U.S.S.R. moved in directions Honecker was unwilling to follow, despite having religiously held up the Soviet Union as the great model for the GDR. East Germans could see every day on television the prosperity and greater freedoms enjoyed by fellow Germans in the Federal Republic. Labor productivity remained well below that of West Germany, as many citizens went along with the system, but without enthusiasm. Efforts to indoctrinate youth met increasing indifference and opposition. A confidential survey by the regime's own Central Institute for Youth Research in May 1989 reported 9 percent strongly believed in Marxism, 35 percent believed with qualifications, and 56 percent held little or no belief in it.[38] For many the GDR became a "niche society," as people retreated as much as possible into some private niche among family and friends, with books, hobbies, gardening, or other private interests becoming a sort of protective shield from the monotony and constraints of public life. Others tried to break out of their closed circle of compliance by seeking out alternative groups and their activities.

## THE STASI EMPIRE

Repression, not reform, continued to be the regime's principal mode of response to dissent as it became more active in the mid-1980s.[39] The major responsibility for dealing with dissent rested on the Ministry for State Security, the Stasi. From its inception the Ministry for State Security acted as the foremost among the guardians of the Party and State. Other guardians existed: army and police with their reserve units; the armed party militia; certain offices within the Ministry of the Interior; the mass party-controlled youth and labor organizations. None of them came close to performing the multifarious functions of the Stasi.

The GDR created this political police modeled on the Soviet Cheka in 1950.[40] After the fiasco of 1953 this unit, a first part of the criminal police, was extensively reorganized and expanded. By 1957, when Erich Mielke took command, it operated with 9,000 full-time employees; by the mid-1970s the total passed 60,000; by 1989 it surpassed 100,000, while the number of part-time "unofficial co-laborers," which is to say informers, grew in like manner. At the end it probably approached 200,000.[41]

The insignia of the Stasi summed up its mission aptly enough: the sword and shield of the Party, indeed, a "sharp sword and reliable shield," as the Leipzig party first secretary described it on its 30th anniversary in 1980.[42] Its mission included not only security in the conventional protective sense of a shield guarding the persons of the leadership and state secrets, but in an active sense of aggressively ferreting out all sorts of information to checkmate the "hostile-negative forces" within the GDR. A list of some of the missions assigned to the thirty-some major divisions and departments offers insight into all aspects of this activity: espionage; investigation; information evaluation; security of persons; guard regiment; postal watch; monitoring arts and cultural activities and the underground; watch for terrorists; telephone watch; political education; tourism and pass control; penalties and detention; codes; radio; training schools; and in defense work in army and border guard. The Stasi maintained its own sort of army including hundreds of tanks, as well as training schools, 2,000 secret "safe" houses and apartments, plus a savings bank, medical service, and special housing for its full-time employees.[43]

In order to carry out all these assignments, the State Security ministry utilized this vast apparatus with its sophisticated and varied methods. It involved heavy expenditures. Operating on an annual budget of over 4 billion marks, Mielke and his "firm" became in a sense one of the largest "industries" in the GDR, and certainly the best informed. The headquarters complex on Berlin's Normannenstrasse contained not only offices and barracks, but also a windowless annex containing personal files on over 4 million of the GDR's 16.5 million citizens, plus files on 2 million other Germans in the Federal Republic. After dissolution in 1990, citizens' committees estimated the macabre legacy of records in Berlin to equal 100 running kilometers, with another 80 or more kilometers in the fifteen district headquarters! Over 300 archivists had worked full-time in Berlin to receive and file this massive inflow of information.[44]

Egon Krenz described the Stasi empire as a state within a state, and some scholars also suggest this view. Krenz, even though a member of the Politburo responsible for security, claimed to have been largely unaware of the extent of Stasi activities. He remembered that Mielke, also a Politburo member, closeted himself with Honecker after Politburo meetings rather than submitting reports on Stasi activity to that body.[45] Still, the Stasi remained an arm of the Party, dependent on it. Stasi officials could gather, evaluate, and pass on information; agents could harass, interrogate, and detain troublemakers; but the Stasi did not make major policy decisions, just recommendations. Lack of response on the part of Honecker and the Politburo to the belatedly alarmist Stasi reports from Leipzig and elsewhere in the summer and fall of 1989 demonstrates this.[46]

Joachim Gauck, head of the special agency created after the *Wende* to deal with Stasi records, offers perhaps the most informed opinion. The answer to the question of whether the Stasi was a state within a state or merely an arm of the party, according to Gauck, is that it was both and still more. The Stasi's vast, pervasive network blurred the lines between Party, State, and society, but, Gauck believes, the Politburo, not the Stasi, made policy and should be held responsible.[47]

One became a Stasi employee by invitation only, after careful screening and a thorough program of training. The training reflected both the regime's paranoia and its insatiable desire for total knowledge of the activities of everyone who might pose a security risk. Any contact with the west, any unguarded word of criticism, appearance at an unlicensed meeting or acquaintance with anyone involved in such could spark a "profiling operation" to create a Stasi personnel file. Trainees learned to suspect everyone as a potential risk and to assume capitalist opponents in the west encouraged and financed all significant oppositional activity. The Stasi held tenaciously to this false assumption to the very end. Security needs must take priority over legal procedures when "enemies of the peace," the "hostile-negative forces" in bureaucratic jargon, threatened trouble.[48] Trainees learned not to use the physical force and torture methods of the infamous Gestapo, but to be subtler. Primarily they gathered and evaluated information, extensive, minutely detailed personal information on the "target," to be used indirectly to prevent job promotions, limit educational opportunities, or on occasion to persuade or blackmail the target into becoming an informer. In a culture where every activity was to be synchronized with the goal of advancing socialism, any activity outside the official parameters automatically drew Stasi attention and efforts not only to obtain information, but to infiltrate, divide, and destroy. Stasi agents also spied on government officials and agencies, on businesses, schools, and factories. By 1990 at least 3,000 individuals installed as vice chairmen of boards, special consultants, coworkers, etc. were submitting regular reports on their colleagues.[49]

Most information gathering was done by many sorts of "unofficial co-laborers" ("IMs"). One sort were the "social colaborers for security," not exactly spies, but loyal SED members in key positions expected to provide the Stasi information upon request. Personnel officers in plants, professors, and teachers often fell into this category. Some persons such as high church officials regularly had visits from "officials," not known by them to be Stasi, wanting a general discussion of people and events.[50] A teenager caught in a minor violation might be excused from penalty and publicity upon promise of future availability to answer questions about his church youth group, schoolmates, teachers, friends, or even relatives. Many other informers worked on a much less informal basis, regularly receiving extra pay and perquisites for hours spent in surveillance or infiltration of a suspect group. Some went further to stir up dissension ("the IMBs") filing regular reports on certain individuals. Stasi spies served for a variety of motives ranging from patriotism or party zeal to expedient desires for personal gain or revenge, to coercion.[51] An individual caught in a personal indiscretion, or attempting to flee the country, or who refused military service might be visited by Stasi and offered a choice of prison or informing, if he or she held some key position or had contacts with suspicious persons. Some accepted, believing they could protect colleagues by submitting innocuous information and overlooking activities that might lead to official reaction. The evidence remains thus far unclear whether some informers were more victims than villains, or perhaps some of both.[52] The Stasi cross-checked their reports by assigning multiple informers to spy on activities. One activist discovered after 1990 to his surprise that 22 informers, including a cousin, had filed regular reports on him.[53] The file on the prominent activist Gerhard Poppe ran to a fulsome 12,000 pages.[54] Certain spies were assigned to check on other spies. The Stasi even collected the scents of oppositionists by means of personal items, which they placed in uniform jars, carefully organized, so they could be offered to trained dogs.[55]

Stasi informers continued their work throughout the stormy fall of 1989, even attending and reporting on meetings of New Forum and the growing number of new activist groups. Activity and morale declined, however, and dropouts apparently multiplied. The government finally dismissed the 109,000 informers remaining on the official list in March 1990. Out of every twenty inhabitants of the GDR, one had served at one time or another as a Stasi spy.[56]

Stasi attitudes and policies toward the churches naturally reflected those of the SED state. Organized religion remained basically an enemy of the State and an obstacle to the building of socialism. Although the State had abandoned open warfare against the churches and agreed to terms of co-existence in 1978, church leaders, even "progressive" ones, were not to be trusted. Efforts to use the block party Christian Democrats and the state-approved Pastors Association to coopt the church leaders failed to attract more than a handful. So while top leaders of State and Church met to discuss cooperative ventures and exchange occasional, polite criticisms, the Stasi covertly acted in its usual "sword" capacity against the churches, especially the regional Evangelical Lutheran churches. The Stasi infiltrated a huge number of informers into the churches, estimated at between 500 and 1,500.[57]

They followed a multilayered approach: (1) to gather information as detailed as possible on church leaders for use against them; (2) to infiltrate church organizations not only for information but to create divisions and diversions within their ranks; and (3) to have informers reporting on nearly every pastor: where he bought groceries; whom he saw; any church or marital problems; contacts with suspected activists or westerners. Information of a compromising nature could then, whenever desired, be passed along to state officials responsible for church affairs, who would bring it to the bishops or superintendents for disciplinary action. By this indirect chain of action the Stasi informers could keep their cover and could continue to function. It was hoped thus to intimidate pastors—and it actually seems to have worked rather well, with some prominent exceptions.[58] They also employed many spy-provocateurs to create dissension among groups and discredit leaders. Pastors who caused trouble might even be set up. For example, a pastor who openly preached against the "shoot to kill" order to the border guards had had difficulty paying rent on a leased auto and buying gasoline for it to make pastoral calls. A "friendly" teacher offered to sell him cheap gasoline as a favor, gasoline which turned out to be apparently stolen from the Soviet army and the teacher a Stasi spy. The Stasi exposed the pastor and threatened him with public embarrassment and imprisonment unless he signed an emigration application.[59]

## LEIPZIG: THE GDR'S "OTHER CAPITAL"

The City of Leipzig and its surrounding administrative districts reflected the same fusion of Party-State-Stasi as on the national level. The SED claimed 160,000 members led by the long-serving, cautious first secretary, Horst Schumann. Although Schumann was the son of a well-known old-line German Communist, he never attained Politburo rank like his Berlin counterpart, Schabowski, nor did he earn any reputation for flexibility or interest in reform as did his Dresden counterpart, Modrow. On rare occasions when anyone dared to press him for comment on any controversial matter, he prudently referred to speeches by Honecker or members of the Politburo.[60] All this deference did not earn the first secretary any praise from Honecker, who was said to dislike both Schumann and Leipzig and to pay little attention to its other party functionaries.[61] During the crisis of 1989 Schumann fell ill and Helmut Hackenberg replaced him as acting first secretary. The party second secretaries, not a distinguished lot, each had certain areas of responsibility. Dr. Kurt Meyer held responsibility for cultural activities and allowed a little more latitude to writers, artists, and cabaretists than some, despite criticism from party hard-liners.[62] In music at least, Meyer allowed conductor Kurt Masur enough freedom to encourage him to stay at the *Gewandhaus* (Concert Hall). Occasional party reports to Berlin suggesting reform or "a more critical approach as is current in the Soviet Union" received no serious attention.[63] Nor did citizens' complaints about dilapidated houses and apartments, poor quality of goods, long waiting periods for cars and new appliances, and difficulties with spare parts for repairs produce any results. Local party and government officials were left to explain why Leipzig was neglected—except for two weeks a year during the fairs—while the regime spent large sums on Berlin. As the mood soured in Leipzig and the crisis deepened, party bosses became increasingly divided over what to do.[64]

The Leipzig city and district government also lacked leaders of stature. The district and city council members handled only routine matters and referred policy decisions to party leaders. Party leaders very rarely dealt directly with church officials, leaving this responsibility to government. A district council member, Dr. Hartmut Reitmann, held responsibility for church affairs and dealt with the local church superintendents and the bishop's representatives from Dresden. Bishops and superintendents were supposed to supervise the pastors and lesser church officials. Only in very exceptional circumstances did important officials deal directly with pastors and parish councils. It was, for example, most unusual that Senior Mayor Bernd Seidel should come directly to a pastor and parish council, as happened when, upon his request, he met with Pastor Führer and the St. Nicholas Council on 1 September 1989 to plead with them to cancel or postpone the Monday prayer meetings. They denied his request and refused to continue the discussion on the grounds that it wasn't proper for parish councils to meet with high officials.[65]

If Leipzig suffered neglect from high party and government officials, it never lacked attention from the Stasi. Indeed, Stasi leaders long regarded Leipzig as second only to Berlin in being a center for oppositional activity, and they had built up a large operation in the Leipzig District. The district headquarters in the downtown Round Corner building contained a large complex of offices, barracks, detention rooms, and archives. The archives included a card file on more than 300,000 Leipzigers.[66] Some 2,400 full-time employees in about 30 departments, special units, and groups carried out the Stasi's mission under the command of General Manfred Hummitzsch (since 1969) in this district headquarters. Another 200 under Colonel Norbert Schmidt busied themselves in the Leipzig-City subdivision office on Gustav-Mahlerstrasse.[67] The Leipzig-City subheadquarters grew to be the largest of its type in the GDR.[68] The number of informers active in the Leipzig area numbered about 10,000.[69] The Stasi occupied at least 581 apartments, offices, houses, and rooms in and around Leipzig for spying purposes. The Stasi used buildings at the agricultural exposition site in Markleeberg, not far from the city, as a detention center whenever a large number of troublemakers needed to be rounded up and detained temporarily. Between 100 and 150 activists were subject to intense surveillance and another 700–800 to special "person control." The Leipzig Stasi network extended beyond the district and even into West Germany.

The Stasi extended its influence still further through close cooperation with other agencies. At the Leipzig district level the four persons primarily responsible for law and order were Stasi chief Hummitzsch, party First Secretary Schumann, Police Chief Gerhard Strassenberg, and the chair of the district's governing council, Rolf Opitz.[70] The mayor and district prosecutor also operated in close touch with this inner circle. They cooperated to utilize the party militia (*Kampfgruppen*) and could also mobilize the "social forces" (*Sozialkräfte*). These social forces consisted of party members who could be called out to fill up a church or public place, or to confuse or disrupt meetings when the officials did not want to use police.

Leipzig, a large city, center for publishing and the book trade, home of the national book depository and library, had traditionally served also as a center for writers, a breed whom the Stasi regarded with unending suspicion. Stasi spies observed and reported extensively on them, long before the 1980s. Ernst Loest was among the Leipzig literati who suffered under Stasi omnipresence.[71] Leipzig churches and leaders of course merited extensive effort. Both IMs and IMBs functioned within the theological faculty, among the clergy, and in the church-related groups. One even served as chair of the District Synodal Coordinating Committee for the groups.[72] Activist pastors such as Führer and Wonneberger received special code names ("Eagle" and "Lukas"). The Stasi drafted plans for dealing with activists, which they regularly reviewed and updated.[73] The State's policy of official cooperation with the churches made it politically inexpedient to throw pastors in jail or attack them publicly, but it was the Stasi's job to learn every detail of their lives in hopes of catching them in some violation of the law or illicit contact with opposition leaders. Beyond that they sought to manipulate rewards such as travel abroad or punishments such as denial of travel requests to foster more loyalty among the clergy. A report dated 2 October 1989 suggests the failure of such policies. It noted Führer's "self-assured and somewhat arrogant attitude" and regretfully concluded that "all active operational efforts toward disciplining him remain without recognizable effect," a conclusion also applicable to Wonneberger and the other clerical and lay leaders of the Leipzig church-related opposition groups.[74]

The Stasi efforts to keep opposition groups small, divided, and ineffective generally failed in the late 1980s. Mielke laid down hard-line policy guidelines after the Liebknecht-Luxemburg demonstrations of January 1988: toleration of the "enemies of Socialism" and their underground activities funded from beyond the borders had its limits; misuse of churches and politicization of their activities must be stopped. Opposition leaders must choose between long years in prison and joining their bosses in the FRG. The churches must abandon their pretensions to any role as watchman over the state's policies.[75] The Leipzig Stasi engaged in diligent efforts to implement these guidelines with increased surveillance, detailed evaluations, and elaborate plans for suppression of unlicensed public activities and control of the few officially licensed ones, such as the *Kirchentag* (Church Rally) held in Leipzig in July 1989.[76]

"Tried and true" methods, however, no longer delivered the expected results. Despite obvious Stasi presence and relentless harassment, the opposition groups, especially those sheltered by the church, continued boldly to meet and increasingly to network, multiply, and engage in public protest. No one knew better the problems in Leipzig than local Stasi officials. General Hummitzsch, district chief, could back up his words with stacks of reports when he warned Minister Mielke in August 1989 that the situation in Leipzig "is very complicated" and the "mood is lousy."[77]

## NOTES

1. Zwahr, 56.
2. English translation in Heitzer, 244.
3. This is based on Krenz's account (Krenz, 11–19).
4. Krenz's prominent front teeth offered an easily understood comparison. See picture of this poster in Lindner, ed., 58.
5. Charles S. Maier, *Dissolution: The Crisis of Communism and the End of East Germany* (Princeton: Princeton University Press, 1997), xii.
6. Ibid.

7. See, for example, the factory workers' complaint in 1967, quoted in Fulbrook, 161.

8. Zwahr, 56.

9. Maier, 117.

10. Ibid., xii. See *DDR Handbuch*, 2 vols. (Cologne: Verlag Wissenschaft und Politik, 3rd ed., 1984), vol. 2, 1161–74.

11. Gerhard Besier, *Der SED Staat und die Kirche: Der Weg in die Anpassung* (Munich: C. Bertelsmann, 1993), 12. Nancy Wolfe, *Policing a Socialist Society: The German Democratic Republic* (Westport, Conn.: Greenwood Press, 1992), 88.

12. A very helpful explanation is in Oldenburg, 55–77.

13. *DDR Handbuch*, vol. 1, 451–59. For a brief summary in English of party structure and functions, see Henry Krisch, *The German Democratic Republic: The Search for Identity* (Boulder, Colo.: Westview, 1985).

14. For the fascinating account of a church youth worker who after the *Wende* discovered that 22 Stasi spies, including relatives, had filed reports on him, see Klaus Hugler, *Missbrauchtes Vertrauen: Christliche Jugendarbeit unter den Augen der Stasi* (Neukirchen/Vluyn: Aussaat Verlag, 1994), 54ff.

15. Krenz; Schabowski; Günter Mittag, *Um jeden Preis: Im Spannungsfeld zweier Systeme* (Berlin: Aufbau Verlag), 1991.

16. Schabowski, 14–20.

17. Ibid., 41.

18. Various jokes about the age and longevity in office of Politburo members circulated, such as "What has four legs and 60 teeth? A crocodile. But what has sixty legs and four teeth? The Politburo. (Weber, 6.)

19. Peter Förster and Günter Roski, *DDR zwischen Wende und Wahl: Meinungsforscher analysieren den Umbruch* (Berlin: Linksdruck Verlag, 1990), 14–25.

20. Krenz, 126–27.

21. Fulbrook, 45–46.

22. Ibid. Gauck defines a fused trinity of Party-State-Stasi. Joachim Gauck, *Die Stasi Akten; Das unheimliche Erbe der DDR* (Reinbek: Rowohlt, 1991), 72.

23. Zwahr, 14.

24. Ibid., 17–18.

25. Some would argue the question of national identity always remained the GDR's fundamental problem. See, for example, Krisch, 173. In the first free election of 18 March 1990, 53 percent voted for parties favoring immediate reunification with the FRG, 21 percent voted for a more gradual unification, and only 16.3 percent voted for the SED, now calling itself the PDS, Party of Democratic Socialism. Helmut Nagelschmitz, ed., "Procedures, Programs, Profiles" (Bonn: Inter Nations Special Report, December 1990).

26. This is Helmut Zwahr's general interpretation—also that of Mitter and Wolle.

27. See Maier, 5–6; Fulbrook, 36–37.

28. For example, the Basic Treaty of 1972 with the FRG, the first general treaty. Krisch, 76.

29. For an analysis of membership figures and trends, see Wolfgang Büscher, "Unterwegs zur Minderheit: Eine Auswertung Konfessionsstatistischen Daten," in Reinhard Henkys, ed., *Die evangelischen Kirchen in der DDR: Beiträge zu einer Bestandaufnahme* (Munich: Kaiser, 1982), 434ff. See also Goeckel, 9–15, 20–21, 42–43, 50.

30. Membership in the Evangelical churches fell from nearly 15 million or 81 percent of the population in 1946 to 10 million, or 59 percent of the population in 1964, the last year the official census recorded religious affiliation. *Deutschland Archiv* 2/10 (Oct. 1969): 1119, printed in Goeckel, 9. Subsidies from the West German Church Federation (EKD) helped to pay minimal salaries of GDR clergy. Membership declined steadily during the 1970s and 1980s.

31. Besier, 344–46.

32. Klaus Gysi, quoted in Ronald D. Asmus, "Is There a Peace Movement in the GDR?" *Orbis* (Summer 1983), 322.

33. Bishop Schönherr emphasizes the regime's politeness (Schönherr, 355).

34. For a pastor's complaint that the church leadership was too compliant and submissive, see Klaus-Reiner Latk, *Stasi-Kirche* (Uhldingen: Stephanus-Edition, 1992), 54–55, 82–83.

35. Rudolf Mau, *Eingebunden in den Realsozialismus? Die evangelische Kirche als Problem der SED.* (Göttingen: Vandenhoek & Rupprecht, 1994), 109–15.

36. Peter Przybylski, *Tatort Politburo*, vol. 2, *Honecker, Mittag und Schalek-Golodkowski* (Berlin: Rowohlt, 1992), 371–73; Zwahr, 11. Writing after the *Wende*, Mittag explained that he had desired major reforms for 30 years but found no allies and was stymied by "oppositional forces" (Mittag, 19–20).

37. The growing foreign debt had exceeded $18 billion by 1989 (Oldenburg, 58–59).

38. Friedrich, 27.

39. For statistics on the number of political prisoners in the DDR jails, see Johannes Raschka, "Für kleine Delikte ist kein Platz in der Kriminalitätsstatistik—Zur Zahl der politischen Häftlinge während der Amtzeit Honeckers," Hannah-Arendt-Institut für Totalitarismusforschung, Berichte und Studien, Nr. 11 (Dresden: Technische Universität Dresden, 1997), 25, 36.

40. Wolfe, 72; Fulbrook, 47–51.

41. Gauck, 10–12, 62–64.

42. Horst Schumann to General Manfred Hummitzsch, Stasi Chief, Leipzig District, in Bürgerkomitee Leipzig, eds., *Stasi Intern: Macht und Banalität*, 2d ed. (Leipzig: Forum Verlag, 1992), 66.

43. Organizational chart in ibid., appendix. See also Oldenburg, 57.

44. Gauck, 11–12. Only "completed" files were well organized; ongoing cases were not always kept filed up-to-date. An undetermined amount of material was removed or destroyed during the last weeks of 1989 before the national and various district headquarters were occupied and sealed by citizens' groups. See Dagmar Unverlau, "Alles Sehen, nichts wissen?—Zur archivisten Hinterlassenschaft der Staatssicherheit," in Leonore Siegale-Wenschkewitz, ed., *Die evangelischen Kirchen und der SED-Staat—Ein Theme Kirchlicher Zeitgeschichte* (Frankfurt/Main: Haag und Herchen, 1993), 26.

45. Krenz, 123–24.

46. Fulbrook, 53–54. Rudolf Mittig, Mielke's assistant, remembered this as a regular, systemic problem in a 1990 interview. Ariane Riecker, Annette Schwarz, and Dirk Schneider, eds., *Stasi Intim: Gespräche mit echemaligen Mfs-angehörigen* (Leipzig: Forum Verlag, 1990), 179–82.

47. Gauck, 70.

48. Bürgerkomitee, 53–54.

49. Gauck, 68.

50. In the aftermath of charges and countercharges after 1990, prominent officials such as church consistory chairman Manfred Stolpe argued convincingly that they were unaware the Stasi listed them as informers and had regarded contacts with party and government officials as part of their job responsibilities, not as spying. Manfred Stolpe, *Schwieriger Aufbruch* (Munich: Siedler, 1992), 12.

51. Gauck, 64–66.

52. Ibid., 27, 37, 53.

53. Ibid., 36–37. Another interesting example comes from a pastor, whose teacher assistant confided to him that he had been recruited by the Stasi and had accepted because "I am a Christian. If an enemy of the Church undertook this spy work here for the State Security, the church would certainly be in much greater danger" (Latk, 35). In Leipzig the Stasi maintained four observation posts around St. Mark's Parish Hall, meeting place of alternative groups (Interview with Pastor Turek).

54. Joppke, 113.

55. Bürgerkomitee, 147–53.

56. Peter Förster and Günter Roski, "Wieviel inoffizielle Mitarbeiter hatte das MfS?" *Forschungen Aktuell, Mitteilungen des Forschungszentrums zu den Verbrechen des Stalinismus*, Nr. 1 (January 1992), 15.

57. Latk, 122.

58. Ibid., 38–39; Fulbrook, 123.

59. Latk, 68–70.

60. Lutz Löscher and Jürgen Vogel, "Leipziger Herbst," in Stefan Heym and Werner Heiduczek, eds., *Die sanfte Revolution: Prosa, Lyrik, Protokolle, Erlebnisberichte, Reden* (Leipzig and Weimar: Gustav Kiepenheuer Verlag, 1990), 129.

61. Christoph Wielapp, "Montagsabends in Leipzig," Thomas Blanke and Rainier Erd, eds., *DDR—Ein Staat vergeht* (Frankfurt/Main: Fischer Taschenbuch Verlag, 1990), 76.

62. Bohse et al., eds., 282–84.

63. Party report of 11 June 1987, quoted in Fulbrook, 148.

64. Bohse et al., eds., 284–85.

65. Parish Council minutes in Dietrich and Schwabe, eds., 380–82.

66. Some 6,000 running meters of files remained in the Leipzig district headquarters archives in December 1989, even after an indeterminate amount had been destroyed. Bürgerkomitee, 104, 361. The card file with the 300,00 names of both informers and "targets" also survived, as did transcripts of intercepted telephone calls, copies of letters, Christmas cards, and other documents. Information from the archivist in the former headquarters, now a museum and archive, June 1999.

67. Ibid., 374.

68. Ibid., 364; Mitter and Wolle, eds., 49.

69. One careful estimate is 9,821 in early October 1989 with 790 in Division XX, which watched opposition activists and the church. *Forschungen Aktuell*, Nr. 1 (January 1992), 14–15, and Nr. 3 (March 1992), 8.

70. For discussion of how this worked in Dresden, see Modrow, 16–17.

71. Ernst Loest, *Der Zorn des Schafes: Aus meinen Tagewerk* (Künzelsau and Leipzig: Linden-Verlag, 1990), 189–224.

72. Examples include Professor Peter Zimmermann of the Theological Faculty, Dr. Matthias Berger, chair of the Synod Coordinating Committee, and Pastor Wolf-

gang Erler (Dietrich and Schwabe, eds., 566, 553; Besier and Wolf, 680). For correspondence after the *Wende* between church officials and the Citizens Committee on this subject, see Besier and Wolf, 719–33.

73. For examples of plans and reports on Führer, see Besier and Wolf, 667, 671. For Wonneberger, see ibid., 682, 684, 687.

74. Stasi report on operational file "Eagle" in ibid., 672.

75. Mielke to Stasi officials, 9 March 1988 (ibid. 550–59).

76. Ibid., 618–25. For an earlier example of these extraordinarily detailed reports sent to Mielke, see Hummitzsch's report to him on opposition to the demolition of the University Church in 1968 (ibid. 271–73).

77. Mitter and Wolle, eds., 127–29; Hummitzsch's retrospective comments are in Riecker et al., eds., 214.

# 3

## "To Hope or to Give Up": The Churches and the Dissidents

Church bells were ringing in towns and villages all over the German Democratic Republic. It was 19 November 1980, but a Wednesday, not a Sunday. Clock hands all pointed to twelve on this Day of Penance (*Busstag*) on the Evangelical Church calendar. The coordinated, nationwide bell-ringing served a particular purpose this day: The bells pealed "for peace in the world, for the negotiations in Madrid and for the end of peace-threatening strife." They served as audible signals of hope. They also ushered in a decade that would witness the ever-increasing involvement of the churches in the political life of the GDR as it dramatically declined and fell.[1]

Just an hour later, at 1:00 P.M., air-raid sirens sounded in a routine national test, signals of fear of the threat of war. This dramatic juxtaposition of contradictory signals illustrates the situation confronting the churches in the officially atheistic GDR. Heightened tensions of the "new" Cold War along with the state's response of increased military education in the schools influenced church leaders to plan special initiatives for peace including the nationwide ringing of church bells at 1:00 on the last day of the new ten-day decade program of peace prayers. State officials, nervous about recent events in Poland and paranoid about public activity not originating with the Party, viewed the proposed bell-ringing at the same hour as the siren test as a direct challenge to the state's defense policy and perhaps even a call for a general strike. They demanded cancellation of the bell-ringing and stopped publications of church newsletters announcing it. Confronted by state opposition, church leaders divided into those ready to cancel, those determined to go ahead regardless, and those, including the top leadership, who favored compromise—moving the time from 1:00 to noon. In the end, each congregation did as it pleased; many rang at noon, some at 1:00, some at 1:15 or in the evening.[2]

It is impossible to know how many people heard the bells and understood their meaning that November day in Leipzig or elsewhere, or how many cared about the intended message. Yet the "problem of the bells" aptly illustrates the difficulties faced by the churches and their divided responses. The Evangelical churches, heirs of centuries of State–Church tradition, retained the position of public institutions with legally recognized status and felt an obligation to function as the public conscience of society. They lived under many constraints and faced many serious problems. Moreover, they differed sharply among themselves over how to relate to a state seeking to build a society on the principles of scientific socialism, which theoretically left no room for religion.

## THE STATE WAGES "WAR" ON THE CHURCHES

The citizens of the GDR were perhaps the least religious of any population within the Eastern Bloc in terms of the usual measures of membership and church attendance. Despite the long-term secularization trend in Europe, the Protestant church rolls still listed nearly 15 million or 80 percent of the GDR's 17 million as members in 1946. The massive exodus from the churches following the war peaked in the 1950s but continued steadily through the 1980s. The 1964 census, the last official census to include membership figures, listed 10 million, or 52 percent, and by the late 1980s less than 7 million were estimated to have retained their membership. Less than 10 percent of newborn infants were being baptized into the church. Only a small fraction of members frequented the church services regularly.[3] The church in Saxony, Luther's home, suffered an even greater decline, from 4.3 million in 1945 to 1.2 million by 1990, yet it still claimed more members than any other of the eight regional churches. Leipzig was second only to East Berlin among cities and towns in low church membership (less than 20 percent) and low attendance.[4] A further reason for declining membership derived from emigration. In 1984 an estimated 59 percent of legal emigrants were Evangelical Church members.[5] The Roman Catholic Church's membership likewise declined, if less dramatically, from 2.2 million to about 1 million by the end of the 1980s. The free churches' combined membership totaled only around 100,000 and declined less dramatically.

The organizational structure of the Evangelical churches reflected both the theological and political divisions from Germany's past and proved both a strength and a weakness in their relations with the State. Prussian kings had only partly succeeded in bringing the Lutheran and Reformed churches together, while Hitler had failed utterly in the attempt to unite all Protestants into one "German Christian Church." Instead of one united church, the fragment of Germany now forming the GDR contained eight regional churches: five Lutheran-Reformed union churches and three, including Saxony, which remained purely Lutheran. In the early postwar years the eight continued to be members, along with the regional churches of the Federal Republic, in the all-German confederation, the Evangelical Church of Germany (EKD). In 1969 they finally yielded to strong political pressure and seceded to form their own Confederation of Evangelical Churches (BEK) in the GDR. The geographical boundaries of the eight generally followed the old provincial boundaries of Saxony, Brandenburg, Thuringia, etc.[6] The eight were represented in the national leadership conference by the bishops and other representatives, who met regularly and from time to time issued statements on public issues as well as church matters.[7] Such a decentralized structure made it difficult for the church to speak with one voice; it also made it possible for the State to engage in "divide and conquer" policies, which it frequently did, especially in the first two decades of its existence. On the other hand, the regional decentralization did not make it easy for the State to control or manipulate simultaneously all eight regional churches from the top down.

The democratic procedures of church government and decision making also held both strengths and weaknesses. A bishop nominally headed each regional church, but he shared power with the council or synod which elected him, which was itself largely composed of elected representatives. Under the bishop stood district superintendents, each responsible for oversight of several parishes. At the bottom of this pyramidal structure the pastor and the elected parish council over which he presided enjoyed a great deal of autonomy in policymaking for their local congregation. The Saxon regional church[8] for example, was headed by a bishop with headquarters in Dresden, while central Leipzig was divided into two superintendencies, Leipzig-East, centered on St. Nicholas Church, and Leipzig-West, centered on St. Thomas. Bishop and superintendent took the initiative in appointing pastors to vacancies, but they could remove a pastor only for heresy or gross misconduct. In practice, as long as a pastor received the support of his congregation and its parish council, the influence of higher church officials was usually only persuasive, not coercive, on him or her.[9] While laypersons filled the seats of the local parish councils, clergy dominated the higher church bodies, such as the synods.[10]

If declining membership continued to be the greatest worry of the East German churches, finances came in a close second. From the sixteenth century until the end of the German Empire in 1918, the Church had enjoyed State recognition and financial support through the church tax, in addition to income from extensive property holdings. During the Weimar Republic and the Nazi Era, Church and State were officially separate, but the Church retained a privileged status, including tax support. After World War II, the Soviet occupation authorities at first continued the church tax and exempted church properties from expropriation. However, the decision to "build socialism through the GDR" led to a new *Kirchenkampf* (Church–State struggle) in the 1950s and 1960s. Church leaders remembered this period as a "brutal time" that they did not want to live through again. Memories such as that of a minister to youth being prohibited from preaching in the university church haunted them.[11]

The State effectively cut off the church tax in 1956 and delayed or refused to pay many of the rents and subsidies due the church. Repair and reconstruction of war-damaged church buildings generally stood last on the priority list for financial support from the state. Eventually some of the rents due were restored and, using these and donations, plus generous help from the West German churches, the East Germans managed slowly to rebuild, to keep their doors open, and to operate their extensive system of benevolent institutions. By the late 1980s western support had grown to more than one-fourth of all church income.[12] Finances, however, always remained precarious. Pastors had to live in decrepit parish houses on minimal salaries. The forty-year delay in the rebuilding of the Berlin Cathedral, even with proffered western financing, typified the regime's attitude. The State's decision in 1968 to demolish rather than rebuild the war-damaged university church in Leipzig, St. Johns, dating from 1240, provoked strong resentment. It was widely perceived that the State was using finances, allotment of newsprint, and scarce construction materials and even demolitions to harass and limit the churches.[13]

In addition to the problems of membership and finance, the Evangelical Church had to reconsider its position in its relations with State and society in postwar East Germany. In order to define the correct position and policies for the church, some theologians and church leaders looked to Luther, some drew on their experiences during the Nazi Era, and others improvised on the basis of contemporary trends and events. Luther's two-kingdoms theory guided one group to accept the GDR as God's instrument no matter how it defined itself, as soon as it became apparent the regime would become permanent. Bishops Moritz Mitzenheim and Albrecht Schönherr fathered the term "Church within Socialism," basing their position on a modified version of Luther's theory.[14] At the opposite pole, Bishop Otto Dibelius of Berlin-Brandenberg, reasoning from the same theory, denied the GDR's legitimacy as a proper government and thus justified his outspoken opposition.[15] Some disciples of Dietrich Bonhoeffer and Karl Barth also came to accept the regime, although for different and somewhat varying reasons. In comparison to the Nazi regime and its terrors, these survivors of the Confessing Church viewed the state's official recognition of the churches as a far better situation than they remembered. They listened to Barth, who disliked the West German Republic for its "harboring" of ex-Nazis and its renascent militarism, as well as its flagrant materialism; it certainly offered no good alternative.[16] A few "progressive" theologians in the state universities, such as Leipzig's Emil Fuchs, and some pastors in the CDU "bloc" party, discovered common ground in the "humanistic ideals" of both socialism and Christianity.

## THE 1978 CHURCH–STATE ACCOMMODATION

The famous summit meeting of Chairman Honecker with the leaders of the BEK, 6 March 1978, marked a change in the relationship between Church and State. The GDR's desire for international respectability, pressures on the state to fulfill the obligations undertaken in the Helsinki Agreements of 1975, and a rise in internal disaffection appear to have influenced Honecker to discard the divide and conquer strategy. He decided to abandon the more overtly hostile policies of the *Kirchenkampf* and to concede to the churches a legitimate and permanent place in the socialist GDR. However, the summit actually represented more a change of atmosphere than a broad general agreement, an entente of sorts, not an alliance. Several specific matters of great interest to the churches were agreed upon: Church access to State television four times a year; inclusion of pastors and full-time church workers in the state pension plan; compensation for expropriated church properties; permission for building new churches (but only if financed by West German marks). The joint communiqué referred vaguely to trust and cooperation and to protection of all citizens regardless of religious confession. Relations between Church and State were to remain tentative and often troubled, but an era of "peaceful coexistence" had replaced open belligerency. The State granted similar concessions to Catholics.

Most Church leaders and pastors viewed the new relationship favorably and charted a course down a broad middle way between unconditional acceptance of the regime and active opposition to it. They declined to join any of the State-sponsored collaborative organizations or any opposition groups, though some of them might occasionally speak out on some issue of direct concern. The new-style "State Church," as critics sometimes called it, lacked the high status and prestige of earlier times; nonetheless, it had carved out an officially recognized, if modest, niche for itself in the brave new world of real existing socialism in the GDR. It has been argued that among all churches in the Eastern Bloc countries, only the Catholic Church in Poland exercised more influence than the Evangelical Church in the GDR through its 4,000 clergy and 7,000 parishes.[17]

By the late 1970s a new generation had grown up in the GDR, a generation who had not experienced World War II and was less burdened by the past. Most Church leaders and members pragmatically accepted socialism, but a minority chose a more activist, oppositional stance on the issues important to them. Peace remained highly important, and after 1975 with the Helsinki Accords, expectations for more state permissiveness on human rights issues increased. Environmental pollution was worsening notably and

evoked major concern. Successes of the nonviolent civil-rights protest movement in the U.S.A. drew attention to Martin Luther King, Jr., then back
to Gandhi and to the teachings of Christ.[18] The "Luther Year," 1983, inspired a fresh look at the Reformer's successful defiance of authority on the
basis of moral and theological principles, especially in Saxony, Luther's
home territory.

The Luther celebration actually began with Reformation Day in November 1982, and Manfred Stolpe, a lawyer, church leader, and vice chair of
the BEK, came to Leipzig as guest speaker for the annual decade of prayers
for peace. In an address at St. Nicholas Church, he called to mind the
example of Luther and urged the listeners to take risks for peace on the
model of Luther.[19] He did not specify what sort of risks one should take.
Stolpe represented the high Church leadership, which by then had accom-
modated itself rather comfortably to the "Church within socialism." Risk-
taking for them usually took the form of mild protest letters, resolutions,
and oral complaints over coffee or cognac in polite meetings with state
officials.[20] Stolpe spoke a different language from the laity; nonetheless, the
idea of risk-taking out of principle resonated. A great gap was yawning between the high Church leadership and the grassroots discontent growing
steadily in Leipzig and elsewhere. The new generation, familiar with the
words and context of the song "We Shall Overcome," thought of risk in
more than rhetorical terms.[21]

Apart from occasional vague references to risk-taking, church leaders
turned their thoughts to what positive role the church should play in a state
which slowly but surely was achieving permanacy and even international
recognition. Beyond the basic decision on whether to accept the GDR as
legitimate, how should the churches and individual Christians respond to a
basically hostile atmosphere? Four options came to be most favored: (1)
withdrawal from involvement in public affairs; (2) focus on nonpolitical support for charitable causes; (3) reserved acceptance of socialism, but with
comment and criticism of social and political problems when necessary; and
(4) active support for victims of official abuses of power.[22]

The withdrawal option was favored by many clergy, and it was possibly
the most popular. Evangelicals continued to invoke Luther's two-kingdoms
doctrine to support their position. Most Roman Catholics and free church
leaders followed this approach also, at least until the late 1980s.

Support and advocacy for needy members of society offered endless opportunities for good works and an excuse for many to distance themselves
from public, political issues. The idea of "The Church for Others" drew
inspiration from Bonhoeffer. By the mid-1980s the Evangelical churches
operated 51 hospitals, 89 homes for the disabled and retarded, 226 homes
for aged, 32 orphanages and infant homes, 326 kindergartens, and 19 special daycare centers.[23] The 15,000 employees of these institutions did not
have to fear the threat of being fired or of job discrimination if they became

oppositional activists, and quite a number of them did.[24] Some clergy extended their advocacy to political victims: writers and activists under arrest needed church mediation, which often resulted in release or at least expulsion of these "troublemakers." Church mediators sometimes had a role in the ransom or "sale" of political undesirables to the FRG, a practice later much criticized.[25]

The reserved acceptance of the regime or "critical solidarity" defines the attitude and actions of other clergy and laity. The length to which they were willing to go toward accommodation varied greatly. Long before the late 1980s some churches opened their doors to activities that included prayer meetings, seminars, workshops, and musical and artistic events where no censors were present to prevent critical presentations on issues of concern.

The church's guardian role for human rights overlapped with concern for victims of society. Bishop Hans Fraenkel, a survivor of Nazi persecution, was among those who early on argued that the church should actively seek to become the conscience of society and to oppose abuse of power by the state. After the GDR signed the Helsinki Final Act in 1975, the new generation of dissidents increasingly appealed to church leaders to press the regime to live up to its obligations in the area of basic human rights. Church concerns led to new institutional structures such as the Ecumenical Assembly for Justice, Peace, and Protection of the Creation, which grew out of discussions at the Vancouver meeting of the World Council of Churches in 1983. This body put justice even before peace in its title, and its meeting in 1988 focused the Church's concern on human-rights issues.[26] Other church groups and human-rights groups outside the Church also participated. Local groups in Leipzig sent representatives to these meetings as far away as Basel, Switzerland, and established a coordinating committee in 1985 to organize workshops and programs to further this "conciliar process."[27]

The State remained displeased with all these choices, demanding instead the Church's unquestioning loyalty to the building of socialism.[28] Yet as the only autonomous public institution in the land, the church found itself by default the center of most of the oppositional activity. The prominent dissident, songwriter Wolf Biermann once remarked that only three options were open to dissidents wanting to flee the GDR: escape if possible through the Wall, commit suicide, or organize within the Church.[29] Given these choices, many non-Christians also began coming into the churches, attending special programs, workshops, and prayer meetings and asking permission for their own special agenda groups to use the relatively safe shelter of the church or the parish house for meetings. Some pastors, such as Pastor Führer in Leipzig, welcomed them with open arms, but most had reservations and ambivalent feelings. Should advocacy for victims and the needy or guardianship of human rights extend to allowing very miscellaneous crowds, mostly youth, often unfashionably dressed, to fill the pews and dominate church programs? Just as in the case of the bell-ringing in 1980, no clear, unambiguous answer ever received consensus among Church leaders and local pastors. In general groups needed to show some religious purpose that at least complemented or did not conflict with the church's position. As the prominent oppositionist Bärbel Bohley rather cynically put it, Church leaders wanted to regulate and confine the oppositionists.[30] In fairness, it should be noted that Church leaders constantly felt pressure from the State and were vulnerable to the cutoff or diminution of the very limited privileges grudgingly granted to them. They had thrust upon them the thankless tasks both of having to keep the oppositionists from being too openly political and critical, and of having to make excuses for them to authorities in order to get them out of jail, or out of the country.

## THE CHURCHES "WAGE PEACE"

The issue which from the onset of the Cold War garnered the most interest from Church leaders, laity, and nonchurch oppositionists was of course the "peace issue." The regime had constantly used, indeed overused, the word and automatically equated the building of socialism with the advancement of peace. The decisions to build up military forces, introduce conscription, and military instruction in the schools seemed contradictory to advancing peace and provoked criticism and the refusal of some young men to serve. In a concession unique in the Eastern Bloc, the state grudgingly allowed a form of alternative service, the *Bausoldaten*, "construction soldiers," in 1964, partly in response to Church pressure. These men were to construct and maintain military bases, wear uniforms, and be subject to military discipline. These limited concessions failed to satisfy everyone; some "absolute refusers" risked imprisonment by rejecting this option, too.

The Church made the peace issue its own. It supported and publicized the alternative service option while the state kept it very quiet. In 1965 a church statement declared that the construction soldiers and absolute refusers gave a "clearer testimony to the commandment of peace" than those serving in regular military units.[31] A majority estimated as high as three-fourths of those refusing regular military service were active church members. They organized Bible studies and tried to influence the regular soldiers they met while in the alternative service. Facing job discrimination when they finished their 18-month term, they formed their own support networks and held reunions and peace programs, often under church auspices. By the 1980s the 5,000 or more alumni of the construction units offered a fertile field for recruitment into opposition groups and activities.[32]

The peace issue illustrates well the shifts in the oppositional climate in the GDR and the role of the churches in it. Activist pastors increasingly spoke out and initiated activities without first securing prior approval of higher church leaders. The leadership, while often accused of timidity and compromise, actually grew more assertive as the "new Cold War" of the early 1980s elevated their concern for peace. A new chapter in the peace issue opened when activist pastor Christoph Wonneberger and the Initiative Group for Peace in Dresden petitioned the church leadership in May 1981 to reopen the question of alternative military service. Petitions carrying 5,000 signatures urged a new social alternative service (SoFd) that would undertake health and benevolent work and would be for two years instead of the regular eighteen months. The regional church of Saxony and the BEK did bring up the issue to State authorities, who quickly rejected it, but the issue continued to simmer. The peace issue led the regional Lutheran Church in Saxony for the first time to identify itself clearly with the growing peace movement in February 1982. Church leaders, fearing violence, persuaded young people planning an illegal peace demonstration on the anniversary of the 1945 Dresden bombing to opt instead for a program in a church.[33]

At the same time, Pastor Rainer Eppelmann joined with dissident Marxist philosopher Robert Havemann to issue a radical appeal for withdrawal of all troops from all of Germany and for its neutralization. The Berlin-Brandenburg Church hastened to distance itself from this radical Berlin Appeal, which earned Eppelmann a jail term, although Church leaders later expressed sympathy and secured his early release after only eight months in jail.[34] Other self-starting clergy continued in Eppelmann's train and created complications for Church leaders in their relations with the State; lay activists created even more. In 1983, the "Luther Year," Friedrich Schorlemmer, a pastor and professor at the seminary in Wittenberg, arranged for a local blacksmith to make a "swords into ploughshares" figure and set it up in the seminary courtyard while a church convention was in progress there and western media were present to publicize it.[35] How should the Church react to people like Jena's Roland Jahn and the bicycle parades, poster displays, and other activities organized by him and his friends? Or to the jazz and rock concerts in churches? Or to "environmental libraries" in churches, whose collections and publications ranged far afield to criticize the *political* environment?[36]

No easy answers appeared to such questions, nor did any total consensus develop among or even within the eight regional churches. Often Church leaders found themselves reacting to events and carried along by them, but they did struggle to devise positive ways to respond to peace issues as well as other issues. One of their most successful initiatives, if measured by attendance and interest, were the peace decades, the ten-day programs of information, inspiration, and prayer each November, beginning in 1980. The clever slogans such as "Frieden schaffen ohne Waffen" ("Wage peace without weapons") resonated, in contrast to such official counterslogans as "Peace must be armed." The powerful symbol of the blacksmith beating a sword into a ploughshare, borrowed from the Soviet sculpture given to the

United Nations and used for the 1982 decade, proved a lasting symbol of "swords to ploughshares" for the peace movement and greatly discomfited the authorities.[37]

## THE ACTIVISTS COME TO CHURCH

The peace decades produced many offspring. Prayer "watches" and "memorials" were old familiar forms of religious activity in Germany and offered many advantages from the viewpoint of sympathetic clergy and dissidents. They were held in church buildings and were presumed to be religious in nature, so police permits which were difficult or impossible to obtain were not needed. Prayer meetings offered a means whereby some of the energy and zeal of activists might be channeled. They brought nonchurchgoers into the churches and thus could be viewed as a form of "outreach ministry." Even so, in a large city such as Leipzig only a handful of pastors such as Führer, Wonneberger, Turek, and Kaden were ready to support regular peace prayer meetings, and only one church superintendent, Magirius, was willing to tolerate, even protect, them.[38] The attitude and policies of Church leaders toward unlicensed demonstrations and other oppositional activities in public places outside the churches remained much more consistent and clearer, at least until the fall of 1989: They officially distanced themselves from them. The bishops and higher leaders remained intent on preserving the limited and ever-tenuous concessions granted in the 1978 agreement and urged local superintendents and pastors to discourage public protests and disassociate themselves from them. As late as 18 September 1989, attenders at the Monday prayers in St. Nicholas Church were enjoined by Pastor Führer to go home quickly and quietly.[39] Did these injunctions substantially affect in any way the 1988–1989 public protests and demonstrations? Did all pastors really want to stop the demonstrations, or were some speaking *pro forma* in public, while offering private encouragement? When church leaders time and again assured the authorities they were doing all they could to keep the prayer meetings from spawning demonstrations afterward, were they at the least exaggerating their opposition? Was this part of a Church policy one pastor described as "pliant intransigence" toward the state?[40]

There is no simple answer to these questions. Church leaders and pastors disagreed among themselves; some modified their opposition and became more involved as events unfolded. Certainly, what happened on the streets outside the churches was quite different from what happened inside during the prayer hour. Clearly all the church leaders worried about the possibility that the demonstrators might turn violent and provoke massive police retaliation. One may assume the pastoral exhortations to go home quietly influenced many of the congregation inside, but by the fall of 1988, many never came inside and at least some of the emigrant applicants came with the full intention of making a public protest.

In Leipzig, Church leaders did more than discourage unlicensed public actions. In the fall of 1988 the superintendent excluded from peace prayers programming the opposition groups because he believed they had become too openly political. Yet when the state had permitted a public activity, the Olof Palme march for peace in September 1987, some activist pastors had come out and brought their parishioners with them. This was not the first time pastors had come out on the streets—and not the last. However, participation in *unauthorized* marches or public demonstrations of any sort remained officially taboo.

The police raid on the Environmental Library in Berlin's Zion Church parish house in November 1987 marked the opening of a new phase in both official and unofficial Church attitudes toward the activists. The leadership was shocked and grew bolder in their criticism of the whole existing system. Lay response in increased attendance at prayer meetings for those arrested indicated support. The Luxemburg-Liebknecht demonstration arrests further heightened tensions in January 1988.

When Bishop Werner Leich, chair of the Church Leadership Conference, met Honecker in March 1988 on the tenth anniversary of the 1978 agreement, he strongly urged a new dialogue on the issues of the day, but his words seemed to fall on deaf ears. At its fall 1988 synod, the BEK took up the call for public dialogue on social problems. It urged that no area be excluded and that criticisms be taken constructively, not labeled hostility to the state. Manfred Stolpe, widely regarded as the architect of the existing Church–State relationship, echoed this call in a public lecture immediately after the synod. He specifically raised anew the contentious issues of alternative military service and equal educational opportunity. He stated that the Church had an obligation to encourage its members to be active for reform.[41]

Events of 1989 provoked the Church into still more involvement. Church leaders issued a statement demanding investigation of the allegations of fraud in the May elections. By the summer and fall of 1989 the ambiguous slogan "Church within socialism" had lost its original meaning of the Church as a friendly if autonomous partner with the GDR regime.

The attitude of Leipzig's Church officials toward activism and demonstrations continued to parallel those of national Church leaders in early 1989, except that the city possessed a larger than average minority of activist pastors. It also had a proliferating number of opposition groups linked to the church, who grew increasingly militant and began to join, even lead, demonstrations by early September. The superintendent, pastor, and parish councils patched up differences among themselves and with the groups, which resumed their participation in the prayer meetings. Until mid or late September speakers at St. Nicholas continued the official line of urging Monday night attendees to go home immediately, but in fact the emphasis began shifting to admonitions to remain calm and nonviolent if they chose to participate.[42] Police roughness and arrests only pushed Church officials to preach nonviolence more emphatically, but not to oppose the demonstrations. Yet sharp divisions remained. Leipzig pastors, meeting after the demonstrations of 25 September, divided into three camps. About one-third believed that the opportunity to reform society was at hand and that the Church should lead. They were themselves willing to go out into the streets with the demonstrators in spite of the risks. A second third sympathized with the demonstrations but preferred to remain observers themselves. The remaining third considered the whole business too political and outside the duties of a pastor. The question of whether to allow the controversial and still illegal New Forum to meet in the churches was debated, but any decision was postponed.[43] The events of 9 October served as the turning point for the churches. The die had been cast by the time the Saxon church newspaper, *Der Sonntag*, reported with pride that Christians had joined in the demonstrations and added, "we should participate" in future, peaceful demonstrations.[44]

With the fall of Honecker, the entire Church–State relationship would undergo radical change as Krenz and his successors needed and sought Church support. Pastors and Church leaders would participate in and often preside over the public discussion forums and round tables that blossomed all over the GDR, beginning in Leipzig, as early as 23 October.[45] In the elections of March 1990 many Church leaders would enter the political realm. Twenty-one pastors, two theologians, and several prominent laypersons would win election to the GDR's first free parliament. In Leipzig, Superintendent Magirius would be elected president of the Leipzig city council.[46]

All of this was still in the future in December of 1989, a future that must have seemed as shrouded in murky fog as was Leipzig. Bells were ringing again, Monday evening, 18 December, and their tones resonated to the thousands of demonstrators filling the downtown streets to observe a profound silence as they held in hand their candles and remembered the victims of official repression and the tumultuous events of the year, especially the past few weeks. Doubtless the bells and the candles and the prayer service just concluded at St. Nicholas Church led some to think of the role of the churches in all these events. Some remembered with gratitude; posters saying "Thank you, Church" had appeared among the many posters and banners in recent demonstrations.[47] Others felt resentment because the Church leadership had seemed to them too timid and too accommodating to the regime. Still others may have meditated with mixed feelings. No one, however, could reasonably dismiss the role of the churches as insignificant or irrelevant. The Evangelical churches, being the only autonomous institutions in a tightly controlled, coordinated State and society, found themselves pushed and pulled from many sides. Both the State and the various opposition groups had sought to use them for their own purposes. As heirs of a centuries-old State–Church tradition, the Church leadership felt obligated to some involvement in public affairs, yet they were much divided over the nature and extent of it. The complex relationships with the State and the multifarious activities and programs of the Church allowed no escape. No clear boundaries between sacred and secular, the religious and political, existed. Opinions varied widely on whether or how much to theologize or how much to politicize the churches' positions and programs. Opinions had not only varied, they had constantly shifted, as the churches had taken up the peace issue and had extended their concerns for the needy to embrace human-rights issues, political victims, and environmental issues.

Church leaders had generally sought some middle way, to make the Church relevant and to have a positive impact on society without becoming too political or directly challenging State authority. The term "critical solidarity" was broad enough to cover the position of many Church leaders. They accepted the legitimacy of the GDR as a state and socialism as an economic system but insisted on the freedom to offer what they considered reasonable, limited, constructive criticism. A minority went further to shelter and help those even more critical and activist than themselves. They wanted the familiar catchphrase "building socialism" to take on a new meaning, one which included more equal treatment of and opportunities for Christians and other outsiders. They believed the non-Christians gathering in churches were needing and seeking hope for a better future.[48] They wanted the churches to offer hope to people for this world, as well as the next. When in July 1989 an estimated 60,000, two-thirds of them under 40 years old, gathered in Leipzig for a massive *Kirchentag* rally, one of the themes was "To Hope or to Give Up" (Hoffen oder Resignieren), with speakers urging their vast audience to see signs of hope in recent events, not merely to resign themselves to the status quo.[49]

It is beyond question that the churches offered a haven, a shelter for the growing number of oppositional groups. Within this haven the church buildings and parish houses opened opportunities for not only religious inspiration, but for sharing uncensored information and for airing opinions and criticisms.

These opportunities took many forms, but in Leipzig the most enduring, and arguably the most effective, were offered on Monday evenings at St. Nicholas Church. Here played out in microcosm the churches' contribution of haven and forum; here, more than in most places, Christians and non-Christians, groups with varying agendas, those desperate to emigrate and those determined to stay, all found something they needed and wanted. Despite many differences among themselves, they not only talked and prayed within the church walls, they attracted others who stood outside to talk and also to demonstrate. Long before September 1989, prayer meeting attendees began to join the protest marches. Church leaders controlled the prayer meetings only partially and with difficulty; the demonstrations growing out of them went beyond the control of either Church or State. In a closed society which constantly pressed the individual to conform, to go along, to give in, the Church steadfastly reminded the citizens of the GDR that they could rightfully expect more from life; they did not have to give up, to resign themselves to the status quo. They could hope—and they could gather in the churches to share and define their hopes and to find ways to act on them. This, perhaps, remains the churches' greatest contribution.

## NOTES

1. The Madrid negotiations were part of the continuing process set up by the Helsinki treaties of 1975; the strife referred to the Soviet–Afghan War and perhaps to the NATO plan for placement of intermediate missiles in West Germany. Quotations are from the materials prepared by the Confederation of Evangelical Churches (BEK) for the 1980 Peace Decade in Ehring and Dallwitz, 258. "To Hope or to Give Up" was a theme at the *Kirchentag* rally in Leipzig in July 1989. See report on Manfred Stolpe's address in the Church's newspaper, *Der Sonntag*, 23 July 1989, p. 1.

2. Ehring and Dallwitz, 259–60.

3. For an analysis of membership figures and trends, see Büscher in Reinhard Henkys, ed., 434–36. See also Goeckel, 9–15, 20–21.

4. Opp's representative sample of Leipzig citizens showed 18 percent claiming church membership in 1993 (126–27). Church tax cards reported only 13.9 percent (ibid., 257). For Saxony, see Bishop Hempel's comments in Udo Hahn and Johannes Hempel, *Annehmen und Freibleiben: Landesbischof i. R. Johannes Hempel im Gespräch* (Hannover: Lutherisches Verlagshaus, 1996), 41–42.

5. Roger Wood. *Opposition in the GDR under Honecker, 1971–1985* (New York: St. Martin's Press, 1986), 34.

6. See map with boundaries of regional churches in Goeckel, facing p. 1.

7. The five "merged" churches, continuing from Prussian times, retained their own organization, the Evangelical Church of the Union (EKU), while the three "non-Prussian" Lutheran churches had their own organization also, the United Evangelical Lutheran Church of the GDR (VELK). Reinhard Henkys, ed., *Bund der Evangelischen Kirchen in der DDR: Dokumente zu seiner Entstehung* (Wittenberg and Berlin: Eckart Verlag, 1970), 466–68.

8. The regional church of Saxony included the area of the pre–World War I kingdom of Saxony and should not be confused with the "Church Province of Saxony" to the north, centering in Magdeburg and old Prussian Lower Saxony.

9. Interview with Pastor Michael Turek at St. Mark's parish, July 1995.

10. Goeckel, 14–15; Joppke, 84.

11. Joachim Heise, "Kirchenpolitik von SED und Staat. Versuch einer Annäherung," in Günther Heydemann and Lothar Kettenacker, eds., *Kirchen in der Diktatur: Drittes Reich und SED-Staat* (Göttingen: Vandenhoek & Ruprecht, 1993), 126–30. Bishop Hempel in Hahn and Hempel, 27–28. Hempel was serving as youth pastor in Leipzig at this time.

12. Goeckel, 66.

13. Lindner, ed., 36.

14. Goeckel, 173–74. Besier. 13–15.

15. Goeckel, 61–62.

16. See the discussion of Barth's position and his 1958 "Letter to a Pastor" in Besier, 303–6. For a concise summary of the theological views that influenced Church policy toward the State see John T. Burgess; *The East German Church and the End of Communism* (New York: Oxford, 1997), 62–65.

17. Goeckel, 241–46; Kirsch, 122.

18. Pastor Christian Führer noted the irony of American and European Christians relearning principles of nonviolent moral opposition from the Hindu Gandhi. June 1993 interview.

19. Manfred Stolpe, *Den Menschen Hoffnung Geben: Reden, Aufsätze, Interviews aus Zwölf Jahren* (Berlin: Wichern Verlag, 1991), 70–74.

20. Schönherr, 355.

21. Bishop Schönherr, among others, recognized in retrospect this gap between the professionals and the parish people (ibid., 353).

22. Goeckel, 174–75.

23. Goeckel, 21–22. See Martin Reuer, "Diakonie als Faktor in Kirche und Gesellschaft" in Henkys, ed., 219–38.

24. Schwabe, 1995 interview.

25. Besier, 17.

26. See, for example, the lead article in the Church's newspaper, *Der Sonntag*, 15 January 1989, p. 1.

27. Dietrich and Schwabe, eds., 482–83.

28. Burgess, 4–5.

29. Quoted in Joppke, 86, from an article in the West Berlin *Tagezeitung*, 11 December 1987. Biermann was expelled from the GDR in 1976.

30. Comment quoted in Philipsen, 136.

31. John Sandford, "The Peace Movement and the Church in Honecker Years," in Gert-Joachim Glässner and Ian Wallace, eds., *The German Revolution of 1989: Causes and Consequences* (Oxford: Berg, 1992), 132–33.

32. Goeckel 186–87, 237–38; see also Kritsch, 127–29.

33. Goeckel, 260–62; Hahn and Hempel, 16.

34. For the Berlin Appeal text in English, see Woods, 193–97. See also Theo Mechtenberg, "Die Friedensverantwortung der evangelischen Kirchen in der DDR," in Henkys, ed., 393–94.

35. Swoboda, ed., 68–69.

36. For examples, see *Die Umwelt-Bibliothek* 22/24 (January 1987), p. 1ff., reproduced in Rüddenklau, 89–93.

37. Kaufman, Mundus, and Nowak, eds., 166–69ff. See also Latk, 46–47, for specific instances of conflict.

38. Friedrich Magirius, "Wiege der Wende" in Schneider, ed., 10–13.

39. Dietrich and Schwabe, eds., 399–400.

40. Detlef Pollack uses the term "geschmeidige Unnachgiebigkeit" in *Kirche in Sozialismus* 6/90, 240.

41. Stolpe, 166–79.

42. See Katharina Führer's interview with Superintendent Magirius. Führer thesis, 29–32.

43. Pastors' conference of 29 September (Sievers, 49–50). On 26 September New

Forum had publicized the rejection of its application to authorities for official recognition and appealed for the writing of letters to the Ministry of the Interior in Berlin to request a reversal of this rejection (Bohse et al., eds., 39–40.

44. *Der Sonntag,* 29 October 1989, p. 1. See also p. 1 of the 5 November issue.
45. Schneider, ed., 57–58.
46. Richard V. Pierard, "The Church and the Revolution in East Germany," *Covenant Quarterly* 48 (November 1990), 51.
47. Such posters appeared on 30 October, if not earlier. Schneider, ed., 74.
48. Hahn and Hempel, 30.
49. Reported in *Der Sonntag,* 23 July 1989, 1–2.

# 4

## Mosquitoes in the Air: The Church-Related Alternative Groups in Leipzig

As reported by the Press Office of the District Peoples Police Authority, on January 19 a group of persons sought to disturb the law and order of downtown Leipzig with a public gathering misusing the memory of Karl Liebknecht and Rosa Luxemburg. This provocation was halted by the authorities, 53 persons were taken away and after being questioned, were instructed and released.[1] (Front page report of *The Mosquito* [*Die Mücke*] 21–22 January 1989)

*The Mosquito* served aptly as the name for one of the underground publications of the Leipzig alternative groups, indeed the term well describes the groups themselves. Small and invisible most of the time, they nonetheless irritated the regime and attracted public attention with the "buzz" and "hum" of their programs and the "bite" of their public "provocations," such as the one reported above. Throughout its history the GDR had never quite succeeded in enlisting everyone in the "building of socialism" through the myriad of party organizations and state-sponsored groups and activities. The number of illegal opposition groups during the era 1949–1989 would doubtless rise into the hundreds if one counted every illicit group, however small and transient. Literary, artistic, theatrical, and musical groups as well as parish groups sometimes took on political dimensions, forming, dissolving, reforming. The number of participants fluctuated and is difficult to estimate. During the excitement of the early 1980s it peaked at perhaps 10,000; it declined, then swelled to exceed this figure in the spring of 1989.

Some 150–200 church-related alternative groups can be identified as functioning in the GDR during the 1980s, with 20 to 25 active in Leipzig.[2]

Many groups existed but briefly, lacked organization, and kept no records. In Leipzig the groups which can most easily be identified are those which survived by sheltering under the roof of the Evangelical Church and went public as participants in the synod committee charged with programming the peace prayers at St. Nicholas Church. These groups formed the nucleus and cutting edge of oppositional activity despite efforts of the authorities to repress them. They deserve much credit for leading Leipzig and the GDR into the era of mass demonstrations which brought down the regime with so little violence in 1989.[3] Many adjectives have appeared to define these groups: opposition, alternative, grass-roots, church-related, social-ethical. Each is arguably correct, at least in some sense. In this study the terms "alternative," "opposition" or simply "groups," will generally be used.

## ORIGINS, MEMBERSHIP, AND ACTIVITIES

Several questions concerning the Leipzig groups need to be addressed: what were their origins, their *raison d'être*, their agenda? Who joined and why? How did they function? What were the nature and significance of their ties to the churches, the prayer meetings, and the demonstrations? to other groups in the GDR? And most important, how significant was their contribution to the epic events of 1989 and 1990?[4]

Origins of the groups in the GDR can be traced back at least to the 1960s, although direct personal or organizational links with groups of the 1980s are difficult to document.[5] Tiny conspiratorial groups met secretly in apartments to show their discontent. Most often they were intellectuals and leftists, critical of the party, reacting to specific events such as the building of the Wall or the GDR's participation in invading Czechoslovakia to end the "Prague Spring" in 1968. Klaus Hugler, a youth pastor in Potsdam, recalled the meetings of church study groups and the influence of the "Jesus People" and charismatic groups from the west.[6]

Faced with a rigidly controlled society, whose governors aspired to complete domination of both public and private life, individuals in the GDR could find but few options to respond. They could of course enthusiastically accept, "get on board," and work for the rewards offered by the regime; or they could publicly conform and go along but without enthusiasm, keeping any reservations to themselves—*Anpassung* was the word for this practice, which apparently a great number of people followed. Official practices of surveillance and discrimination toward persons and groups who hesitated to go along achieved much success, but for a certain minority they failed. Indeed, if one accepts the views of reactance theory, oppressive policy can actually nurture oppositional thought and action, at least in some cases.[7] Among those who thought otherwise, some reacted with an inward migra-

tion, a "closet in the head," and led a sort of double life of outward conformity and secret dissent.[8] They sought refuge from their public world in
family, gardening, hobbies, or private sessions for sharing with a tight circle
of close friends. Young people turned to western rock music and deviance
from the cultural norms, especially with the wearing of long hair and blue
jeans. Pressures of the need for education and jobs, however, compelled
most youth into at least outward conformity, into subordinating their opposition. Many intellectuals confined themselves to the private niche they
could carve out in what some called a niche society.[9]

Yet for other individuals the private niche failed to suffice; they needed
social space as well as private space. It has been argued that resistance to a
dominant order finds no reality in pure thought; it exists as it is articulated
in a social process and in some sense, therefore, practiced.[10] Detlef Pollack,
the prominent Leipzig professor in the sociology of religion, has distinguished four specific motives that led individuals to take the risks of joining
alternative groups. First, some felt a desire to do something about contemporary problems such as threats to peace, the arms race, environmental damage, world hunger, or violations of human rights. These began as global
concerns and often paralleled organized efforts in the Federal Republic and
elsewhere, but as time passed more and more individuals focused on specific
issues in the GDR. Second, individuals joined groups for therapeutic reasons, that is, to find a setting in which to articulate their personal frustrations
and thus lessen them by some sort of activity among sympathetic peers.
Third, the desire for freedom for autonomous self-expression instead of
merely going along, and thus to find some meaning in life and sense of self-
worth. Fourth, curiosity, the search for some excitement, for some trendy
activity attracted some who were bored or felt marginalized in such an ordered, rigid society.[11] Pollack recognizes the fact that many Christians participated in the alternative groups, but his findings suggest that their
Christian faith and church membership did not serve as prime motivators
to join groups.[12] Others have argued for the importance of religious motivation, for religious dimensions to the secular agenda, and that a convergence of religious ideals and secular reform demands can be noted among
individuals participating in the groups.[13] Probably, many joined out of a
mixture of motives which shifted with time and events.

Motivations to overthrow the regime, or to resolve the "national question" by some sort of reunification, scarcely appear at all. The alternative
groups strove to gain a voice in reforming the regime; but they offered their
recruits no opportunities to make bombs or engage in any violent, revolutionary activities. The young people who composed the overwhelming majority of the groups had grown up with and accepted socialism in the GDR.
As Christian Joppke points out in his study of East German dissidents, one
of the triumphs of the regime was to convince most of its opponents of the
validity of socialism as a quasi-nationalist imperative only a traitor would

deny.[14] Moreover, any idea of merger with capitalist West Germany remained very distasteful, not an option for consideration.[15] For those who rejected the "voice" option offered by the groups the "exit" option to nearby West Germany remained. The more radical East German intellectuals and potential leaders of a more militant opposition regularly appeared in the west, either by expulsion or by choice. Groups formed by exit applicants generally focused only on how to expedite their departure, and many alternative groups shunned them as "quitters."

Very little evidence can be offered to demonstrate the primacy of explicit economic motivations. Despite complaints about shortages, long waiting periods for automobiles and appliances, and the absence of various imports such as the lack of bananas (which became proverbial), individuals did not join these groups or participate in actions aimed specifically at improving the national economy or increasing their own prosperity. Indeed, the demands of the environmental groups concerning, for example, the mining and use of lignite coal, if implemented, would have hurt production. Nor did the groups favor introduction of western-style capitalism; they remained overwhelmingly socialist revisionists.

## ISSUES AND ACTIONS

What then, did the groups hope to accomplish? What was their agenda for East Germany, if not revolutionary overthrow of the regime or economic betterment? Peace-related issues galvanized the groups that formed in the early 1980s. The introduction of conscription and the initiation of military studies in the schools especially stirred opposition. Reunions of ex-*Bausoldaten* offered an ongoing setting for criticism of the regime. The acrimonious debate in West Germany over the NATO decision to place intermediate-range ballistic missiles in the Federal Republic in 1979, with its implementation completed by 1983, resonated across the Wall in East Germany very strongly.

The peace issue produced a strong convergence between official church policy and the ideas of youthful dissidents, Christian and non-Christian. By 1983 several thousand people were in some way involved in groups all over the GDR. In March of that year 120 representatives of more than 30 groups met in Berlin under church auspices to coordinate their support for a Swedish proposal to establish a nuclear-free zone in central Europe.[16] Networking remained limited and erratic, however, and interest in peace issues ebbed somewhat in the middle 1980s, with the completion of missile placement and the pressure from the omnipresent Stasi. Nevertheless, various groups survived and continued to meet, finding shelter in the churches.

Some groups shifted their agenda from the peace issue to other concerns. The regime's repressive policies toward peace dissidents, including arrests and detentions, roused interest in human rights, which gained encouragement from the GDR's adherence to the Helsinki Human Rights Declaration. Interest in such issues as Third World poverty and hunger grew, not unrelated to similar interests in West Germany. The obviously deteriorating quality of air and water drew the attentions of some groups. The decaying infrastructure in cities such as Leipzig also aroused concern. Inflexible state policy, combining official denials of such problems, the refusal to enter into dialogue about them, and the severe repressive policies against "complainers" pushed some groups into more activism. The expulsion of prominent dissidents, such as that of Wolf Biermann in 1976, deprived the opposition of leadership but at the same time made a very deep, negative impression on many youthful dissidents-to-be.[17]

Who chose to take the risks involved in group engagement and from what socioeconomic background did they come? Such questions are difficult to answer with precision, since for security reasons groups kept few records and were constantly forming and reforming with overlapping membership. There is agreement that they were youthful, having an average age around thirty, with the most active individuals averaging in their middle twenties. The official description of group members as societal misfits from troubled family backgrounds can be dismissed as propaganda rather than truth.[18]

Class distinctions blurred in the groups. Many were of lower-middle-class origins. Discrimination in admissions to advanced education due to their family's or their own lack of conformity meant that few were university students or held degrees in higher education, except for theology students, who often played prominent roles as group leaders.[19] Other members came out of a proletarian background and, according to one interpretation, groups containing large members from the working class became oriented to an activist agenda sooner than others.[20]

Pollack offers four reasons people went beyond merely joining to become activists: (1) they had lost faith in the regime's rosy promises of future progress as they noted the growing disparity between propaganda and the realities of everyday life; (2) modernization and industrialization in the GDR left individuals sensing themselves to be only small cogs in a great impersonal machine; (3) the regime's effort to dominate all aspects of life and thought bred a sense of helplessness, frustration, and anger among those who "thought otherwise" because more individual freedom of expression was being allowed in the U.S.S.R. with *glasnost*; and (4) broadening contacts with the west due to television, tourism, and imported books provided increasing opportunities for GDR residents to learn how narrow and constricted their world was, and how meaningless for them. Groups offered a means of responding wherein an individual could find a new sense of self-worth, hope for the future, and a practical way to exchange ideas and engage in actions that might make a difference.[21]

A new group often passed through various phases. Members at first felt newborn and experienced a sort of psychological high from the camaraderie with others of like mind, as they pooled ideas and planned their role as the avant-garde for a renewal of society. This phase often gave way to a crisis phase as strong-willed individuals differed in their opinions about how to accomplish this and struggled for leadership. The Stasi's omnipresent informers quickly learned of new groups and systematically worked to infiltrate them and provoke crises.[22] A third phase followed as frustrations set in; attempted programs or actions failed to attract much attention or were aborted by the forewarned authorities; few new converts appeared, or membership actually declined; the general public remained aloof and not easily "reeducated." Being individualistic and suspicious of spies, members shied away from formal organization or regular meetings and meeting places, and thus their response to a crisis was often to withdraw from that particular group and join another or simply act on their agenda on an *ad hoc* basis with like-minded friends. Some groups survived by refocusing their agenda, as for example from rather vague efforts for world peace to local environmental or human-rights issues. Some gave up on any dangerous public activity and confined themselves to informational programs and self-improvement. They offered help and support to members of society in need, including those who refused military service, people suffering discrimination or jailed for their nonconformist actions, or the emigrant applicants. Groups which found consensus on a clear focus that inspired members to invest time and energy despite political risk were those which survived. Until 1989 a condition of survival for nearly all groups was also finding a shelter of legitimacy or quasi-legitimacy under the roof of the churches.[23]

## RELATIONS BETWEEN THE GROUPS AND THE CHURCHES

Isolated and persecuted by the state, the alternative groups sought refuge with the churches and accepted the advantages they gained: a form of legal recognition as church-related organizations; places to meet in churches and parish halls without need of police permits or fear of police raids; and support when they got in trouble or in jail. Sympathetic pastors lent respectability and offered leadership in many parishes, and everyone knew that pastors were almost never arrested. The Church thus served as an "island of separateness in the totalitarian sea," as did the Catholic Church in Poland and to some extent in other countries in Eastern Europe.[24]

In addition to these practical advantages, the groups and the churches shared certain major interests and goals: peace, first and foremost, and also sensitivity to abuses of human rights, to environmental problems, and to people with various economic and social problems. This convergence of ideals and concerns served as a major reason for collaboration between the groups and the churches during the 1980s. Lectures such as the one given by Heino Falcke, a prominent clergyman, in Leipzig on the "ambivalence of progress," which questioned the priority of technological advance at the expense of the environment resonated well among the groups.[25] Other churchmen, such as Ehrhart Neubert, discovered strong Christian motivations behind the causes to which the groups devoted themselves, which brought groups and churches increasingly together. Even though the institutional church had been marginalized by the regime and suffered from declining membership and stagnation in its traditional organizations, people could experience their religious-political values confirmed, expressed, and acted upon within the church-related alternative groups. Churches nearly empty on Sundays might be bustling with activities during the week as groups met there.[26] Some sociologists view the groups as acting almost exclusively from secular political, not religious, motives and see their alliance with the churches as generally a marriage of convenience. However, they agree that the tie with Christianity and the churches offered renewed hope and stability to the groups and encouraged them to seek positive nonviolent courses of action.[27]

Much of the disagreement about the role of the groups and their relationship with the churches grows out of the difficulty in generalizing about them. They remained quite diverse in philosophy and actions with shifting memberships and changes in focus. A regular church parish youth group, sponsored by its youth minister, which took up controversial issues might be light-years away from a gathering of Marxist intellectuals, even as both expressed discontent with the status quo in the GDR. Group diversity and changeability also made it difficult for the Evangelical Church to formulate any precise policy or even general guidelines about the groups, and indeed it never did. The decentralized nature of church government left most of the decision making on such questions to local superintendents, pastors, and parish councils, not the bishops or their national leadership conference. Perhaps that was fortunate for the groups, because it shielded them from any uniform control from above by state-pressured high Church officials. Also it seems that some pastors and parish councils remained more open-minded toward the groups than did the higher clergy.[28]

Cogent reasons persuaded the Church, or more accurately, churches, to shelter and encourage most of the groups: they came as people in need, seeking help, and their agenda corresponded or appeared to correspond to Christian ideals about peace, justice, and respect for human dignity and for God's Creation. Some pastors, enduring a marginalized life in a hostile society, with only a few elderly parishioners in near-empty buildings, found a new *raison d' être*, a confirmation of purpose, as they worked with excited young people in the groups.

Officially recognizing the groups and allowing them to use church facilities proved a good deal easier than integrating or controlling them. Strong-willed, determined group members who were taking serious risks to challenge state policy had no intention of submitting meekly to bishops, church superintendents, or pastors. Moreover, their tactics and style often came in conflict. Church leaders preferred quiet diplomacy, while some groups looked for dramatic ways to make public statements and attract media attention in the west. The churches wished to preserve the 1978 agreement and the status and security it offered them, while the groups cared little about such things. The churches favored small steps through occasional, carefully worded resolutions, while some groups wanted to bring about comparatively drastic, immediate change through bold public actions, and they expected the churches to bail them out when they ran into trouble.[29]

Thus, the relationships between churches and groups experienced continuous tension and no little acrimony. Church leaders complained that they and the church buildings, especially St. Nicholas Church, were being "used" for politicized programs and questioned just how Christian some of the groups and their members actually were. Activist group members engaged in criticism of the regime, unfurled political banners at prayer meetings, and protested Church restraints imposed on them. Yet underlying these tensions lay a broad basis of general agreement and mutual interest which held them together.

A minority of the clergy accepted the groups as arms of the church for social involvement even if they were not all Christian, nor their agenda motivated specifically by Christian principles. The groups in turn accepted the sponsorship of the churches not only from stark necessity, but because of their respect for certain pastors, because of shared goals, and because of the appeal of the nonviolent approach, both ideologically and practically. Even though the demand "When we march the bishop ought to be marching in the front rank" failed to bring any bishops out into the streets, some pastors did march, while others encouraged marching, and the bishops did intercede with authorities to have marchers who were arrested released.[30]

The most difficult generalization of all to make about the groups is an evaluation of their nationwide impact on the decline and fall of the GDR. Their membership was never large, possibly no more than 10,000 to 15,000 in a country of 16 million, even as late as the summer of 1989.[31] The general public was unaware of their existence and almost never saw their newsletters. The surprisingly small vote for the Alliance 90 combination of groups in March 1990—only 3 percent—might lead one to dismiss them as noisy but very minor actors in events in the GDR. Interpretations focusing more on qualitative than on quantitative information have, however, evaluated their role as extremely important, even essential. The most effective method to arrive at an accurate evaluation can be studies which focus on groups in given localities. Berlin, the GDR capital, deserves study, as do other major cities such as Dresden and smaller towns such as Jena and Plauen.[32] However, Leipzig remains arguably the most important place, due to its prominent role in the events of 1989. Many argue that Leipzig was where the "revolution" of 1989 really began.[33]

## GROUP ACTIVITY IN LEIPZIG

The choice of Leipzig for focus on the groups can be defended for several cogent reasons: this large city, the "other" or "unofficial" capital of East Germany, suffered from the problems that beset the country, often in aggravated forms; the "Leipzig scene" of group activity developed early and, along with atypical Berlin and occasionally Dresdan, gained national prominence. Leipzig led the whole GDR by mid-1989 in oppositional activity. Those interested in the relationship of the churches to the political opposition can find in Leipzig a rich opportunity for investigation due to the more structured and generally more intense and friendly relationship there. Ties between Leipzig groups and those clamoring to emigrate grew closer than elsewhere, and the would-be emigrants played a dramatic part in 1989. The failures and successes of the groups' efforts to network among themselves and with groups elsewhere can also be instructive. Thus, the goals, the activities, and the diversity of the Leipzig groups can serve very helpfully to illuminate the national oppositional scene in the 1980s.

The situation in Leipzig offered all the elements that were most likely to breed opposition in the GDR, and several in an intensified form. The Leipzig historian Helmut Zwahr writes of a process of self-destruction in the city during the postwar era, while Kurt Drawert compares the city to an organism suffering from cancerous metastasis.[34] The regime's notions of socialist renewal included demolition instead of reconstruction of a number of buildings that had constituted a prominent part of the city's cultural heritage, even the demolition of some that had survived wartime bombing, such as the thirteenth-century Gothic university church. Less-than-minimal maintenance allowed the entire infrastructure to deteriorate. The Pleisse River became so foul and odorous from industrial pollution it had to be put underground. Coal mining advanced right to the city limits. At the same time, East Berlin enjoyed priority as the GDR's capital and showcase and Dresden's famous palaces were carefully rebuilt. Population declined steadily in this smoggy, dreary setting, down 70,000 from 1970 to 530,000 by the late 1980s.[35]

Yet the second city in a country generally without "windows" did possess its special "window" to the outside world: the international trade fairs held annually in March and September, during which citizens could see for themselves examples of the growing gap between the world economy and their own; and experience a little more freedom or at least tolerance from officials under the bright light of the presence of 100 or more reporters from the international media. Fair weeks were marked by opera premieres and special cultural events and by guest lectures in St. Nicholas Church, but also by a second economy skirting the edges of legality in private room rentals to visitors, influx of foreign currency, private deals for scarce goods and banned books, even special arrangements for prostitution.[36]

Being the cultural, educational, and economic center for a large part of the southern GDR, Leipzig not surprisingly became a center for opposition groups. Indeed, the city could trace a long history of nourishing oppositional thinking and organizing back to Martin Luther and in modern times to the rise of the Social Democratic Party in the late nineteenth century, and the Goerdeler circle and Confessing Church in the Nazi era. It is fascinating to speculate on the influence of this weighty heritage, but no direct organizational continuity can be documented. Nevertheless, it may be argued that a certain independence of spirit lingered in Saxony and particularly in Leipzig, where unlicenced groups met and public protests occurred long before the 1980s. Writers, intellectuals, and artists, many employed in Leipzig's publishing trade, formed private groups to discuss subjects too sensitive for public discourse and books banned by authorities. Sometimes they mimeographed newsletters with interesting titles such as *Sno-boy*. A few engaged in actions such as surreptitiously posting slogans for peace and justice in streetcars or in prominent public places such as the "Battle of the Nations" monument or distributing selections from banned books such as Rudolf Bahro's *Alternative*.

Some music groups utilized folk music, slipping in their own references to current political problems, while others skirted or defied official prohibitions on western rock music. Official efforts to break up these groups and stop their public activities generally succeeded through use of arrests, fines, imprisonment, and discrimination in education and employment. As early as 1964, Leipzig police had used brutal force to break up youthful "hippie" protests in the prominent Leuschner Square.[37] Music held a very strong attraction to these youth and offered opportunities for protest. In the 1970s the *Musikgruppe Renft* in Leipzig attracted a considerable following, making two LPs before its ties to oppositional groups led to imprisonment of some of its members, who were then regarded as martyrs. Protest music also early sought and found refuge in those churches whose pastors welcomed the influx of youth into a place where the police could not arrest them for illegal assembly.[38]

The groups of the 1980s in Leipzig generally followed the patterns of composition, focus, and activity discussed above. By early 1989 some 20 to 25 groups existed, with a following estimated at 300. Age of members averaged around 25 to 30 and size of the groups around 15 with males outnumbering females in a ratio of about 70 to 30 percent. Rarely did persons over thirty involve themselves. Many worked in service jobs for church-sponsored institutions, where they did not face dismissal or discrimination. Few university students joined, since any participation meant certain expulsion. Only the theological seminary students could safely participate, and many did, providing a large share of the leadership; indeed, theology students led in the founding of several Leipzig groups. However, it should be noted that more than a few had entered theological studies because all other doors to education were closed to them; after the *Wende*, some shifted to other areas of study or to politics.[39]

This new generation of alternative groups that began emerging in Leipzig and elsewhere drew members from several constituencies, perhaps the first and foremost being the ex-*Bausoldaten* and those who refused even that military alternative service. Ever since the reintroduction of military conscription in 1962, a few had refused to serve and usually received prison terms. When the alternative service option of "construction soldier" was created in 1964, some chose that option. Others continued to refuse even alternative service, since it utilized military discipline with uniforms and involved construction on military bases. By the late 1970s between 4,000 and 5,000 in the GDR had either gone through the *Bausoldaten* program or endured the penalties of total refusal. As outsiders to the official order, they had already suffered multifarious discrimination and therefore were accustomed to meeting together for mutual support. Since many of these had refused on religious grounds, they sought and found a haven to meet in their churches.

## PROMINENT LEIPZIG GROUPS AND THEIR AGENDAS

In Leipzig, ex-*Bausoldaten* and total refusers had formed a very active group, the Working Group in the Service of Peace (*Arbeitsgruppe Friedensdienst*) or AGF. Events after 1978 stimulated this group to organize peace "circles" within several of the youth parish groups. Its agenda focused on prayers and informational programs for peace, especially the establishment of a genuine, nonmilitary alternative service program. The city youth pastor, Wolfgang Gröger, encouraged and sponsored this group between 1981 and 1987. Its leaders were the prime movers in organizing the continuation of the St. Nicholas peace prayer meetings in 1981–1982 and in some of the earliest demonstrations, including the candlelight demonstration in 1983. They also organized peace seminars from 1982 to 1985, which drew in people from areas well beyond Leipzig.[40] They popularized the "Swords to Ploughshares" insignia as badges sewn on jackets and on other clothing which so bothered the regime. Members of this group were among the first in the 1980s to suffer heavy fines and imprisonment of up to two years for their activities.

It would be difficult if not impossible to list every group that ever functioned as part of the oppositional scene in Leipzig during the 1980s. There is need, however, at least to mention some of the more prominent groups and the umbrella organizations of their networks if one is to begin to understand their role in the earthshaking events of 1989. The "group scene" remained ever fluid, as membership and focus changed and new groups split off. Nonetheless, one can distinguish groups according to their agendas: some continued to focus on peace issues; some sought to help the "victims" of society, prisoners, ex-prisoners, sufferers of discrimination, and the needy at home and abroad; some worked for recognition of human rights and for a more open society; and some focused on environmental problems. The emigrant applicants' groups flourished but changed continuously in 1988 and 1989 as many members were expelled or allowed to emigrate. Then there were the coordinating groups, which sometimes fulfilled missions of their own. Some drew from the city, some from the Leipzig district and beyond, some functioned only within the boundaries of one of the two church superintendencies or a parish in Leipzig and its suburbs.

In addition to the AGF, the Working Group for Military Service Questions at the Church Youth Office (*Arbeitsgruppe Wehrdienstfragen beim Jugendpfarramt*), founded in 1985, agitated for a "social peace service as a nonmilitarist alternative" to military service. They also wanted to establish the right for a conscientious objector to refuse totally. The group sheltered under the protection of Youth Pastor Gröger and his successor Youth Pastor Kaden, with encouragement from Pastor Wonneberger of St. Luke's. Many of the members were apparently ex-*Bausoldaten* or total refusers.

The Gohlis Working Group for Peace (*Arbeitsgruppe für Frieden Gohlis*) became one of several parish groups actively promoting peace issues. This group was founded in 1985 and led by Gotthard Weidel after he became pastor of the Peace Church of Leipzig-Gohlis. They planned programs in the parish hall on peace issues, and their concerns broadened to include environmental problems and consumerist lifestyle. They withdrew from programming the St. Nicholas prayers in June 1988. They cited readers' letters in *Kontakte*, an underground publication, to support their concern about too much influence on the programs coming from the emigrant applicants to the neglect of their agenda.[41] Peace issues continued, of course, to hold special importance for them as for many other groups, even when not their only focus.

Concerns for human rights and a more open, less censored society grew out of peace concerns quite logically and naturally for some of the groups in Leipzig. The advent of Gorbachev and *glasnost* in the Soviet Union brought them hope for change in the GDR. Also, a new generation too young to remember the repressive years of the 1950s and 1960s was coming of age. The status quo policies of the Honecker regime based on old agreements such as the 1978 Church–State settlement seemed to them antique and inadequate, at the least. "The generation of the late 1980s wasn't content with that anymore," according to one of its Leipzig members.[42] Their role models were not the geriatric Politburo members, nor did well-worn slogans about "building socialism" through conformity hold any appeal.[43]

One of the strongest and most effective groups to take up human-rights issues was the Working Group for Justice (*Arbeitskreis Gerechtigkeit*), the AKG. Theology students and former students founded this group in December 1987. They modeled their organization on the Berlin-based human-rights group Initiative for Peace and Human Rights (*Initiativ Frieden und Menschenrechte*), the IFM, and maintained close ties with it. The leaders of AKG skillfully organized subgroups which indicate the breadth of their activities: Eastern Europe repression, emigration, political prisoners, environment, newsletter, and media. Each subgroup consisted of five to ten members with a coordinating committee of six to oversee them all and sponsor branch groups in nearby towns. This group pioneered in bringing together those wanting to exit the country with those intending to stay, but wanting a voice in reforms. In Berlin and other places, suspicion and recriminations marked the relations between "exit" and "voice" dissidents, but much less so in Leipzig, which by 1989 had surpassed all other cities in the number of legal and illegal emigrants. As one member recalled, his group "always particularly worked with those people who were wanting to leave the country because we shared many of the same ideas. Our motivations were the same, except we wanted to stay and change things, and they said, 'We just can't stand it any longer.' "[44] AKG developed extensive contacts with opposition groups in other Eastern Bloc countries and sought to publicize human-rights violations there as well as at home, using contacts with the western media. Tensions developed within the group over whether to give priority to informational programs or engage in riskier conspiratorial activities such as distributing leaflets or smuggling information to western reporters. Unlike many of the groups, AKG possessed its own (unlicensed) duplicating equipment for publishing and after November 1988 a full-time coordinator.[45] Although not large in numbers and with extremely ambitious plans, AKG accomplished amazing things, including distribution of a mail survey to determine the difficult situations of would-be emigrants—to which over 2,000 people responded. Its inclusion of the would-be emigrants enabled it to mobilize more people than other groups. It worked closely with a group called AGM (see below), collected a sort of library of information on human-rights issues in cooperation with them, and ultimately merged with it in September 1989 to form the Leipzig branch of the IFM.[46]

The AGM, Working Group for Human Rights (*Arbeitsgruppe Menschenrechte*), shared many of the goals of the AKG, but it was tied more closely to the Church, indeed to one church and one pastor. In 1987 Pastor Wonneberger organized it in his parish, St. Luke's, where it remained headquartered. It serves as a prime example of a church group which reflected closely its pastor's interests yet succeeded in a cooperating with other groups

on projects of common interest. Wonneberger had close ties to Czechoslovakia and Eastern Europe and great concern about persecution of dissidents.
He was also very interested in the establishment of a social service alternative
to military service, and so these became the priority items on the group's
agenda. Not only informational programs but bold petitions and open letters to public officials and to *Volkskammer* (parliament) members issued
from this little group, which rarely exceeded 15 members but attracted considerable attention. In addition to the joint library, they helped organize the
alternative *Kirchentag* (Church Day Rally) and published a newsletter, *Forum für Kirche und Menschenrechte (Forum for Church and Human Rights)*
in 1989.[47] They also joined with AKG to publish *Die Mücke* (the Mosquito),
a lively newsletter, and with AKSK (discussed below), and four groups outside of Leipzig to organize a national human-rights group.[48]

The formation of national groups proved quite difficult in the GDR due
to the efficiency of the Stasi and also to differences among the groups. The
call for a national human-rights group, issued in December 1988, led
quickly to the arrest of the individuals involved. In spite of this, the AGSM,
Working Group on Human Rights in the GDR (*Arbeitsgruppe zur Situation
der Menschenrechte*), did organize and it facilitated exchange of information
about human-rights violations throughout the country. Its leaders were theology students and it sponsored monthly meetings in the theological seminary in Leipzig for representatives from all over the GDR. In 1989 it also
merged into the Leipzig Chapter of the IFM.[49]

Another human-rights-oriented group, AKSK or Working Group for Solidarity in the Church (*Arbeitskreis Solidarische Kirche*), held to a slightly
different focus even as they shared many of the concerns of other groups.
Theology students from various parts of the GDR organized it in 1984 and
claimed 400 members by 1988, some 25 of them in Leipzig. They gathered
in Leipzig twice a year at the theological seminary to discuss how they and
the other church-related groups might achieve more voice in the affairs of
the Church—and also of the State. Leipzigers dominated the editorial staff
of the group's publication, *Solidarity Church*.[50]

Theology students in Leipzig seemed to find time to work in many organizations. The activity of a Berlin group inspired formation in September
1987 of the Working Group on Delimitation and Openness (*Arbeitskreis
Abgrenzung und Öffnung*). The members, numbering about 10, held programs to discuss concerns about the exclusion of most GDR citizens from
the real political process and the official policy of delimiting, that is, totally
separating East Germany from West Germany.

Several other groups concerned with human rights and political reform
operated on the fringes of the church-alternative-group scene; generally they
also favored direct action. Mockau Action (*Offene Arbeit Mockau*) groups
developed in parishes in Mockau, a suburb of Leipzig, as early as the late
1960s but were only very loosely associated with the churches. By the mid-

1980s nine groups offered youthful discontents places to meet and opportunities to engage in political protest actions.

The Democratic Initiative Group (*Demokratische Initiative—Initiative zur demokratische Erneuerung* or DI), organized and distributed fliers in January and February 1989, becoming one of the new nonchurch political movements of that year. Members cooperated with the other groups in observing the May elections and contesting the results and in the fall merged into New Forum.

Expressions of discontent finally even reached into the sacred precincts of the Party. Some 15 young people, many of them Party members, arranged a lecture series in November 1988 at the League of Culture building to discuss the changes in the Soviet Union. To escape official restraints, some of these later organized their own group, New Thought (*Neues Denken*), in the spring of 1989. Although never tied officially to the churches, one of their leaders had spoken at a St. Nicholas prayer meeting in June 1988, and several were regular attendees.[51]

Discontent over the ever-worsening environmental situation in the GDR gave birth to alternative groups focusing on this problem. The leading group, the Working Group for Environmental Protection (*Arbeitsgruppe Umweltschutz* or AGU), organized in 1981 under sponsorship of the district youth pastor's office, drawing inspiration from the church's Environmental Research Center in Wittenberg. At first its efforts were directed mainly toward education, with the hope of raising the awareness and altering the behavior of individuals. They encouraged the use of bicycles instead of cars and promoted tree planting. They also began to address the environmental situation more generally, calling attention to the very lax enforcement of the weak antipollution laws. Unresponsiveness of state officials hardened into hostility in the face of embarrassing questions raised by this group. The group itself, while continuing its educational work, joined with other groups in unauthorized public actions on Earth Day in June each year, such as the pilgrimages along the polluted Pleisse River. The group's newsletter, *Streiflichter*, pointed out that the state's policy toward the once-scenic Pleisse illustrated all too typically its general policies. When the pollution stench became too heavy to ignore, the river had been channeled through Leipzig underground and thereafter ignored with the hope that citizens would react according to the old saying, "Was ich nicht weiss, macht mich nicht heiss" ("What I know not, won't make me hot"). This group grew to more than 70 members with nine subgroups, quite large in comparison to the others. It developed extensive contacts with environmental groups in the Federal Republic.[52]

Some members thought the AGU had focused too much on discussion and not enough on action. About 30 broke away to form the IGL, Group Initiative for Life (*Initiativgruppe Leben*), in May 1987. They earned the distinction of being the first and for nearly two years the only group whose main purpose was public action. They met in private apartments, not churches, though still tied with the church groups and encouraged by Pastor Wonneberger. Undeterred by Stasi harassment, criticism from more cautious groups, or the reservations of church leaders, they embarked on one project after another. They also expanded their concerns to include human rights and other issues. They initiated the Pleisse marches, distributed leaflets, posted placards, and unfurled banners in churches and even in public places. The street music festival they sponsored in June 1989 drew nationwide attention—and as usual detention of participants by authorities. They ran a sort of café in one of the city's innumerable abandoned buildings. The IGL remained individualistic to the extreme, with no chairperson or formal organization, indeed many if not most of their public actions were carried out by individuals on an *ad hoc* basis without any formal group approval or plan.[53]

Other groups appealed to certain constituencies. Bärbel Bohley, the "mother of the underground," organized the women's peace group Women for Peace (*Frauen für den Frieden*) in Berlin in 1982, paralleling women's groups in the FRG and Western Europe, to oppose conscription of women and the accelerating armaments race. The Berlin group preferred to be outside the churches, yet they often held prayer services and other activities in a Berlin church. A Leipzig chapter formed in 1984. Never large, the 15 or so members focused on opposing military studies in schools and kindergartens and on women's rights and family issues so vigorously that they quickly attracted the attention of the Stasi. Non-Christian women joined the Christian founders as the group obtained a room for its headquarters within St. Nicholas Church.[54] Christians out of Leipzig's small Catholic population formed a peace group also, the Grünau-Lindenau Peace Group (*Friedenskreis Grünau/Lindenau*), which worked closely with the Protestant groups and extended its concerns to human rights all over Eastern Europe, especially Czechoslovakia.

The groups that drew their members from the emigrant applicants fluctuated in size and leadership, due to the their transient nature as members received their exit visas, were expelled, or somehow escaped. However, those groups that interested themselves in supporting emigrant applicants, political prisoners, and other "victims" in society grew in numbers and activities. In 1986 Pastor Führer sponsored a group called Hope for Those Wanting to Emigrate (*Gesprächskreis "Hoffnung für Ausreisewillige"*) at St. Nicholas Church; District Youth Pastor Kaden early in 1988 organized the so-called Kaden Group (*Kadenkreis*), which sometimes attracted as many as 100 to its meetings. Groups such as these offered venues for the would-be émigrés to share the problems that had led them to apply for exit visas and also the frustrations and discrimination they suffered as they waited. They also continually lobbied Church and State officials to help them get out.

Victims of the regime such as these emigrant applicants and other malcontents whose activities landed them in jail found help and encouragement from groups who advertised their arrest, prayed, and worked for their release, then offered support after they went free but faced discrimination. The Working Group for Released Prisoners (*Arbeitskreis Treff für Haftentlassene*) became one such example. It began in October 1987 with the goal of helping reintegrate ex-prisoners, especially political prisoners, into society and later extended its concern to prisoners' rights and prison conditions as part of the churches' social ministry. After the raid on Berlin's Environmental Library in late November 1987, special prayer meetings and new groups sprang up all over the GDR, including, of course, Leipzig. The Coordinating Group for Peace Prayers for the Prisoners (*Kontaktgruppe Friedensgebet für die Inhaftierten*) formed in Leipzig in January 1988, when some young people began to meet for prayer and information at the district youth parish office. They took up the role of Leipzig representatives in a nationwide campaign to free the captive Berliners. After these prisoners were indeed released, the group attempted to maintain a network of contacts and draw other groups into helping maintain a "contact center" (*KOZ Trägerkreis*) but with limited success.

Several groups formed out of concern for needs in Eastern Europe and the Third World. Action for Reconciliation (*Aktion Sühnezeichen* or ASZ) pioneered in this area as early as 1958, sending members on their vacation time into the east to work as Christians in reconstructing or in helping victims of Nazism. Superintendent Magirius had led the Berlin chapter before coming to Leipzig. Among the new generation of groups, the Initiative Group for Hope in Nicaragua (*Intiativgruppe Hoffnung Nikaragua* or IHN) began in 1981 to raise money to support development projects in Sandinista Nicaragua. The group encountered State resistance to sending money abroad and to its independent art shows, but it found common ground with other groups. The Leipzig chapter of some 20 members enjoyed support from the Leipzig-East Church District. The lecture series the group sponsored in the summer of 1987 moved from hope for Nicaragua to hope for reform and for freedom for opposition in the GDR.[55]

## GROUP COORDINATION AND NETWORKING

Coordination among such diverse groups with divergent goals never proved easy. The negative factor of their discontent with the regime united them, while the chief positive uniting factor remained their common ties with the churches. Overlapping memberships in various bodies tied together, at least loosely, an increasing member of Leipzig groups and offered opportunities to network among themselves and with other groups around the country. Three such umbrella groups particularly influenced events: the

"Peace Concrete" conferences, the Ecumenical Assembly for Peace, Justice, and Protection of the Creation, both national bodies, and Leipzig's own District Synodal Committee for Peace and Justice.

Peace Concrete (*Frieden Konkret*) served as the interesting name for a series of nationwide gatherings of representatives of peace groups from all over the GDR. These gatherings allowed members to break out of their isolation by meeting and sharing ideas and information with activists from other places. Leipzig groups were always well represented. Efforts to convert the conference into an organized political group never succeeded, apparently because of the divergent opinions and goals of those attending. The conference met in Leipzig-Connewitz in February 1987 and inspired the formation of Leipzig's AGM.[56]

Although the Peace Concrete conferences gained the nickname of alternative group "synods," the Ecumenical Assembly with its conciliar process offered a more structured umbrella and regularized means for intergroup activity. The GDR regime had allowed, even encouraged, representatives of its churches to participate in international church organizations such as the Lutheran World Federation and the World Council of Churches (WCC). It hoped thereby to promote its long campaign for diplomatic recognition, to enhance its image as a peace-state, and remove some tarnish from its reputation on human rights. At the Vancouver meeting of the WCC in 1983, GDR church representatives proposed that the council undertake a special effort to promote peace and justice and to protect the creation, i.e., the environment. The council adopted their proposal and planned for a world meeting on these subjects. Member churches were encouraged to sponsor programs—the conciliar process—to inform members in preparation for the world meeting, scheduled for Basel, Switzerland, in May 1989. In East Germany the Evangelical Church Federation encouraged member churches and local parishes to become involved and planned three nationwide assemblies, which were held in 1988 and 1989 in Dresden (twice) and Magdeburg. This series of meetings played a major role in stimulating and drawing together the various groups.[57]

The conciliar process proved to be much more than just another series of church meetings, especially for Leipzig. A special committee for the Leipzig-East Church District called the District Synodal Committee for Peace and Justice (*Bezirkssynodalausschuss für Frieden und Gerechtigkeit* or BSA) came into existence in November 1985 to implement the conciliar process. The Leipzig-East Church superintendent, Magirius, initiated this committee in response to the national church federation's call for participation; however, in Leipzig this committee served another purpose as well. Tensions had developed between some of the more activist groups and their pastor sponsors and also their membership had extended beyond any one parish. The new arrangement allowed the groups to send representatives to the BSA and so be considered church-related without having to be tied to one parish and its pastor. Thus, the BSA tied most of the alternative groups to the churches; it also tied them to each other, offering opportunities for exchange of ideas. Nine groups adhered to this committee from the outset, and others later joined. Magirius put the committee in charge of programming the Monday peace prayers at St. Nicholas Church, which became one of its most important functions.[58] The three-member executive committee of the BSA stated their view of the purposes of the BSA to Superintendent Magirius shortly after it began: to include all the groups interested in issues concerning peace, justice, the environment, women, and homosexuals and helping the Third World; and to program the peace prayers more effectively.[59]

The BSA served to bring the Leipzig groups together, but it did not control them. Indeed, their attitude toward it remained ambivalent: they needed the protection offered by the church connection, yet they disliked any constraint that might come with it. The status of the BSA depended on the church superintendent, yet he exercised only limited influence. State officials viewed the BSA with suspicion and continually urged the bishop and the superintendent to discipline the groups. Perhaps the State's willingness to let the BSA function at all related to the policy of using the Church to channel oppositional activity. The fact that Matthias Berger, the pastor elected as the BSA chairman, also worked secretly as Stasi informer "Carl" even made BSA meetings useful information sources for the Stasi. On the other hand, church officials already suspected this pastor of spying and treated him accordingly in this complex game of cat-and-mouse.[60]

The importance of the BSA as well as the tensions and ambiguities surrounding it surfaced in August 1988, when Magirius took programming of the peace prayers away from it. He charged the prayer meetings with straying too far from their original purpose in the conciliar process and with becoming too controversial. After a heated dispute and boycott by the groups, a compromise returned programming to the BSA in April 1989.[61]

## SIGNIFICANCE OF THE CHURCH-RELATED GROUPS

The final phase for most of these groups began in late 1987 and ended in late 1989. Aggressive new official efforts to arrest group leaders and suppress their publications and activities began with the raid on the Berlin Environmental Library in November 1987. An accelerated series of arrests and fines, followed by prayers and demands for release, followed by a spiral of more activities and more arrests, continued unabated with increasing attention from the western media. Activists became bolder, posting signs, putting out leaflets, and engaging in acts of protest. The climactic events of the summer and fall of 1989 caught up the groups in the mass gatherings in and around St. Nicholas Church and the demonstrations on Monday evenings. Hopes were raised and thoughts turned to more sweeping reform than most groups had ever dared to contemplate.

The new situation produced a new set of political movements and parties outside the churches, yet they were often founded and joined by members of the church-related groups. It is not the purpose here to study these groups—New Forum, Democratic Awakening, the New Social Democratic Party, Democracy Now—except to point to their close ties to the older groups, many of which merged or simply faded into these newer groups in late 1989. By early 1990 nearly all the older groups had "turned" along with the national "turn" or *Wende*. The new movements enjoyed a heady existence and much influence through the roundtables and citizens committees that virtually assumed power during the last months of the GDR. Yet when election day came in March 1990, the poor showing of the new movements and parties revealed that public opinion had moved away from them. Or, how much had the general public ever really supported them? or the church-related opposition groups before them?[62]

Questions concerning the significance of the groups in relation to the events that brought down the SED regime in late 1989 will doubtless continue to be debated as more documents become available and can be evaluated. Also, the complex relationships between the churches and groups must be sorted out further. Before definitive judgments at the national level can win a consensus, further studies at the local level need to be done. The group activity in Leipzig did not typify that of the GDR. The groups were arguably more active and diverse there. They clearly appear to have enjoyed better relations with the churches and with the would-be emigrants. Perhaps, for all their differences, they got along at least as well with each other as the groups in Berlin and other cities, if not better.

Evaluations of the groups and their significance have varied widely. Honecker and company, for all their paranoia and their bitter attacks on "otherwise-thinking" people, regarded these groups as a minor irritation, continuing to exist only due to western provocateurs and financial support. Group members, on the other hand, tended to regard themselves as the wave of the future and not surprisingly often overstated their importance.

One can be reasonably certain about a few matters: their numbers were small, a few hundred in a city of over 530,000; they were very loosely organized and not centered on one or a few charismatic leaders.[63] In spite of all the regime's accusations, the groups acted without western backing, except for the attention of western media, which they had learned to cultivate by 1988–1989. Their numbers swelled with the peace movement, 1979–1982, then waned in the mid-1980s. The rise to power of Gorbachev with his ideas of *glasnost* brought renewed hope for change, and the arrival of Pastor Wonneberger in Leipzig added badly needed leadership in 1985. The intransigence of the regime and its increasingly aggressive efforts at repression provoked a backlash of resentment and activity that steadily grew, especially after the fall of 1987. Other factors, such as the gross deterioration of the infrastructure, the dangerously high levels of air and water pollution, and the masses attempting to emigrate, multiplied the groups' discontent. Ties with opposition groups in Eastern Europe brought information and, by 1988, encouragement to the Germans.

It is equally clear that the ideas and acts of these groups were never revolutionary in any conventional sense. Nearly all of them accepted socialism and simply wanted to reform it. Informational programs, prayers, candlelight vigils, and petitions were favored methods. Until 1987 and 1988 only a few attempted public group actions such as marches.

As late as October 1988, after the regime had raided the Berlin Library, arrested numbers of people there and elsewhere, censored church publications, and stopped a "march of silence" in Berlin, a group of about 200 people met informally outside St. Nicholas Church after the prayer meeting. This was also during the time the groups had been excluded from programming the prayer sessions. After some discussion, the strongest action they could agree upon was to send a letter to the state secretary for church affairs in Berlin, stating, "We are of the opinion that in the GDR peaceful demonstrations must be allowed," then they went home and back to their jobs the next day.[64]

Many reasons for the lack of revolutionary fervor have been given, from the old notion of the stereotypical "obedient German" to the fact that the regime systematically expelled the most radical troublemakers to the "other" Germany. This question will be addressed later.

The significance of the groups cannot, however, be dismissed simply by reason of the small number involved or the mildness of their opposition. Leipzig sociologist Karl-Dieter Opp concedes only a minor role to them as far as the mass demonstrations are concerned, but is that enough?[65] Although few of Leipzig's citizens ever attended their meetings, read their clandestine leaflets, or participated in their activities, the public did become increasingly aware that some brave souls were voicing discontent over problems that were widely perceived. Their mosquito-like "buzzing about" and occasional "bites" became known through word of mouth and through western media, which established regular contacts in Leipzig during the fair weeks, and through West Berlin. Drastic measures by the regime only created solidarity among them and sympathy for them from a widening audience. The public ultimately followed the example of the boldest of them and joined them in the streets. The courage of group members and their stubborn adherence to nonviolence evokes admiration even among those who consign them to a minor role. Yet was it so minor, or was it essential? Perhaps Detlef Pollack is closest to the truth when he writes that no matter how many other factors one includes, there can be no doubt that "the political-alternative groups played a not insignificant role" in the epic events of the *Wende* and even before 1989. They deserve recognition for presenting serious options for change in an otherwise static, closed system.[66] They relentlessly sought to spur the broader public to an awareness of problems and to a hope that change could occur and occur peacefully. Perhaps their one greatest achievement was to transform the Monday night meetings in St. Nicholas Church from simple prayers for peace to programs that inspired hope and provoked action for political change.

## NOTES

1. *Die Mücke (The Mosquito)*, front page, 21–22 January 1989. This underground newsletter was published by two Leipzig groups, AKM and AKG. A large number of such publications are filed alphabetically by name in the ABL.

2. Dietrich and Schwabe, eds., 495.

3. Debate continues over the significance of the church groups in the events of 1989. Some groups functioned more outside than inside the churches. This study does not attempt to include New Forum and the secular groups that organized in late 1989.

4. Numerous studies based on interviews with group members, archival materials, and statistical surveys have appeared. See, for example, Detlef Pollack, ed., *Die Legitimität der Freiheit: Politisch-alternative Gruppen in der DDR unter dem Dach der Kirche* (Frankfurt/Main: Peter Lang, 1990); Christian Dietrich, "Fallstudie Leipzig 1987–1989" in *Material der Enquete-Kommission "Aufarbeitung von Geschichte und Folgen der SED Diktatur in Deutschland*," vol. 2: *Widerstand, Opposition, Revolution*, 558–667; Friedhelm Feldhaus, "Politisch-alternative Gruppen in sozialen Raum der DDR—ein Beispiel politischer Dokumente und Erklärungen Leipziger Oppositionsbewegungen," unpublished dissertation, University of Hannover, 1993. For studies in English, see Joppke, Philipsen, and Opp.

5. Helmut Zander, *Die Christen und die Friedensbewegungen in beiden deutschen Staaten* (Berlin: Duncker & Humblot, 1989), 231–37.

6. Hugler, 33–34.

7. James Scott, *Domination and the Arts of Resistance: Hidden Transcripts* (New Haven: Yale University Press, 1990), 108–13.

8. Wolfgang Büscher, "Die evangelischen Kirchen in der DDR—Raum für alternatives Denken und Handeln?" in Dietrich Staritz, ed., *Die DDR von der Herausforderung der achtziger Jahre: Sechzehnte Tagung zum Stand der DDR Forschung in der Bundesrepublik Deutschland, 24 bis 27 Mai 1983.* (Köln: Deutschland Archiv, 1983), 162.

9. Joppke, 58–59.

10. Scott, 118–19.

11. Detlef Pollack, "Ursachen des gesellschaftlichen Umbruchs in der DDR aus systematischer Perspektive" in Grabner, Heinze and Pollack, eds., 129–139.

12. Ibid., 146–48.

13. See, for example, Ehrhart Neubert, *Gesellschaftliche Kommunikation im sozialen Wandel: Auf den Weg zu einer politischen Ökologie* (Berlin: Edition CONTEXT, 1989), 32–35.

14. Joppke, 29, 185–86.

15. Rüddenklau, 12–13.

16. Büscher in Staritz, 158–159.

17. Grabner, Heinze, and Pollack, eds., 9–10.

18. Ibid., 134–35.

19. Some nonconformists entered theological study because it remained the only avenue open to them.

20. Feldhaus, 146.

21. Pollack in Grabner, Heinze, and Pollack, eds., 147–49.

22. One member of two groups, Ernst Demele, recalled in a 6 November 1989 interview that the Stasi succeeded quite often in disrupting group plans. (Anja Kettler, "Von Friedensbewegung zur Oppositionsbewegung—Die 'Arbeitsgruppe Friedensdienst' und die Initiativgruppe Leben in Leipzig in den achtzigen Jahren" [*Diplomarbeit*, University of Münster, 1999], 120–22).

23. Ibid., 135–38.

24. A phrase used in Carl F. Friedrich and Zbigniew K. Brezezinski, *Totalitarian Dictatorship and Autocracy* (Cambridge, Mass.: Harvard University Press, 1965), 279. See also Joppke's discussion, 83–84. This description of the role of pastors was confirmed in 1995 interviews with Protestant pastors Rolf-Dieter Hannsmann, Kaden, Turek, and Sievers and Catholic Monsignor Hanisch.

25. Büscher in Staritz, 161–62. See also Falcke's article, "Unsere Kirche und Ihre Gruppen: Lebendiges Bekennen heute?" in Grabner, Heinze, and Pollack, eds. Falcke was a church dean (*Probst*).

26. Neubert, 7–8, 31–33: Burgess, 52–55.

27. Pollack in Grabner, Heinze, and Pollack, eds., 120–22, 147.

28. Wielapp in Blanke and Evd, eds. 72–73.

29. Günter Krusche, "Gemeinden in der DDR sind beunruhigt—Wie soll die Kirche sich zu den Gruppen stellen?" in Pollack, ed., 58.

30. Joppke, 97–99. Grabner, Heinze, and Pollack, eds., 141–42.

31. Grabner, Heinze and Pollack, eds., 222–23. Politburo members estimated only 2,500. See Przybylski, 116.

32. A very useful survey of group activities and demonstrations in many cities and towns all over the GDR is in Schwabe, "Wir waren doch das Volk?"

33. Opp, 2.

34. Zwahr's book title about the *Wende* in Leipzig translates as *The End of Self-Destruction*. See Kurt Drawert's essay "House without People" ("Haus ohne Menschen"), *Der Spiegel*, 5 July 1993, 149–51.

35. Christian Dietrich, "Fallstudie," 24. Dietrich was a theology student active in the groups. For statistics, see also Günter Fischbeck, ed. *DDR Almanach '89: Daten, Information, Zahlen* (Bonn: Bonn Aktuell, 1989), which lists 549,000.

36. Dietrich, "Fallstudie," 24–26.

37. Ibid., 26.

38. Knabe in Lindner, ed., 32–34.

39. These numbers derive from memories of participants; see Dietrich and Schwabe, eds. Letter from Schwabe to the author dated 10 June 1998. See also Detlef Pollack, "Sozialethisch engagierte Gruppen in der DDR," in Pollack, ed., 134–139.

40. For information on AGF and the following Leipzig groups, see especially Dietrich and Schwabe, eds., 495–504 and Dietrich, "Fallstudie," 25–30. The AGF apparently continued the work of a 1960s group, *Arbeitskreis Friedensdienst*.

41. *Kontakte*, June 1988 (held in ABL), published in part in Dietrich and

Schwabe, eds., 170–71. The letter from the group to the Synod Committee follows, 171–72.

42. Interview with Katherina Führer, July 1995.

43. Joppke's interviews with *Arbeitskreis Gerichtigkeit* (AKG) members support this (Joppke 145–46).

44. Interview with Rainer Müller, July 1995.

45. Thomas Rudolph, theology student and a confounder of AKG became the coordinator. As was the case for many of the leaders, he belonged to another group, also, "Solidarity Church." Dietrich and Schwabe, eds., 498–99, 562.

46. Joppke 146–48; Feldhaus 171–73.

47. Copies are held in ABL.

48. Initiating groups were AGM, AGK, AKSK, in Leipzig, AKSK in Thuringia, the Environmental Library in Berlin, IFM, and the Naumburg peace group. Dietrich and Schwabe, eds., 497.

49. Copies of IFM's underground newsletter, *Grenzfall*, circulated out of Berlin to Leipzig (Joppke 107–8). Copies are held in ABL.

50. Copies are held in ABL. Documents and interviews relating to the Leipzig activity of this group can be found in Joachim Goertz, ed., *Die solidarische Kirche in der DDR: Erfahrungen, Erinnerungen, Erkenntnisse* (Berlin: BasisDruck, 1999), 145–56.

51. Dietrich, "Fallstudie," 49–50.

52. See especially the article "Optimistisches Ausblick" signed Christoph and Peter in *Streiflichter* 23 (May 1987) and 54 (10 July 1989), 3. Copies are held in ABL. Whenever arrests occurred, this newsletter quickly published names and reported the circumstances. See, for example, the 29 November 1988 issue, p. 9. The ABL holds copies.

53. Feldhaus, 169; Kettler, 123–25.

54. Interview with Marianne Ramson, a member, in Leipzig in 1995. For Bohley's comments in English on Women for Peace and on oppositional activity in general, see Philipsen, 131–39.

55. Dietrich, "Fallstudie," 33–34.

56. Joppke, 139.

57. Pollack, for example, believes that these meetings had a very significant impact among the attendees, as they realized they were no longer isolated or alone. Interview, Leipzig 1995.

58. The nine original groups in order of their joining were Christian Peace Conference, Youth Group (youth arm of the State-sponsored organization); Work Group for Justice and Ecumenism; Work Group for Released Prisoners; Leipzig Chapter of Action for Reconciliation; Conciliar Process in Pre-school; Leipzig chapter, Solidarity Church; Work Group on Delimitation; Work Group for Justice; Work Group for Military Service Questions. Later Women for Peace, AGU, AGF, peace groups from suburban districts, and others joined. Dietrich, "Fallstudie," 32, notes 43 and 45.

59. Minutes of BSA Executive Committee meeting of 27 February 1986. Dietrich and Schwabe, eds., 94.

60. Documents made public after the *Wende* revealed that Berger, who was also a lawyer, had functioned as a Stasi informer since 1978. Examples of Stasi reports based on his information are in Besier and Wolf, 429 (see note 231), 431, 677, 682,

and 684. For Bishop Hempel's account, see ibid., 717–18. For information gathered by the Leipzig Citizens Committee on Berger and others, see ibid., 722–26.

61. For Magirius's position and the protests from the groups, see Dietrich and Schwabe, eds., 178–84. For the compromise, see correspondence in November and December 1988 between the BSA and the St. Nicholas parish council in ibid., 251, 254, 255. See also Wonneberger's letter of 29 December, 263. The program schedule for April–June is also there, 298.

62. Opp's population sample yielded a figure of 5 percent who later claimed any group involvement. In the present author's sample nearly half the participants in prayer meetings and demonstrations belonged to one or more groups.

63. Pastor Wonneberger came nearest to being a charismatic leader. Many interviewees, including Professor Pollack, remembered his powerful sermons and his effective work as coordinator of the prayer meetings. Interviews, Leipzig 1995. Demele interview in Kettler, 124–25.

64. Reported in *Die Mücke*, 21–22 January 1989, 7–8. Copies are held in ABL.

65. Opp, 162.

66. Pollack, ed., 13.

**Figure 1**. A critical view of the German Democratic Republic as a prison without doors and windows. Illustration by author.

**Figure 2**. "Swords to Ploughshares," the emblem for the 1981 prayer decade, often used by the protest movement during the 1980s.

**Figure 3.** Monday evening in St. Nicholas Square. The crowd waits for the prayer service to conclude. Courtesy of Martin Naumann.

**Figure 4.** Monday prayer service in St. Nicholas Church. Courtesy of Waltraud Grubitzsch.

**Figure 5**. Uncensored news. Lists of people recently arrested are posted in St. Nicholas Church windows along with protests and demands for their release. Courtesy of Martin Naumann.

**Figure 6**. Placard in St. Nicholas Church window: "freedom" and "immediate release of the prisoners" is demanded. Statement on the left reads: "In the newspapers of this country one reads, 'Here Freedom reigns.' That is either error or lies: Freedom does not reign." Courtesy of Martin Naumann.

**Figure 7.** A police cordon across St. Nicholas Street, Monday, 18 September 1989. A familiar sight during the fall of 1989. © Gerhard Gäbler.

**Figure 8.** Police move from Karl-Marx Square along Grimma Street toward the Saint Nicholas Church to dispurse demonstrators on 7 October 1989, the 40th anniversary "celebration" of the GDR. Courtesy of Martin Naumann.

**Figure 9.** The mass demonstration of 9 October 1989. More than 70,000 people march along the Ring Boulevard, passing Karl-Marx Square and the Opera. Photo by Heinz Löster. © Gustav Kiepenheuer Verlag GmbH, Leipzig 1990.

**Figure 10**. Marchers carry banner: "Jesus Christ—The Way." Photograph by
Gerhard Weber. © Gustav Kiepenheuer Verlag GmbH, Leipzig 1990.

**Figure 11.** Demonstrators occupy the "Round Corner," Leipzig District Stasi headquarters. Monday evening, 4 December 1989. Members of the Citizens Committee stand on the balcony to assure protesters no force is needed. Courtesy of Martin Naumann.

**Figure 12**. The "Leipzig Six" hold the first dialogue session, 22 October 1989, in the Concert Hall. (Left to right) Bernd-Lutz Lange, Roland Wötsel, Peter Zimmermann, Kurt Masur (standing), Jochen Pommert, Kurt Meyer. © Bernhard Eckstein.

**Figure 13**. "We Are the People." St. Nicholas Church, the mass demonstrations, and the city of Leipzig are honored by one of the last postage stamps issued by the GDR.

# 5

## "Not a Spirit of Fear, but of Power and Love and Self-Control": The Peace Prayer Meetings at St. Nicholas Church

"I went to the St. Nicholas Church prayer meetings whenever it was possible. It was very important to have the prayer meetings at a central place where everyone could know where it was, where they could go on Mondays at five o'clock and meet people with the same interests. There they also met those who wanted to leave the GDR and who had lost their fear, because they had sort of finished with the GDR, had lost their friends, were isolated. The only place they could meet and talk with like-minded people was at the peace prayer meetings." (Rainer Müller)[1]

The doors of St. Nicholas Church stood "open to all," just as the familiar sign outside announced, as over 600 people filed in for the usual 5:00 P.M. Monday prayer service on 20 March 1989. The time was usual, but unusual happenings often accompanied the programs. Three weeks before, on 27 February, Pastor Führer and members of the emigrant applicant group calling itself "Hope" had directed the program into a critique of the status quo in the GDR, a critique which upset some high Church leaders and which State officials had protested as a "massive attack against state and society" in angry sessions afterward.[2] The week before, 13 March, had been Fair Monday and immediately after the service 300 people had marched without a police permit from the church to the nearby market square. When security forces intervened and broke up the march, a few had shouted "Stasi pigs!"[3]

The program for the evening of 20 March proceeded in a less political vein, but those in the congregation who expected something unusual were not disappointed. Just as the service concluded three young men climbed over the ropes closing off the side balcony and unfurled a banner over the railing reading "Freedom for Havel and all political and religious prisoners in Czechoslovakia!" A fourth quickly photographed the banner. The film would be smuggled into West Berlin through an established conduit to be given to the western media.[4]

This episode illustrates the well-known fact that the Leipzig prayer meetings became much more than quiet times to pray for peace, indeed they functioned increasingly as the locus of extraordinary events of protest. A detailed narrative of these events and the persons involved would offer most interesting reading. However, questions about the prayer meetings and their significance in the sudden, nonviolent decline and fall of the GDR need to be addressed. First, Who came to these meetings? Why did they come and why did so many nonchurchgoers join in? What were the obstacles imposed by the state? What constraints, what encouragement came from the church? What did oppositional activists expect to accomplish through them? Why and how did they become institutionalized with a broadening political agenda, and by 1988 steadily growing attendance? Finally, then, the most difficult question: How should one evaluate their relationship to the mass demonstrations of the fall of 1989 and their place among factors in the collapse of the GDR? There is a temptation to postpone research into questions about such recent events until the masses of extant records can be fully gathered and organized into archives, until personal memoirs, diaries, and other documentation become more readily available. The hazard in postponement is, of course, that time inevitably fades and distorts memories of participants. Also, if one can "learn from history" and if there is anything of significance to be learned here, tentative answers to these questions can serve better than no answers at all.

## WHO ATTENDED THE PRAYER MEETINGS?

One method of seeking answers to the above questions is to begin by surveying the participants. In 1995 the author mailed questionnaires to 312 known "oppositionists." A total of 101 (32.4 percent) responded, 81 of whom had participated in the prayer meetings. Open-ended questions were primarily used in the survey. Follow-up interviews were conducted with 35 respondents in Leipzig.[5] These results will be compared with the results of the survey of a representative sample of 1,300 Leipzigers, and of 209 members of opposition groups, by Leipzig sociologist Karl-Dieter Opp and associates in late 1990 with a response rate of 40.3 percent. Since Opp's and other surveys focused on the demonstrations, not the prayer meetings, additional comparisons will be possible when the demonstrations are discussed in the next chapter. Such surveys document the mood and mindset in Leipzig at this critical time.

Who came to these prayer meetings? Contemporary accounts refer to youth-dominated congregations, but with a considerable mix of older people. Church members formed the initial core, but by the fall of 1988, if not before, alternative group members and nonchurchgoers swelled the attendance from a handful to several hundred. The third component consisted of the emigrant applicants, who by the fall of 1988 began to attend in large numbers or stand outside during the service in order to rally and march afterward. Pastor Führer's sympathy and hospitality toward these frustrated applicants drew them into contact with the oppositionists not interested in leaving. These contacts led to increasing cooperation, which remained rare in other cities.

Surveys to investigate the prayer meeting attendees could not, of course, include the emigrant applicants who scattered westward after the barriers came down. Of those remaining in Leipzig, the 81 attendees responding to the 1995 survey provided interesting information concerning themselves, their motivations, education and occupations, and participation in opposition groups and activities. The survey did not specifically ask for age, but information from the interviews and indications from other questions support the idea that most were in their twenties in 1989, yet other age groups were represented. Men outnumbered women 60 percent to 40 percent, not so much as the 2–1 ratio often speculated for demonstrations and group members.

What were the occupations and socioeconomic class of the attendees? Among the two-thirds of the attendees surveyed who came "regularly" or "often" over an extended period, most (55 percent) were engaged in a wide variety of lower-middle-class occupations such as readers and workers in Leipzig's book-publishing business, social workers, and salespersons. Some (11 percent) worked in technical-mechanical or factory jobs, including construction. Engineers (5 percent), medical doctors (4 percent), and a few (1 percent) employed in science and research constituted nearly all of what might be considered "middle-middle" or "upper-middle" class. Clergy were 15 percent, while 5 percent taught in church kindergartens or worked for church-run institutions and 2 percent were theological students.[6] Only 2 percent indicated they were housewives; no one was unemployed. Among the other third who "seldom" attended, there was no significant occupational difference from the above.

Educational levels of all the attendees of course corresponded with their occupational status: 27 percent had only a basic education (5 percent completed 8th class, 22 percent 10th class); 22 percent had gone further on the trade school–technical school track equivalent to finishing high school; 28 percent had earned the *Abitur* to qualify for university-level education, and 16 percent possessed a university degree or equivalent. Some 5 percent had completed their theological education. Responses were not always perfectly clear, but study and comparison of both the responses to education and to occupation questions suggest strongly that nearly all the university-level education was in fact "university-equivalent" polytechnical training, such as engineering. None could clearly be identified as having a classical liberal arts university degree and none were university students at the time, except theological students. During the interviews, several mentioned being denied opportunity for advanced education because of their political nonconformity, especially their refusal to take part in the state's secular youth confirmation, the *Jugendweihe*, or their refusal to serve in the military or their opting for the alternative service as *Bausoldaten*. Interviews also revealed that some of the theological students had chosen seminary because it was the only advanced education open to them. A comparison of educational levels of regular/often attendees to seldom attendees shows the latter had slightly higher educational credentials, but probably not enough to make a significant difference.

The prayer meeting attendees were not only rather well educated; three out of four belonged to a church (76 percent) and over half indicated they attended services regularly or often. Lutherans naturally predominated: 63 percent were Lutheran with 40 percent attending regularly and 23 percent seldom. Roman Catholics were 11 percent, Reformed 2 percent, while another 3.5 percent considered themselves religious, but nonaffiliated.[7] The remaining 18 percent marked no membership, while the responses of 2.5 percent were unclear or lacking. Do these figures overrepresent church membership among attendees? This is of course possible, since the survey could not include the emigrants and since there seems to be consensus that the number of nonchurchgoers in attendance swelled in 1988 as the prayer meetings gained increasingly notoriety. On the other hand, the predominance of church members at least until late 1988, if correct, fits the strong assertions of well-informed participants that the prayer meetings always remained distinct from, even if related to, the mass demonstrations of 1989.[8] One means to investigate this further is to inquire into the motivations of the attendees and when they began to participate.

## WHY DID THEY COME?

Why did people come to St. Nicholas Church on Monday evenings? Inside a church building religious programs could be held legally without a permit, but everyone believed in the omnipresence of Stasi informers and could observe the unblinking eye of the security camera posted squarely across the street from the church's front door. So why take this risk?

Prayer meeting attendees who responded to this survey often listed multiple motives for attending, with more offering religious motives than any other. It was concern or duty as a Christian and/or church member that moved 32 percent; a desire to protest publicly and press for change primarily moved 15 percent; an interest in promoting the cause of peace and justice came first for 13.5 percent; and a need to come together with like-minded people was prime motive for 7 percent. Other motives included general interest, curiosity, a desire to obtain information, a felt need for hope and for strength, environmental concern, and sympathy for emigrant applicants. Eleven percent listed no specific motive. In contrast, a few during the interviews mentioned that they came less or stopped coming when they felt the meetings were being politicized by the groups or dominated by the would-be émigrés. It is curious to note that a larger percentage of those who came "seldom" listed a specifically religious motive (41 percent), than those who came "regularly" or "often" (28 percent). However, some of those among the "regular/often" group who listed peace, justice, or hope may have had a religious motive they did not happen to put first in the survey response (22 percent of the regulars listed peace, justice, or hope as compared to 34 percent of the seldom attendees). That many church people did come because of a religious motivation should not be a surprise.

Although motives for the Leipzig emigrant applicants cannot be surveyed, it seems safe to infer, as did their contemporaries, that they had given up on the GDR, wanted out, and saw in the prayer meetings an opportunity to meet and encourage each other with pastoral support. Afterward, the opportunity to demonstrate outside might irritate the authorities enough that they would expel them! Yet what of the motives of the nonchurch members who attended but were uninterested in leaving the GDR? Survey responses revealed mixed, multiple motives. Some 17 percent of this group came out of curiosity, which developed into interest in the proceedings. An equal number came for information, since no newspaper or media reports were allowed to publicize oppositional happenings as did the announcements during services and on the bulletin boards inside St. Nicholas Church. Eleven percent primarily came to make a public demand for change. Other motives included the desire to meet and gather with like-minded people, promote peace, relieve anxieties, pray for peace. By the spring of 1989, if not before, these motives melded together for many in the intense, highly charged Monday night hour in the church. As one nonchurch member, a printer at a publishing house, described it, "There was a spell-binding atmosphere which gave one strength to endure many things such as possible [repressive] acts against the demonstrations."[9]

Nearly half the survey respondents had begun attending the prayer meetings when attendance was small, long before they became notorious and tied with demonstrations. Over 17 percent started coming during the early 1980s; 26 percent began in the middle and latter 1980s; 21 percent first came in early 1989 as tensions mounted, and 28 percent joined in by the fall of 1989 when attendance peaked. A larger number among those who came "seldom" (40.7 percent) first appeared in the fall of 1989; the "often" and "regulars" began earlier (22 percent first began attending in fall 1989). Less than 5 percent of the respondents noted that they dropped out or came less frequently over time. Those who did gave as reasons the politicizing of the meetings or the influx of the would-be immigrants. The great majority—whether they began to come out of religious duty, general concern for peace, justice, or other issues, peer invitations or curiosity—indicated that their interest deepened and they experienced satisfaction; as a result they attended more frequently. Several who marked "seldom" explained that work or family obligations made it difficult for them to be at the church at 5:00 P.M. every Monday.[10]

Another approach to the question of motivations is to divide them into internal and external. Internal motives would include a sense of religious duty, which was most prominent, and a desire to find peer support, inner strength, and hope. External motives would include a desire for information and for interaction with peers. The belief that attendance would be a statement of public concern which could make a difference, that is, would be politically influential, constituted another external motive. Many more than the 16 percent whose responses related to making a public statement for changes included or implied that among their motives was the belief that attending the prayer meetings was a significant way to exert political influence. Responses to the Opp survey confirm this: 46 percent of respondents believed participation in prayer meetings and in other church activities were "politically influential," as compared to 33 percent who favored opposition group activity for that purpose, 22 percent who listed refusal to vote, and 19 percent refusal of SED party membership.[11]

## RESPONSES OF PARTY, STATE, AND CHURCH OFFICIALS

Party and State officials certainly regarded the prayer meetings as having a dangerous political potential and used various means, subtle and not so subtle, to discourage attendance. After the first peace decade of November 1980, even before the weekly prayer services began, officials in Leipzig called in the two church superintendents to warn that another such "decade" would not be tolerated because speakers had called into question the military institutions of the GDR; had drawn comparisons with old Prussian militarism; had used slogans that came near to incitement to violence; and had criticized State officials. The superintendents defended the programs and refused to cancel them.[12]

Failing in a frontal attack, the regime turned to other methods: camera surveillance, new personal Stasi files on attendees, and Stasi informants in the prayer meetings as they developed into regular Monday night happenings. Police blocked off streets and set up checkpoints around the church. Although arrest and detention did not become common until 1989, attendees felt the pressure. Among survey respondents, 44 percent reported experiencing explicit harassment or discrimination for participating in prayer meetings and demonstrations. Another 8 percent had suffered arrest. Officials selected alternative group leaders and emigrant applicants for special attention but made no effort to distinguish prayer meeting attendees from other "troublemakers." It is not surprising, then, that survey respondents could not clearly say whether harassment they experienced came only from prayer service attendance or from other activity or at least suspicion of it. Protests by Bishop Hempel, Pastor Führer, and others that the authorities were failing to make a distinction went unheeded.[13]

Among those reporting arrest or some form of harassment, 24 percent experienced job discrimination, 15 percent denial of educational opportunities for themselves, and another 6 percent reported that their children's education suffered. Twenty percent received direct warnings from the Stasi and another 11 percent noticed Stasi surveillance of them. Another 2 percent remembered denial of permission to travel outside the GDR, while 13 percent referred to an atmosphere of general intimidation they felt as they came on Monday evenings. The Leipzig newspaper, the *Leipzige Volkszeitung*, reinforced this sense with accounts of "rowdies" and "ruffians" in St. Nicholas Square; the Stasi's position that the church had become the scene of "negative activities by the political underground and reactionary church forces" financed from the west was often repeated.[14]

Those who persisted in coming thus had to reckon with serious consequences for themselves and their families. Those whose purposes went beyond the purely religious exercise of praying for peace also faced constraints imposed by Church leaders. As mentioned above, the higher leadership and a large majority of the pastors had no desire to see the Church transformed into a political opposition. They regarded such as outside the church's mission and moreover as risking the relatively privileged, autonomous status the Church had enjoyed since the 1978 "Edict of Toleration," as one pastor called it.[15] Church leaders disagreed on where to draw the line between protecting the victims of society and nurturing political opposition. In Leipzig Superintendent Magirius proved willing to extend the protective shelter of the Church to opposition groups by admitting them to membership in the District Synodal Committee and allowing them to coordinate programming for the prayer meetings. This went further than most superintendents or bishops wanted to go. As state actions irritated the groups and speakers became bolder and more political, as nonchurch attendees swelled attendance or stayed just outside, church leaders became increasingly nervous. Unauthorized unfurling of political banners and handing out underground news sheets and leaflets during and after the services led to exclusion of the groups from programming from August 1988 to April 1989. A compromise requiring every group to have a responsible clergyman to advise them ended the exclusion and constrained the programming—for just a little while—that spring. Some of the most militant activists left the prayer meetings to meet clandestinely in apartments. Nevertheless, the prayer meetings remained the only public venue for gatherings even remotely connected to political reform and could never completely be "theologized."

## THE PRAYER SERVICES BECOME INSTITUTIONALIZED

Thus the Monday meetings assumed a life of their own, despite State disapproval and constraints attempted by the higher Church leadership. By the mid-1980s they were clearly institutionalized, with an increasingly broad agenda marked by political overtones. How did this happen?

Among major factors were support from clergy, need for a forum where the growing discontent could be articulated, the rise and multiplication of the alternative groups, and the alliance formed between Church, groups, and emigrant applicants. The availability of St. Nicholas Church as a centrally located forum or safe place for regular meetings helped hold this uneasy alliance together.

Many prayer meeting attendees did come in response to pastoral encouragement. Over one-fourth of the survey respondents remembered that the prime reason they involved themselves in prayer meetings or demonstrations was due to encouragement from clergy. Some pastors acted publicly, opening their church buildings and parish halls to the groups and for special services; others quietly advised parishioners or informally sponsored groups; some set an example by attending and speaking at the Monday services.

Pastors who engaged in such activities, no matter how quietly, knew that the Stasi would find out, and that they risked sanctions. Official policy never included arresting pastors, but there were other ways. Denial of construction supplies for desperately needed repairs of church buildings, refusal of permits for outdoor activities—even simple ones like tree-planting—served to bring pressure. Perhaps the most feared was denial of educational opportunities for children of clergy.[16] Undaunted by all this, not to mention minimal salaries and declining church membership, the determined minority, Catholic and Reformed, as well as Lutheran, gave crucial support to the prayer meetings and similar activities. The only alternative where one could break out of isolation or gain more reliable information and, above all, inspiration and hope resided in the churches and especially in the open-to-all prayer meetings. A landmark in institutionalizing them came with the incorporation of the groups into the District Synodal Coordinating Committee in November 1985.[17]

Some groups had participated and even led in programming since the inception of the prayer decades in 1981. The AKF (Working Group in the Service of Peace), AKU (Working Group for Environmental Issues), the ASZ (Action for Reconciliation), and the ESG (Evangelical Student Congregation) participated in the 1982 decade. As interest lagged and groupings shifted in the early 1980s, involvement of groups outside St. Nicholas remained rather *ad hoc*. Renewed interest and increase in group activity in the mid-1980s provoked new suspicions from authorities, who pressed Church officials to define the loose, ambiguous ties between groups, Church, and peace prayers. Superintendent Magirius sought to define these relationships by offering a share in programming the Monday services to the groups. This established an official relationship that served to legalize their existence as "church groups," allowed to meet and work inside the church building without special license from the state. From the viewpoint of Church leaders, this arrangement allowed a much-needed measure of coordination and—hopefully—control of activists, many of whom already met at least irregularly on church premises. From the viewpoint of the regime, this arrangement could be tolerated as a lesser evil than having underground activist groups meeting clandestinely anywhere with unknown and perhaps more radical agendas. Officials continued right up to October 1989 to think erroneously of the arrangement as a "chain of command": bishop—superintendents—pastors—groups, which they could utilize for control.[18]

Pastor Wonneberger, when he became the sponsor in September 1986, encouraged more planning and organization for the prayer meetings, yet the format and actual happenings in the church remained somewhat irregular and varied. After the 1986 peace decade, Wonneberger proposed an approximately equal focus on peace, environment, and justice, with programming by interested groups. In practice, the emphasis on human rights seemed to develop earlier and more strongly in Leipzig than elsewhere, probably due in part to Wonneberger's influence.[19] He listed ten elements to be included in each service, including Bible readings, hymns, prayer requests, exchange of information, meditation, and free time for an address or other presentation.[20] The flexible format for the prayer services became both their strength and their weakness. The elements of religious exercise reassured Church officials that they had a *bona fide* Christian purpose and form appropriate to a church and thus defensible to suspicious state authorities; activists saw in the "free time" and in opportunities for information-sharing and prayer requests the means to further their political causes. At the same time, the services, being neither regular church worship nor political program, held the potential to veer from the one toward the other. Neither State officials nor Church authorities or political activists always found the services meeting their conflicting expectations.[21] So at times State officials complained the services had become too political and oppositional, even while activists chafed under Church restrictions and sometimes defied them with unauthorized banners and leaflets and political attacks on the system thinly veiled as prayer requests or announcements. Church officials alternately strove to reassure State officials and cajole or somehow restrain the militants.

The fall peace decades continued to attract several hundred participants throughout the 1980s; participants in the continuing Monday services rarely numbered over a dozen until late 1987. No detailed records remain of the first peace decade in 1980 with its theme "Wage peace without weapons" at St. Nicholas Church. The 1981 decade with the theme "Justice-Disarmament-Peace" drew 800 to its closing service and inspired continuing prayers on Mondays.[22] The 1983 decade produced the first attempt at a candlelight demonstration as mentioned above. By 1984 in Leipzig, the Stasi elevated the peace decades and continuing prayer services to a major concern and discussed plans to hinder or stop them.[23]

## "HOT MONDAYS" IN LEIPZIG

Actions of the regime in Berlin, moreover, gave a fresh impetus to oppositional activities in Leipzig. The police raid on the Environmental Library in November 1987 and the arrests in January 1988 relating to the Luxemburg-Liebknecht parade provoked widespread resentment and many special prayer services all over the GDR. On the first Monday in February more than 700 people came to St. Nicholas Church for prayers, and thereafter the Monday night crowd continued to be in the hundreds. These events also roused groups all around the country to coordinate and network with each other as never before. The bulletin board in St. Nicholas carried names and news about prisoners. A coordinating committee, Peace Prayers for the Prisoners, formed and used the long-distance-connected telephone at the city evangelical youth office to exchange information with other groups in the GDR. St. Mark's parish also had a long-distance phone which activists used.[24] Some individuals had also learned—possibly from associates in East Berlin—how to contact the western media by telephone. The Stasi were well aware of these developments and dutifully tapped the telephones and reported up through channels to Leipzig's first secretary, who quickly forwarded information to Berlin,[25] yet, strangely enough, no effort was made to cut off the long-distance connections. Perhaps the Stasi phone-tapping operations and insatiable thirst for information discouraged any cut-off? The two Leipzig superintendents were called in once again and told to suppress "political-negative activities" in their churches. The superintendents conceded that the services should be primarily religious, not political, but countered with comments that wide discontent within society naturally would be reflected in Church activities and named specific State policies that were increasing this discontent, such as the award of the Karl-Marx Order, the GDR's highest honor, to Romanian dictator Nicolae Ceaușescu.[26]

The boldest malcontents, the emigrant applicants, flocked to the prayer meetings in 1988 and, more than any other element, deserve responsibility for the large increase in attendees. Both Church leaders and the groups reacted rather negatively at first to this influx of people who had given up on the GDR and who appeared to come, not to pray, but to attract attention, even create disturbances in St. Nicholas Square with the hope of being expelled from the country. However, Pastor Führer and others reached out to them, offering special programs and a sympathetic hearing, even while they were being excluded from the new group network. His efforts gained a ready response; one special meeting, planned for 50, drew 500![27] Relationships continued to experience strains throughout 1988 and 1989, but the emigrant applicants continued to come to St. Nicholas on Mondays, in contrast to many places, where open hostility grew up between them and the "staying-home" oppositionists.

Thus three elements fused, or at least allied together, to expand the agenda and greatly swell the attendance on Mondays: regular churchgoers, alternative group members, and emigrant applicants. A fourth element also began to appear in early 1988: citizens previously uninvolved who came to show their concern for those arrested and continued attending to become part of a weekly event that offered them something meaningful. By early 1989 some came just to stand outside and others came to demonstrate, or to cheer on those who did. The widespread reaction to the rigged communal elections in May 1989 converted oppositional activity from marginal to almost respectable and substantially increased the numbers of this fourth element.

## THE TIME, THE PLACE, THE PREACHERS

A factor in the success of the prayer meetings not to be overlooked is that of place and time: St. Nicholas Church, 5:00 P.M., Mondays. St. Nicholas Church enjoys the most central location of any downtown church in Leipzig, no more than four to seven short blocks from the encircling Ring Boulevard in any direction. Only one block to the east lies the vast Karl-Marx (now again Augustus) Square with the Opera House, Karl-Marx University, Concert Hall, post office, and a major junction of streetcar and bus lines. To the north only four blocks away stands the huge train station, three blocks to the west the Market Square and old *Rathaus* (town hall), and to the south other university buildings and the new *Rathaus*, all in easy walking distance. Built in 1165, the church building has experienced Romanesque, Gothic, and baroque phases in its various reconstructions and additions. The 2,000-seat classical-baroque interior with two encircling balconies is world-famous for its rich ornamentation and palmate columns. An unusual "angel of peace" painting hangs over the main altar. For over a quarter of a century St. Nicholas shared J. S. Bach with St. Thomas Church as choirmaster and organist with their congregations hearing premieres of several of his most famous works. The regime could demolish St. John's, the war-damaged university church, and refuse to rebuild St. Matthew's, an obstacle to Stasi expansion at the Round Corner, and St. Mark's, a nineteenth-century church, but it had to permit repair and renovation of this imposing artistic monument. Numerous side chapels served as places for Monday prayers in the early 1980s and for workshops and special programs during the peace decades. Even nearby St. Thomas Church, though more famous due to its better-known Bach connection and choir school, could not equal St. Nicholas in centrality and commodious facilities.[28]

The 5:00 P.M. hour suited many Leipzigers well. They could come directly from work by public transportation, then go on homeward for the evening meal. More important, the regularity of the services became a major asset. In a country where all media were strictly controlled, it was obviously very difficult to publicize the time and place for oppositional activity. Alternative groups in Berlin and other cities held many prayer services and meetings in various churches, but they shifted in time and place; in Leipzig from the beginning it was Monday, 5:00 P.M., St. Nicholas, and everyone knew it.

Given the existence of these prayer meetings, the people who came, and their motivations plus the context of discontent, one can understand the broadening agenda of the services. General concerns for world peace and justice continued to be popular, but more specific items such as greater freedom to travel, openness of the media to criticisms of existing society, creation of a new alternative peace service for draftees not wishing to enter the military, and other quite political matters slipped in, thinly veiled under biblical topics and texts. Each group which in turn arranged a program used the occasion to promote its particular cause. The Old Testament prophets, especially Jeremiah, with their attacks on sinful and corrupt kings, became favorite sources of reference.[29] The temporary exclusion of the groups from programming proved to be only an interlude, not an end to these sorts of programs, when the groups were readmitted to the program process in April 1989.

Why did attendance grow, steadily and then spectacularly? Again one must refer to the repressive acts of the regime. Ironically, the more active the Stasi became in detaining activists, the longer grew the lists posted in the church windows and the larger the crowds who crowded in to hear the latest news and to pray for their release! Not only arrests stirred discontent, but other acts, such as the banning of *Sputnik* and statements by officials sympathetic to the notorious Romanian dictator and hostile to Gorbachev's *glasnost* and *perestroika*, aroused people. Pastor Wonneberger and others had contacts in the restive Eastern Bloc countries and shared news of oppositional activities as they multiplied more rapidly there than in the GDR. Even apart from external events, one can detect a certain snowballing effect as those finding satisfaction for various reasons passed along the word to family and friends. As the Monday evening crowds grew to fill and overflow the church, the intensity of feeling and electricity of those moments seemed to increase exponentially.[30] As crowds poured out of the church to mingle with the increasing crowds filling St. Nicholas Square, some felt ready to translate their concerns into action—to march, to demonstrate!

## FROM PRAYERS TO MARCHES

No one can deny that the prayer meetings became somehow related to the demonstrations, but considerable differences of opinion exist about the nature and significance of this relationship, even among participants. Were they "two sides of one coin" of protest? Is the analogy of a small spring of water to a great river more apt? Or is it best to refer to the one as the essential prerequisite to the other and go no further?[31] Discussion of the demonstrations in the next chapter can shed more light on this question. From the perspective of the prayer meetings, there are already several points that are clear enough and deserve mention here.

It is well to remember that the Monday prayers grew out of the autumn peace decades which from the beginning had a political and to a degree an oppositional dimension. Opposition to NATO deployment of missiles quickly also became opposition to the new requirements for military studies in GDR schools; discussion of alternatives to military service soon entered the agenda. Supposedly nonpolitical concerns for such issues as the environment, women's rights, and injustice in general filtered into the Monday prayer services, which shifted more and more toward political opposition as the regime's hostility and intransigence repeatedly frustrated reform efforts.

Also, the prayer meetings became a venue for the convergence of people and ideas. St. Nicholas Church offered more than a roof and relative safety from police action. The institutionalization of the services there gave a "religious legitimacy" to alternative modes of thinking and to opposition groups, many of whose members later led or joined in demonstrations. Although the higher leadership of the Church and often the clergy who led the services urged attendees to go home quickly and quietly, not all obeyed. Indeed, by September 1989 not only the would-be émigrés and non-Christian activists, but church people, even clergy, went out after the service to march. Everyone in the author's survey who attended prayer meetings also demonstrated.[32] Of the thirteen clergy surveyed, all had marched. The remarkably pacific nature of the crowds, even as they swelled to many thousands, can most probably be attributed to the nonviolence preached at the prayer meetings, which set the tone at the beginning of each demonstration.

The increasing crowds in church in a country with low and declining church membership and attendance confirm the fact that this was no purely religious revival. The meetings reflected—and arguably stimulated—the political engagement of the congregation.

It is also clear that no other activity or agency in the GDR came forward to inspire opposition, and certainly not demonstrations. In contrast to neighboring Eastern Bloc countries such as Poland, Czechoslovakia, and Hungary, no reformist faction within the Party or its youth movement or other supplementary organizations for the arts, sciences, etc. came forward, no union movement with a Lech Wałęsa organized marches or oppositional activities, no university student group took leadership.[33] Indeed, one reputable survey suggests that university students remained loyal to the system longer than any other group![34] Demonstrators doubtless gained courage to march from other sources: writers, artists, Leipzig's political cabarets, clandestine small-group meetings in homes and apartments, and by September from the new, secular groups organizing outside the Church, such as New Forum. Nonetheless, the coalition of church people and alternative groups, augmented by the would-be émigrés and "staying-home" protesters, formed the primary constituency of both the prayer meetings and the demonstrations.

Most Church leaders never wanted the Church and activities it sponsored to become a center, and certainly not *the* center, of political opposition and demonstration. The prayers on Monday remained during the early years focused on peace and the improvement of "real-existing socialism." The Monday congregations thought in terms of incremental reform and clearly never regarded themselves as rebels. Not in their wildest dreams did they anticipate a collapse of the whole system and country. Western critics chided them after the *Wende* not for being too revolutionary, but for being too accommodating. The connection with church and prayer meetings helps explain why this was so. They envied the west for its respect for individual freedoms, but not for its materialist-capitalist system. Most did not want to be an opposition alongside socialism, nor an opposition against socialism; they at most wanted to be an opposition within socialism.[35] Only after the demonstrations took on a life of their own in October–November 1989 did more radical demands appear.

Definition of the relationship between prayer meetings and demonstrations turns out to be no simple task. None of the three analogies or interpretations mentioned thus far seems fully satisfactory. The "two sides of one coin" approach suggests a close identity of participants and a congruity of ideology. Yet the prayer meeting congregations and programs, while increasingly large and diverse, always retained a strong religious dimension and remained little interested in overt political action before 9 October 1989. These were not Protestant revolutionaries, caucusing to conspire for overthrow of the regime.

On the other hand, the view that the safe haven offered by the Church was an essential prerequisite, or prelude, and nothing more also falls short by failing to comprehend the intense feelings of the attendees and the large percentage that did join in the demonstrations. This leaves the third view, which favors the "small wellspring to a great river" analogy. This can be more attractive, since it moves somewhat beyond the "prerequisite only" view without subscribing to the identity of the two. If pressed, however, it may be flawed in that it would imply that the constituencies and aims of the two differed only in quantity or intensity. A fuller, more precise definition of the relationship requires a close look at these demonstrations and a search for answers to various questions about them and their participants.

## CONCLUSIONS

The Monday prayer meetings cannot be dismissed as a mere prelude to the mass demonstrations, or some insignificant appendage deserving little attention. They functioned in a unique and influential way and their achievements made a major difference in the outcome of the *Wende* in Leipzig. First, they offered a specific channel in a metaphysical sense to bring to the attendee the hope for a better future that is part of the fabric of Christianity. Such hope, always present if vaguely in the services of the churches, found focus in the subjects of peace, justice, protection of God's Creation (that is, environment), and others. A communion of hope shared with others inspired those who saw little hope in the controlled, conformist, drab society in which they lived. Skeptics who reject the reality of religious faith should accept the fact that for whatever ultimate reason, this sort of function operated for many.

The prayer meetings also facilitated a convergence of interests.[36] Those who came eluded the official barriers intended to isolate individuals and preclude any alternatives to the regime's organizational network and stated agenda. Religious, personal, political needs and grievances mingled and merged among the attendees. Courageous and sympathetic leadership of a few key clergy translated St. Nicholas's sign, "Open to All," into meaningful reality for many.

Out of these converging interests—churchgoers, group members, emigrant applicants, "staying-home" discontents—the prayer meetings created a culture of resistance of a special sort. Nonrevolutionary and nonviolent, and at first not exactly political in the usual sense, the prayers did arouse concerns from Party and State officials, but not until too late did they begin to comprehend the depth and potential of this sort of resistance. They never expected "harmless" religious rituals, candlelight vigils, and prayers for peace to relate seriously to major political resistance, but in the end they did.

The influx of group members, then emigrant applicants, transformed the meetings into religious-political events and provided these oppositionists a respectability, legitimacy, and publicity they would not otherwise have enjoyed. The groups, small in number and with few resources of their own, cleverly managed their programming of Monday services to present their respective agenda to a growing and sympathetic audience. The would-be émigrés, cast out of society but denied exit permits, were numerous but only a conglomeration of isolated, disaffected individuals until they began to gather on Mondays to swell the crowds inside and outside the church.

It is not too much to argue that their loss of fear of arrest, their bravado in waving banners and staging protests and marches, affected the more reserved and timid attendees.

Finally, on a very practical level the prayer meetings offered a discontented individual something positive to do and a certain sense of empowerment in doing it with the feeling one just might make a difference for the future. For those who have always lived in the west this may be hard to understand. In the GDR, however, the individual experienced a sense of being controlled, being isolated and being without knowledge or input into society; a sense of helplessness in the face of problems and constraints that impinged on one's personal life. The air one breathed, the travel restrictions, even to attend family weddings and funerals in the west, the restricted, highly slanted news from the controlled media, the fear of being "disadvantaged" by a report of some supposed friend or colleague employed by the Stasi, were among the most common problems. Acts of protest or resistance rarely happened and remained largely negative. One could avoid party membership, participate only minimally and perfunctorily in activities of one's official union or professional organization, or absent oneself from the polls on election days. One could thus protest in these ways or try to be "nonpolitical" in one's own little niche in a highly politicized society and probably get away with it. However, those ambitious for job advancement or for their children's educational opportunities had best avoid such behavior. Positive acts of protest such as joining illegal groups or attending clandestine meetings could easily lead to arrest, loss of job, and imprisonment. Services held inside church buildings possessed legal approval, however, and one could attend without joining an illegal group or having to give up the ordinary course of one's life. It would be doing something positive for a change with the reassurance that it was religiously a good thing, or for the nonbeliever, politically attractive. Being with others of like mind created a sense of hope, encouragement, and empowerment very meaningful to one grown accustomed to a feeling of powerlessness and lack of control over one's life. The growing crowds by late 1987 increased this sense of hope, courage, and empowerment.

The snowballing effect of rising attendance, the impact of the increasingly political programming, and news of external developments in the U.S.S.R. and the Eastern Bloc appear to be major factors in leading an increasing number of attendees to think the unthinkable, that is, to add to the public statement of concern made by their presence *inside* the church by joining the crowds to make some statement of protest *outside* the church. By September 1989 the unthinkable was not only becoming thinkable, it was considered doable as the mass demonstrations began.

## NOTES

1. Rainer Müller, born into a Christian family, refused the secular confirmation ceremony and military conscription, even the alternative *Bausoldat* service. He became active in various church and environmental groups. Denied the opportunity for advanced education, he came to Leipzig in 1987 to study in the theological seminary and joined one of the groups, the AKG. He was the subject of constant Stasi surveillance and spent time in jail. Interview, 1995. See the Stasi report on him in Dietrich and Schwabe, eds., 307–9. The chapter title is a quotation from II Timothy 1:7 used by Bishop Werner Leich in his pastoral letter of 14 October 1989, which is housed in ABL.

2. K. Führer, 26–27; text of 27 February program is in Dietrich and Schwabe, eds., 281–86; minutes of meeting of Church and State officials and minutes of St. Nicholas parish council meeting in ibid., 286–93.

3. Stasi report of 14 March in ibid., 295–96; K. Führer, 27. Mielke's summary to Honecker and Politburo members is in Mitter and Wolle, eds., 28.

4. Rainer Müller and Uwe Schwabe unfurled the banner. It had been made for use the day before for a nationwide "action" day meeting in behalf of the Czech opposition, held in the St. Mark's parish hall. The banner was quickly photographed, and Michael Arnold, another veteran activist and IGL member, passed the film to Thomas Rudolph, who regularly smuggled such items out of East Berlin. Letter from Schwabe to the author dated 10 June 1998. See Stasi report in Dietrich and Schwabe, eds., 307–9.

5. For survey information, see Note preceding the Appendix. The author is much indebted to Herr Uwe Schwabe, participant and archivist, for securing names and addresses for the survey and interviews.

6. Among the clergy were five Lutherans, two Catholics, one Reformed.

7. One Lutheran member indicated coming from a free church upbringing.

8. A viewpoint espoused by pastors Turek and Sievers and by IGL cofounder Schwabe, among others. 1995 interviews.

9. Questionnaire of respondent 94.

10. The response categories were 1982–1985; 1985–1988; early 1989; and fall 1989. The data do not show how many of the rather large number who began in 1985–1988 came only after the raid on the Environmental Library at Zion church in Berlin in November 1987 and the Luxemburg-Liebknecht arrests in January 1988, but it is likely many began then. Although the questionnaire consistently referred to "Monday prayer meetings," it is possible a few marking the early 1980s thought of the fall prayer "decades" in November, not the continuing Monday services.

11. Opp, 74, 79.

12. Kaufmann, Mundus, and Nowak, eds., 130–31.

13. For an example of Hempel's protests, see Rein, ed., 148. An example of Führer's is published in Dietrich and Schwabe, eds., 399–400. For a Stasi version see Dietrich and Schwabe, eds., 400–402.

14. Leipzig District Stasi Chief Hummitzsch to Mielke, 31 August 1989 in Armin Mitter and Stefan Wolle, eds., *Ich liebe euch alle! Befehle und Lageberichte des MfS, Januar-November 1989* (Berlin: BasisDruck, 1990), 128.

15. Heym and Heiduczek, eds., 102.

16. Pastor Führer's wife mentioned this as one of her special worries. Interview, 1993.

17. K. Führer, 14–15. The nine original groups were later joined by others.

18. See for example Politburo member Jarowinsky's declaration to Bishop Leich, chairman of the BEK, and to party leaders, 19 February 1988, printed in Gerhard, Rein ed., *Die Protestantische Revolution 1987–1990: Ein deutsches Lesebuch* (Berlin: Wichern Verlag, 1990), 87–88.

19. Neubert, 783–84.

20. Wonneberger's proposal and accompanying letter to the groups are in Dietrich and Schwabe, eds., 101–3.

21. K. Führer, 17.

22. The 1982 theme was "Angst-Trust-Peace." Themes of succeeding years were 1983, "Build Peace upon the Strength of the Weak"; 1984, "Life above Death"; 1985, "Peace Grows Out of Justice"; 1986, "Peace Be with You"; 1987, "Living Together"; 1988, "Peace for Those Near—Peace for Those Afar." K. Führer, 10ff.

23. See Leipzig District Leader Hummitzsch's draft of 10 December 1984 for the 1985 plan of action in Besier and Wolf, 434–35. The Stasi were also concerned at the increasing number of topics discussed in small group workshops during the decade week. For example, in 1987 small groups met in the side chapels of St. Nicholas and at the Reformed church to discuss topics such as "Friends of Peace and State Power," "Women and Power," "Latin America," "Education for the Future," and Wonneberger's social peace alternative service (to military)—see K. Führer, 17.

24. Few telephones in the GDR had a long-distance capability. Individuals normally had to go to the post office to call long distance.

25. See, for example, First Secretary Horst Schumann to Horst Dohlus, secretary to the SED Central Committee and Politburo member, encoded telex dated 26 January 1988, reporting on the 25 January peace prayers and related events (Dietrich and Schwabe, eds., 108–9).

26. Dietrich and Schwabe, eds., 109–12.

27. K. Führer, 18.

28. Wolfgang Hocquél, *Leipzig: Baumeister und Bauten von der Romanik bis zur Gegenwart* (Berlin and Leipzig: Tourist Verlag, 1990), 43–45.

29. See, for example, the programs summarized in K. Führer, 20–21.

30. Many recalled these feelings in the interviews.

31. The "Protestant Revolution" discerned by Neubert and others tends to identify the two very closely. See Neubert, 785–88. Pollack admits a connection, but of limited significance. See Pollack in Grabner, Heinze, and Pollack, eds., 86–88. Förster and Roski do not mention any connection, 19.

32. Interviews confirm this.

33. Sigrid Meuschel, "Revolution in a Classless Society" in Glässner and Wallace, eds., 155.

34. Friedrich, 25ff.

35. John Sandford's point in his article, "The Peace Movement and the Church," in Glässner and Wallace, eds., 140.

36. Meuschel uses those terms in Glässner and Wallace, eds., 151–56.

# 6

## "Time to Voice Our Convictions Bravely and Openly": The Mass Demonstrations in Leipzig

"It is time to voice our convictions, bravely and openly," a time "to stand up for a democratization of our Socialist State." (Leipzig leaflet, 15 January 1989)

"We'll be here again next Monday!" (Shout of demonstrators to each other and to police heard at the end of demonstrations).[1]

Leipzig activists secretly picked up their allotted shares of thousands of leaflets and quietly began their clandestine distributions into mailboxes all over Leipzig around midnight of 11–12 January 1989. The leaflets boldly called for an open demonstration the next Sunday afternoon in front of Leipzig's old *Rathaus* (City Hall). The occasion, the 70th anniversary of the murders of Rosa Luxemburg and Karl Liebknecht, offered the opportunity to publicize Luxemburg's famous statement that "freedom means always freedom for those who think differently." The Berlin activists' efforts the preceding January to join the official parade with banners of their own no doubt inspired the Leipzigers. The Leipzig event would be different, however; it would be independent of any official ceremonies. The wide distribution of thousands of fliers by several alternative groups should rally so many people that the authorities would be unable to abort the event as they had very nearly done in Berlin with preemptive arrests.

The authors of the flier signed themselves. "The Initiative for Democratic Renewal of Our Society" and were active in several of the alternative church-related groups, especially the Initiative Group for Life (IGL) and the Working Group for Justice (AKG), two of the most militant.[2] The signature on the leaflet represented no one group; it simply signified the general concern about how things were in Leipzig and a determination to take the concern out onto the streets. Obviously this involved risks; to participate in an unlicensed public demonstration violated the law. The authorities had not interfered, however, with the unlicensed Earth Day march along the polluted Pleisse River the preceding June, and the third meeting of the Conference on Security and Cooperation in Europe, nearing conclusion in Vienna, would make this, perhaps, a moment too awkward for drastic police action. Nonetheless, the crackdown in Berlin, beginning with the raid on the Environmental Library in November 1987 and the 120 arrests of Berlin opposition leaders in January 1988, boded ill for Leipzig, which had hitherto drawn little attention from top GDR leaders.

Official response did come, swift as lightning. Before dawn on Thursday, 12 January, police descended on several known leaders; arrests continued Friday and Saturday, totaling 11 or 12. Police and Stasi searched apartments thoroughly, sometimes more than once.[3] When Sunday afternoon came, the area around the old *Rathaus* was sealed off and numerous police vehicles, including a water cannon, had parked conspicuously in the area. Undeterred by this show of force, a crowd estimated at up to 800 gathered nearby, and one of the leaders made a quick speech denouncing the arrests and calling for unrestricted freedom of speech, press, and assembly. Some 500 of the group then attempted to carry out the planned "march of silence" from the *Rathaus* to the Liebknecht Monument, responding with whistles to police loudspeaker demands that they disperse. Before they had gotten halfway, police wielding nightsticks moved in, scattering the marchers. A large number, 50 to 100, were "taken away," the euphemism officials used for such arrests, but released later that evening. Within a few days the leaders arrested earlier regained their freedom, too.[4]

The January 1989 "march of silence" never reached its destination, and the number of participants seems not very impressive when one recalls the tens of thousands that would be in the streets by October. Yet it resonated across the GDR and can serve as a beginning point for study of the Leipzig demonstrations. As Bernd Lindner has noted, the Leipzig activists succeeded that January, whereas the Berlin activists a year earlier had failed.[5] Perhaps failure is too strong a term, because the Berliners' attempt to join in the official Liebknecht-Luxemburg parade, while thwarted by arrests, had inspired others, especially the Leipzigers. It had also drawn oppositionists together in various cities and towns in an unprecedented network of prayers for the prisoners. The exit of many Berlin leaders, by expulsion or choice, left the opposition movement in Berlin temporarily leaderless and also divided within, as some criticized those who had decided to leave the country.

## LEIPZIG BECOMES THE NATIONAL CENTER
## FOR OPPOSITION

The January 1989 demonstration marked the beginning of Leipzig's emergence as the new national center for opposition. Prayer and informational meetings drew crowds to churches all over the GDR to intercede for the "march of silence" prisoners and to discuss problems.[6] The leaflets had widely publicized the plan to demonstrate and, despite four days' advance notice, the authorities had been unable to prevent it. Moreover, this demonstration went beyond the limited agenda of one group; members of several groups joined to demand a general democratic renewal, albeit within the socialist state. Photographs were taken and passed westward to the increasingly interested western media. This pattern would recur regularly.

The demonstrations also forced the Church leadership to reconsider their position. The bishop and superintendents disavowed any prior knowledge of or connection with the event and wrote the pastors to say that engaging in demonstrations was not an appropriate activity for the Church to support.[7] Yet they expressed Christian concern for the prisoners and allowed circulation of their names through Church channels for prayer. When State officials pressed for cancellation of the Monday prayer services and transfer of the church day rally (*Kirchentag*) scheduled for Leipzig in July to another city, the bishop and Church leaders emphatically refused.[8]

Although the 15 January demonstration did not begin after prayers on Monday as later demonstrations usually did, both Church and State authorities acted on the assumption that there was a strong tie between prayer meetings and demonstrations. For example, on Monday evening, 23 January, Superintendent Magirius allowed one of the recent prisoners a moment at the beginning of the service to thank the congregation for its prayers for the prisoners' release. The ex-prisoner used the opportunity to protest the arrests and defend the demonstrations. Before the service adjourned, another activist stood up, uninvited, to urge everyone to come to a concert and to a planning meeting for a public street music festival, a special sort of quasi-protest event.[9] So a symbiotic relationship had developed between prayer meetings and protest events. People flocked to church to pray for prisoners from the last event, only to be recruited for the next.

Many questions need responses if one is to understand and evaluate the Leipzig demonstrations. They are similar to the questions already asked about the prayer meetings in chapter 4. Among the most important are: Who participated and what motivated them? Why were the authorities unable to suppress them so that they continued to grow? What was the nature and extent of the connection between prayer meetings and demonstrations? How and why did the demonstrations of November and December 1989 begin to differ from earlier ones? And finally, Did they accomplish what the demonstrators hoped?

In seeking answers, one must first of all distinguish between the different phases. Early demonstrations—that is, before January 1989—happened infrequently; remained small, isolated, and parochial in their concerns; and were usually so thoroughly suppressed that the general public only occasionally even heard that they had happened. In Leipzig the 15 January 1989 march opened a new, second phase in that it grew out of increased cooperation among members of several groups; it focused on a general reform agenda, not just peace, the environment, or any single issue; and the publicity it generated through the leaflets and subsequent public prayers for prisoners significantly raised the level of public awareness of oppositional activity. Public awareness increased further with the cooperative efforts of the groups to observe the May communal elections and their exposure of election fraud. The mass exodus of the summer fueled public concern even more. The third stage, the mass movement stage, began on 4 September with the coming together of "exit" and "voice" oppositionists, soon joined by rapidly growing numbers of hitherto uninvolved citizens. After the opening of the Berlin Wall on 9 November, observers noted a shift in tone and emphasis from reform of the socialist state to demands for a radical change in leadership and direction and for reunification.[10]

Protest in Leipzig had occurred in various forms from the early days of the GDR, sometimes as part of national events as in 1953, sometimes in response to local events, such as the demolition of the university church in 1968. The first phase of renewed public protest opened with the public candlelight demonstration in 1983. Since this is the first related to the peace prayers, our study can use it as marking the beginning of demonstrations as understood and remembered by participants in the surveys and interviews used.

## WHO DEMONSTRATED?

Who demonstrated and why? Answers to these two basic questions cannot be determined with the precision that one desires, but survey responses and other data offer useful clues. The author's survey respondents nearly all participated in the 1989 demonstrations (100 out of 101), most of them regularly (88 percent). Their ages fell mainly between 25 and 55, with the highest representation from the age group 25–30, especially in the spring and summer demonstrations. Males outnumbered females by more than three to two.[11]

Three other very significant surveys have yielded similar conclusions on age and gender and will be used for comparison here and elsewhere. Peter Förster and Günter Roski, staff members of Leipzig's *Zentralinstitut für Jugendforschung* (Central Institute for Research on Youth), took advantage of their new freedom from official restraint and surveyed 2,597 demonstrators on the streets on two Mondays, 4 December and 11 December 1989, and another 1,147 on 12 February 1990.[12] Kurt Mühler, Steffen Wilsdorf, and a group of Leipzig University sociology faculty and students passed out a thousand questionnaires to demonstrators twice in November, once in December, once in January, and once in February.[13] Then Professor Dieter Opp and his associates surveyed a representative population sample of 1,314 Leipzigers and an additional sample of 209 oppositionists in late 1990. Among the individuals on Opp's population sample, 39 percent had participated in demonstrations and 7.7 percent belonged to groups. Among the individuals in the opposition sample, all had demonstrated and 38 percent belonged to groups.[14] In the author's survey, 47.5 percent held group membership and all but one had demonstrated, so it is most comparable to Opp's opposition sample.

How well educated were the demonstrators? Those in the author's sample were rather well educated. Nearly 7 percent had completed the eighth class, that is, elementary and middle school; 27 percent had gone on and completed a trade school or nonuniversity-track high school; 25 percent had earned the prestigious *Abitur* (diploma) from a university-track high school (Gymnasium); 11 percent had an equivalent from a technical high school; 5 percent had a seminary degree; and 22 percent reported a university education or advanced technical school equivalent.[15] Thus, they were somewhat less well educated than respondents who regularly attended the prayer meetings. The strict demand for party loyalty as a prerequisite for university studies apparently failed to assure continuing loyalty from all university alumni, although threat of expulsion kept current students out of the demonstrations. The opinion of 77 percent of the respondents was that university students played little or no role in the demonstrations. Opp's survey found that the extent of one's education had only a weak correlation to participation in demonstrations and it showed that the higher the education, the more frequent the participation. Students in the Church's own Leipzig seminary faced no risk of expulsion and frequently served as leaders in the groups and in their protest activities.

If the demonstrators were not university students, what was their occupation and socioeconomic status? Nearly half the demonstrators in the author's sample may be loosely described as lower-middle-class: salaried employees in various businesses, especially the book trade (30 percent); teachers of some sort, often in the church kindergartens (10 percent); and some technicians, university support employees, nurses, museum workers and so on. (5 percent). Some were blue-collar workers (30 percent); clergy (10 percent); students, all or nearly all the theological (8 percent); and a few in unspecified church-related jobs (5 percent). None were unemployed, and only 1 percent were retired. The other two surveys also note a predominance of the lower middle class, but Förster and Roski discovered a significant shift to working-class predominance by February 1990.[16] In the author's comparison of prayer meeting attendees with demonstrators, a larger number of demonstrators came from the working class, fewer from the lower middle class, and still fewer from the middle or upper middle class. It is also clear that the unemployed or uneducated did not generate the demonstrations. These demonstrators had worked all day; they planned to march and then go home for a proper night's sleep in order to appear at work on time the next morning. Pollack described this as the "after-hours revolution."[17] In interviews and surveys, many remembered frustrations they had earlier experienced in being denied university admission or job promotion because of lack of conformity to established norms. A rather good education and secure job thus did not assure contentment; rather, they carried with them daily reminders of the discrimination many activists had personally experienced in their schooling and careers or were still experiencing.

## MOTIVES FOR PUBLIC PROTEST

Why then did they march? Further discrimination in the workplace, Stasi harassment, possible arrest, heavy fines, or imprisonment awaited any oppositionist who went out on the streets to demonstrate. Lingering in St. Nicholas Square or even just coming into the general downtown area out of curiosity or for unrelated personal business could lead to arrest on Monday evenings. What then could motivate sober, educated, middle-class and working-class citizens to take such risks? Various surveys have revealed a complex mixture of motives, often interlocking. Responses to the author's survey indicated that far and away the strongest motives were political and centered on the desire for greater freedom (49.5 percent), by which respondents meant freedom of speech and association and for input into public policy. An additional 3 percent listed freedom to travel as their overriding motive. The next-largest group, 16.8 percent, recalled that they were just fed up with the whole system. Follow-up questions in the interviews produced explanations such as feelings of helplessness, marginalization, and isolation in the society, a sense that things were getting worse and that the regime remained aloof and indifferent to the situation, stirring itself to activity only to suppress opposition. This general sense of being fed up included economic problems such as difficulty in obtaining consumer goods, but the economic problems remained clearly secondary. Not one respondent specifically listed any economic motive as the prime reason for demonstrating. Another political reason, reform of socialism, moved 6 percent, which seems rather small unless one understands that the desire for more freedom rested on the assumption of the vast majority of demonstrators that they could obtain all the freedom they desired under a reformed humane socialism, not by overthrowing the regime. Few if any marched for western-style capitalism in the demonstrations before November.

A surprisingly large number of respondents, 11.9 percent, reported their chief motive to be the desire for Germany's reunification. This seems to contradict the usual interpretation that very few thought seriously about it until after the Berlin Wall opened on 9 November; then only a limited, if growing, number of demonstrators are supposed to have advocated it through the remainder of 1989 with majority support developing only in 1990. Did these respondents favoring unification join in the demonstrations late in the fall after slogans like "Germany, One Fatherland" resonated increasingly among the crowds? No, these veteran marchers typically joined in September and October, or even earlier. Three percent were early demonstrators, before 1985. Another 3 percent began in 1985–1988, while another 8 percent joined in early 1989. Most (78 percent) joined when the mass demonstrations began in September and October, but none joined in 1990. During the interviews, a few volunteered that they had stopped marching by late November or December due to the shift in demands by the crowds.[18]

Another explanation could be that respondents' memory lacked reliability six years after the events. Opp and his associates used sophisticated statistical analysis to probe this possibility among their respondents. They concluded that those who actively participated in the events of 1989 remembered them quite clearly and accurately.[19] There is no reason to think otherwise of the respondents to the author's survey. These epic events remained etched indelibly on their minds even through less than half (41.6 percent) still felt the optimism they had nourished about change in 1989.

A more credible explanation for the unexpectedly large number remembering they favored unification derives from responses to another survey question. Respondents were queried as to their expectations before 9 October about what the demonstrations could achieve, and then their expectations after 9 October. The same percentage, 11.9 percent, included some expectation of unification before that date, but thought of some *limited, gradual confederation* of the two Germanies. After 9 October the number favoring unification increased to 46.5 percent, but in the interviews the prevailing sentiment held that reunification as it actually occurred was not at all what they had favored. It was too hasty and very different from what they had marched to demand.

A variety of reasons motivated smaller numbers. Religious motives were primary for 5 percent, not so much to demand freedom for the institutional churches, which already enjoyed considerable freedom, but out of religiously inspired reasons of conscience which opposed the injustice, discrimination, and repressiveness in the existing system. Family influence, environmental concern, hope inspired by Soviet reforms, and honest curiosity were each mentioned by 1 percent of the respondents as their prime motive. Follow-up interviews clearly showed that concern for Leipzig's environmental problems and hope springing from Gorbachev's *glasnost* exercised a larger influence than the 1 percent suggests; they often appeared among secondary political motives after general mention of freedom. Gorbachev played a very significant role, according to 90 percent of survey respondents.[20]

The Opp questionnaire responses suggested different motives. Reasons for dissatisfaction were separated into three areas: political, social, and economic. Using a scale of 1–5 with 5 indicating highest discontent, he found that the major political dissatisfactions were environment (4.45), lack of fairness in political trials in courts (4.32), lack of freedom to express one's opinion (4.30), and Stasi surveillance (4.28). The two items provoking most social discontent were lack of gender equality (2.68) and lack of educational opportunities (2.58). In the economic realm, respondents expressed highest dissatisfaction with lack of choices of goods in stores (4.26).[21] How does one explain the differences between the two surveys? Different samples, times, and formats are factors. Also, the Opp respondents referred to their general attitudes and perhaps less to their specific motives for going out on the streets. They were not on average so active in the demonstrations as the respondents in the author's sample. The mean number of times Opp's respondents participated in the demonstrations was .84 before 9 October and after that date was 1.18.[22]

## CAN SOCIAL SCIENCE MODELS EXPLAIN THE DEMONSTRATIONS?

Social scientists frequently use models to help understand human behavior. Opp reviews models that might be applied to these demonstrations. The organization model assumes a person or group plans and organizes such events. The threshold model assumes that after enough very brave individuals experience some sort of success, others may decide to join in a sort of chain reaction. The spontaneous cooperation model assumes that more or less isolated individuals with similar discontentment may coincidentally decide to do the same thing at the same time. The rational actor model focuses on the individual and assumes that he or she will thoughtfully weigh the benefits and costs or risks and then think through a course of action accordingly. None of these alone can fully explain the Leipzig demonstrations. No charismatic leader or well-organized group planned them. No evidence exists that people assumed "safety in numbers" until after 9 October. The spontaneous cooperation model fits best, but only with considerable modification. Nonetheless, each of these models can be useful. The earliest protest actions and demonstrations resulted from the plans of the emigrant applicants, then the alternative groups and their leaders. Attendance at the prayer meetings provided an organization of sorts and offered the first "threshold" of safety for some overt action by discontented persons. According to the Opp survey, before 9 October oppositionists regarded participation in the prayer meetings and other church events as the action *most likely to bring change* (a median of 2.32 on a 1–4 "unlikely–very likely" scale), ahead of working in an opposition group (2.06) or negative actions such as refusing to vote (1.84) or to join the SED or its affiliates (1.82).[23]

Those protesters who moved beyond negative protest and church-related events to public protest had to hold convictions strong enough to outweigh for them the considerable risks involved. Although a higher percentage were young and may have had fewer family commitments than did the general population, the possibility of sanctions against family members as well as against themselves always had to be considered.[24] Respondents not only perceived the *possibility* of sanctions, they experienced them! Nearly half the respondents had been personally affected. Eleven percent had undergone arrest or detention by police; of these 4 percent for a few hours, 3 percent for a few days, 4 percent for a longer period. The laws of the GDR allowed police to detain anyone they wished without charges for 24 hours and then by a simple filing of a charge like disturbing the peace for longer periods. Although no torture methods in Gestapo style were reported, detainees had to endure strip searches, long waiting periods, sometimes without being allowed to sit down, and long interrogations without opportunity to notify family of their fate. Detainees spent tedious hours, even days, waiting and wondering whether imprisonment, a heavy fine, or just a warning awaited them.[25] Those coming to demonstrations who escaped arrest risked physical injury from Stasi and police roughness, which could include a clubbing with rubber nightsticks or an unpleasant dousing from a water cannon. They feared that they could not rule out police dogs or even firearms.

## PROTEST INCENTIVES AND DISINCENTIVES

These risks remained all too real and escalated in September. Yet a greater source of anxiety for many derived from Stasi surveillance and the knowledge that Stasi spy reports could bring reprisals at one's workplace or in various ways. Uncertainty grew and intensified, based on rumors that Stasi agents were omnipresent and from such obvious occurrences as agents conspicuously present at demonstrations with video cameras. Those gritty activists who steeled themselves against their Stasi shadows felt anger if not fear, as well as anxiety.[26] Nearly half the respondents to the author's survey (43.6 percent) remembered suffering some form of surveillance or harassment resulting from their participation in demonstrations. The desire to be freed of such angst actually served in itself as a powerful motivation to push hitherto nonpolitical people into protest activity.[27]

Given the strong disincentives to demonstrate, and given also the fact that there seemed little prospect for immediate success, one must ask all the more, Why did the demonstrators *continue to come*? After the 1989 summer break, many wondered whether the prayer meetings would be allowed to resume in September and whether there would be new efforts to demonstrate afterward. No hint of any slackening of repressive official policies appeared. The general public, outside the narrow circle of the groups and Monday service attendees, seemed to remain too fearful or too indifferent to join in any meaningful way in any public protest.

Two questions relating to the fall 1989 demonstrations need further consideration: Why did the core group continue? Why did the general public after all and rather suddenly begin to appear in large numbers? The first may be easier to answer than the second. Despite arrests and harassments, the core group had already weighed the costs and benefits. Moral incentives drove them, inspired them, and enabled them to continue. Detention, arrest, and denunciation as rowdies, punks, and disturbers of good order tended to radicalize them, not stop them.[28] Suppression of the street music festival in June and of the attempted demonstrations during the summer had only deepened their resolve. The well-publicized exodus of GDR citizens during the summer raised hope that renewed public protest would at last force the regime to listen and to enter into the dialogue the groups had long demanded.

Responses to the author's survey support the thesis that moral incentives predominated among the core groups. The prime motivation that drove them—freedom—was a moral issue. Their ties to religion and the churches reinforced their moral stand. A higher-than-average number belonged to and actively participated in the churches: 52.6 percent explicitly named religious reasons as important, and 37 percent as *very* important reasons why they demonstrated. The other surveys show similar findings.[29] These are rather impressive figures in a city where only 18 percent belonged to any church with only a small fraction of those attending regularly. The words of Martin Luther, used by Pastor Schorlemmer to preface his own "Twenty Theses from Wittenberg" in 1988 still resonated: "The time for silence has passed and the time to speak out has come."[30] There were, of course, those whose moral incentives derived from secular sources. The influence of moral principles offers the most plausible reason for such determined, sustained efforts. Surveys have found group members showed little or no interest in economic gain, harbored no ambitions for political power through revolution, nor were much moved by any other reason.

## THE PHENOMENON OF "PEOPLE POWER"

The question of what pulled so many of the general public out on the streets is more difficult to answer. The various reasons mentioned above operated for some. Publicity in the western media of the 4 September demonstration informed a wide number already discontent and now alarmed by the continuing mass exodus. Sympathy for the core demonstrators and curiosity brought some downtown on Mondays. Events in Poland, Czechoslovakia, and the U.S.S.R. may have at least indirectly influenced others to believe that for the first time there was a real chance to push the regime to reform.[31] By the time of the first massive demonstration on 25 September, a snowballing effect became evident, as the demonstrations grew and took on a life of their own, even drawing in some who had only intended to be onlookers.[32]

Zwahr reports another factor that deserves recognition: these massive crowds, while peaceful, developed a sense of enormous power, a rhythm of their own, a communal oneness, which he, an eyewitness, remarks cannot be fully appreciated by those who did not experience it.[33] The crowds clapped, sang, chanted slogans, carried banners, and learned to follow a ritual march route around the Ring. Their sheer numbers exhilarated the participants and confounded and paralyzed the security forces called out to control and disperse them. Their peacefulness and growing confidence and cheerfulness week by week through September and October continue to amaze marchers as they look back on those Mondays. The crowds brought flowers, lighted candles, and chided the security forces attempting to disperse them. Occasionally they got hold of police caps and tossed them around, but usually candles, derisive whistles, clever banners, and chanted slogans were their only weapons. The sheer surge of the multitudes sometimes broke police lines, but in general the crowds avoided direct confrontations. Observers at the early demonstrations recalled that the crowd in St. Nicholas Square sang "We Shall Overcome" and the last three verses of the Communist "Internationale"; and chanted the French revolutionary slogan, "Liberty, Equality, Fraternity"; yet as they hesitantly began to march, those in front waited at the first street for the green light and walked only in the pedestrian crosswalk as they headed for Karl-Marx Square.[34] Police used arrests, nightsticks, and water cannon from time to time in an erratic, piecemeal fashion sufficient to irritate and perhaps radicalize demonstrators, but not enough to deter them from coming back the next week.

Leipzig officials reported to Berlin that 2,000 people were in St. Nicholas Church and another 1,000 awaited them outside on 25 September.[35] On 2 October they reported that the church was again packed, with 3,000 persons outside filling the square and overflowing into side streets. Still more people filled the Reformed Church not far away in a second prayer service. Even more joined as the demonstrators marched, an estimated 6,000–8,000; chants became louder and bolder with cries of "Stasi out!" added to repetition of earlier slogans. The demonstrators marched farther and lingered longer before dispersing. As late as 8:30 some 1,500 gathered again in front of St. Thomas Church, where the unnerved security forces pounced on them with nightsticks and police dogs in a melee lasting an hour.[36]

The events of 9 October are recounted in chapter 1, when more than 70,000 marched after prayer services in four downtown churches adjourned. The next week, no longer fearing any police reaction, at least 120,000 came out. Figures for these weeks, all approximations, are

9 October 70,000+
16 October 120,000

23 October 150,000

30 October 300,000 (in the rain)

6 November 300,000+ (in the rain)

13 November 150,000

20 November 200,000

27 November 100,000+ (cold, damp)

4 December 150,000+

11 December 150,000+

18 December 100,000+ [37]

The growth and massive numbers of the Leipzig demonstrations, as well as their determined nonviolent boldness quickly became the inspiration and model for demonstrations all over the GDR, from East Berlin to the smallest villages. It is probably no coincidence that the size of the crowds peaked on 6 November and declined somewhat after the opening of the Berlin Wall allowed emigrant applicants to leave.

## THE CONNECTION BETWEEN THE PRAYER MEETINGS AND THE DEMONSTRATIONS

Official reports from Leipzig to Berlin about the demonstrations usually began with information about the prayer meetings and often provided for copies to go to Party and government officials responsible for church affairs. Officials always assumed a close tie between the prayer services and the demonstrations. Were they correct? Participants and those who have studied the demonstrations differ rather widely on the nature and closeness of the connection. As late as 18 September, Church leaders were insisting that prayer meeting attendees did not stay to demonstrate. [38]

Regional and national Church leaders officially distanced themselves from public protests. No evidence exists that pastors or Church leaders—or anyone else for that matter—planned and orchestrated the mass demonstrations. On the other hand, Ehrhart Neubert, Gerhard Rein, and others view the prayer meetings and demonstrations as essential, integral parts of a whole, which can in a sense be described as a "Protestant revolution." [39] Pollack, Opp, and others recognize only limited connections, seeing the prayer meetings as a significant, perhaps essential, prelude to the mass demonstrations.

Participants' responses to the author's surveys and interviews suggest that they believe the ties between the two were always very close and very significant, even though prayer meetings and marches remained two distinct and separate phenomena. St. Nicholas Church and its square offered the relatively safe place, programmatic structure, personnel, reference group, and critical mass absolutely essential to generate the early demonstrations. The most important tie of all, however, remained the moral incentives, at least until late November or December, when the composition of the demonstrating crowd altered.

The peace movement which spawned the prayer meetings in the early 1980s based itself on moral principle. When the churches made the peace issue their own, it assumed an authenticity beyond the manipulative peace propaganda served up by the regime. Other moral causes provided motives which moved people onto the streets: concern for social injustices, human rights, and freedoms; protection of the environment (as God's creation). Most respondents to the author's survey (58.4 percent) marched because they were fed up from some combination of the above. Others (23.8 percent) listed specifically human-rights concerns and a general sense of being oppressed. Only 11 percent mentioned economic or job-related incentives, while 4 percent admitted they just wanted to be part of the movement. Christian principles derived from the churches and preached in the prayer meetings provided foundational moral incentives undergirding these concerns and thus motive for participating in both prayer meetings and demonstrations. Just as the demonstrators waited patiently for the doors of St. Nicholas Church to open at the end of the Monday night service before marching, so they depended on the moral principles enunciated in the church to inform and inspire their marches. The principle of nonviolent protest serves as a prime example. Perhaps the most familiar and often-chanted slogan heard in Leipzig that fall was "*Kein Gewalt!*" (No violence!) When, on 25 September, a large number of prayer meeting attendees poured out and *openly* joined the waiting crowd to march, they escalated to a new level the series of mass demonstrations that would unhinge the whole political structure of the GDR.[40]

The authorities only belatedly realized that their decade-long effort to co-opt and manipulate the churches had backfired. When the usual methods of combating opposition—propaganda, surveillance, discrimination, and detention of key leaders—failed, they stayed in denial without the nerve to use all-out force. A peaceful, hymn-singing crowd, carrying candles, not weapons or rocks, did not fit into any of their scenarios. Honecker was unwell and determinedly focused only on the Fortieth Anniversary and the other Politburo members were divided and so uncertain that they left a wide discretion to local authorities in Leipzig. And if they had indeed decided to use force on a large scale in Leipzig? They would likely have created martyrs and radicalized the crowds. The large number of spontaneous, simultaneous demonstrations all over the country suggests that the regime had so lost credibility that it was doomed in any case and sooner rather than later.

## SHIFTS IN SENTIMENT AFTER THE FALL OF
## THE WALL

After 9 October, the "Day of Decision" in Leipzig, the regime's inability
to stop the demonstrations became apparent to all. On the 16th, an im-
mensely larger crowd marched around the Ring Boulevard, secure in the
knowledge that they no longer needed to fear. Crowds continued to grow
throughout October into November despite worsening weather. After the
Christmas break, they resumed in January and the cycle of mass demonstrations continued until the March 1990 elections. However, by mid-
November both the composition and the attitude of the crowds altered
noticeably. When a foreign visitor, Timothy Garton Ash, attended the prayer
service and watched the demonstration on 21 November, he noted that
inside St. Nicholas Church the theme was understanding, tolerance, and
reconciliation, but that he heard little of that outside. There, speakers de-
nounced forty years of corruption and lies, all sorts of groups with special
agendas clamored for attention, and the crowds repeatedly roared, "Germany, One Fatherland!" No longer did anyone sing the *Internationale* or
talk much about the reform of socialism.[41]

What happened to produce such a change? The dramatic events of October and November affected public opinion. The resignation of Honecker
and later the entire Politburo, followed by revelations of corruption, the
opening of the Berlin Wall on 9 November, and an influx of persons and
political programs from the Federal Republic, obviously influenced the situation. Sentiment in Leipzig again ran ahead of the rest of the country.
Förster and Roski's survey of demonstrators on 4 December found that 75
percent of them favored immediate reunification, while only an average of
48 percent of demonstrators in other cities favored it.[42]

The change in composition of the crowds derived primarily from the addition of many new participants, not any substantial withdrawal of the original ones except for the émigrés, at least not until January. Half the 2,000
participants Roski and Förster surveyed on the streets on 4 December and
11 December reported that they were veterans, having marched already
seven Mondays or more. Thirty percent of these 2,000 had also attended
the prayer meetings.[43] Some veterans indeed dropped out in late November
and December, but the great majority kept coming. The advent of the newcomers with their loud shouts gave the crowds the appearance of a greater
change than had actually occurred.

The next logical question is, Did the agenda of the veteran demonstrators
change, even as they kept coming and were joined by so many newcomers?
The author's survey results suggest a qualified "yes" is the answer. A large
majority, 70 percent, demonstrated for political reform of the GDR before
9 October, while few, 11 percent, advocated or expected reunification. After

that date, as events unfolded, their sentiment shifted, until before 1989 ended 47 percent wanted reunification, while the number still hoping to reform the GDR fell by half, to 36 percent.

This "yes" must be qualified by the results of the interviews, which indicated that their idea at that time had been some sort of gradual convergence or confederation of the two Germanies. Nonetheless, at the time of the survey (1995) only 27 percent remained generally disillusioned by the outcome of the demonstrations. Interviewees shared their numerous disappointments and concerns, but few came close to Bärbel Bohley's view of a revolution betrayed.[44] The composition and agenda of the demonstrators had clearly changed by November, primarily with the addition of demands for reunification and the shift away from reform of socialism within existing GDR structures. However, the basic goal of more freedom, the primary motive for 51 percent of the demonstrators, and the desire to turn around a system with which they were overwhelmingly "just fed up," which drove another 17 percent, was achieved, thanks in large part to the demonstrations. It is no exaggeration to say that according to the survey more than two-thirds of the veteran demonstrators achieved what they wanted most.

## CONCLUSIONS

One may conclude, then, that the mass demonstrations in East Germany and especially Leipzig played a significant role in the Eastern Bloc scene in the autumn of 1989, as people power in various forms pulled down one communist-led regime after another, while the Soviets remained aloof. The demonstrations grew out of long-festering discontent and earlier oppositional activities. Young adults in their twenties and early thirties of lower-middle-class background led the way, with slightly more males than females, but the composition of the demonstrations became increasingly diverse as the crowds grew. These demonstrators were not motivated by charismatic leaders or large, well-organized labor or political groups, indeed they evinced an amazing spontaneity and courage in the face of official harassment and discrimination. After the arrests and scattering of opposition leaders in Berlin in 1988, Leipzig became the national focus of oppositional activity. Greater cooperation among the small alternative groups sheltering under Church protection and a converging of interests and activities among staying-home dissidents and discontent emigrant applicants strengthened the citizens' movement in Leipzig more than elsewhere and allowed them to take the lead. Even more, the connection between the prayer meetings with their increasingly politicized, critical programs and the marches that began from St. Nicholas Square brought a unique moral incentive and strength to the Leipzig demonstrations and promoted a nonviolent, massive mode of protest which ultimately confounded the regime. Although most

Church leaders remained opposed to or ambivalent toward public demonstrations until the end of September, they preserved the prayer meetings, while a minority of the clergy gave much-needed leadership and inspiration.

Outside events of the summer and fall doubtless influenced growing concern among the general public, especially the mass flight of people from the GDR and Gorbachev's shift in Soviet policy. When the staying-home oppositionists joined the emigrant applicants in early September to march, they escalated the demonstrations and gave them a legitimacy and publicity that made it easier for the general public to participate, as indeed they began to do in late September and October in vast numbers. Collapse of the regime's opposition on 9 October meant a diminution of danger for Monday marchers and fostered a massive increase in numbers as Leipzig continued to lead the nation. With the swelling of the crowds, the opening of the Berlin Wall on 9 November, and revelations of corruption among GDR leaders, the crowds became more critical and more interested in reunification, moving beyond, even leaving behind the early leaders. One has heard much about East Germans' disillusionment and feelings of betrayal after the end of the GDR and reunification; indeed, few of the Leipzig dissidents gained prominence in the new order. The "democratic renewal of our Socialist state" never happened. Yet, the author's survey results suggest that veteran demonstrators remain more pleased than displeased with the outcome. Many incentives motivated the demonstrators, but most basic were moral principles, especially the desire for more freedom and more respect for basic human rights. The demonstrations succeeded in helping to achieve both.

## NOTES

1. See the text of the leaflet in the Appendix. For report of the shout see Grabner, Heinze, and Pollack, eds., 51.

2. Rüddenklau, 314–20.

3. Ibid.

4. Dietrich and Schwabe, eds., 266–68, 527. See the Stasi Report in the Appendix.

5. Bernd Lindner, *Die demokratische Revolution in der DDR 1989/90* (Bonn: Bundeszentrale für politische Bildung, 1998), 8.

6. Dietrich and Schwabe, eds., 527.

7. See the position paper of the Leipzig church superintendents in Dietrich and Schwabe, eds., 266–67, and the forceful rebuttal of Berlin group members in Rüddenklau, 321–22.

8. See excerpts from the five-page report by State Secretary Löffler on his meeting with Bishop Hempel on 23 January in the Appendix. The full German text is in Dietrich and Schwabe, eds., 269–72.

9. K. Führer, 27–28; the text of the prisoner's declaration is in Dietrich and Schwabe, eds., 267–68. Michael Arnold read the declaration; Jochen Lässig issued the invitation from the floor. Both were prominent activists.

10. The 1989 demonstrations may be further subdivided into: (1) 15 January–May elections, growing discontent but few and small demonstrations; (2) May–9 October, election protests escalate discontent and size of crowds; (3) 9 October–9 November, the heart of the movement; (4) 9 November–18 December, rapid shifts in focus and composition of crowds; (5) mid-January–18 March, Election Day, focus on the coming election. See, for example, Philipsen, 333–34.

11. To be precise 60.4 percent were male, 39.6 percent female. In Leipzig's total population females outnumbered males 54.4 percent to 45.6 percent. See Opp, p. 255, and *Statistisches Jahrbuch Leipzig*, 1992.

12. Förster and Roski, *DDR zwischen Wende und Wahl*, 18–19; 159ff. Opp, 253–61.

13. Kurt Mühler and Steffan Wilsdorf, "Meinungstrends in der Leipziger Montagsdemonstrationen," in Grabner et al, eds., 159–63. Their focus was primarily on the trend favoring reunification.

14. Opp, et al., 253–61.

15. No response was 3 percent. From interviews, it appears a few of those marking "university education" intended to indicate university-eligible, that is, *Abitur*.

16. Förster and Roski, *DDR Zwischen Wende und Wohl*, 161. Responses reported by Mühler and Wilsdorf were very similar. Opp found that neither professional position nor monthly salary made any significant difference in the level of protest activity, 164.

17. Interview 1995. Jochen Lässig, a prominent leader, also held this opinion. Opp, 104–5.

18. The remaining 8 percent did not remember when they joined or did not respond to this question.

19. Opp, 259.

20. Mühler and Wilsdorf report 88 percent to 93 percent responded similarly in all of their five surveys. Grabner, eds., 169.

21. Opp, 263.

22. Ibid., 262.

23. Ibid., 41–43.

24. Activists often expressed such concerns in the interviews. See Appendix.

25. For two graphic accounts in English translation, see Swoboda, ed., 155–67. Numerous excerpts from Stasi policies toward demonstrators can be found in *Bürgerkomitee*; see for example 217–18. See the Appendix for the all too typical account of Karsten Boche.

26. Interviews with Carola Barnschlegel (see Appendix) and Rainer Müller, Leipzig 1995.

27. For the Berlin activist Jens Reich, freedom from such angst was the most important outcome of the *Wende*. Gerhard Rein, ed., *Die Opposition in der DDR: Entwürfe für einen anderen Sozialismus* (Berlin: Wichern Verlag, 1989), 27–29.

28. The Opp surveys found the radicalization effect confirmed statistically (Opp, 175). One demonstrator, Reinhold Tetzner, among others, recalled that his anger at being labeled one of the rowdies in the press made him all the more determined to go to the next Monday demonstration. Tetzner, 16.

29. Opp, 134–36.

30. Schorlemmer's "Twenty Theses" are published in Rein, ed., *Die Opposition*, 199–202. See excerpts in the Appendix.

31. Opp's responses rather discount the influence of these external events. Opp doubts that general trends and events in other countries directly motivated individuals spontaneously to go out and march (Opp, 30).

32. For further descriptions of this effect, see Döhnert and Rummel, in Grabner, Heinze, and Pollack, eds., 150–55.

33. Zwahr, 9.

34. Döhnert and Rummel in Grabner, Heinze, and Pollack, eds., 150–51. Photographs of the first massive demonstration are in Bohse et al., eds., 34–38.

35. The top-secret Stasi report together with proposals for official response to preclude any repetition is in Mitter and Wolle, eds., 174–76.

36. Official report of the Leipzig SED second secretary, Helmut Hackenberg, to Honecker dated 3 October in Dietrich and Schwabe, eds., 437–40.

37. These estimates come primarily from Schneider, ed., which contains many excellent photographs along with a brief chronicle of events. For a chronicle giving highlights of other demonstrations and related events in the GDR, see, among others Links and Bahrmann and Besier and Wolf, eds., 817–41. Opp also includes estimates and believes the correct number for 9 October is more likely 124,000 than 70,000 (Opp, 24).

38. See Pastor Führer's notes on 18 September in Dietrich and Schwabe, eds., 399–400.

39. Neubert, *Geschichte*, 33ff.; Rein ed., *Die Protestantische Revolution*, chapter 1.

40. Zwahr, 79.

41. Timothy Garton Ash, *The Magic Lantern: The Revolution of '89 Witnessed in Warsaw, Budapest, Berlin and Prague* (New York: Random House, 1990), 70–73.

42. Förster and Roski, *DDR Zwischen Wende und Wahl* 163.

43. Günter Roski and Peter Förster, "Leipziger DEMOskopie," in Schneider, ed., 173–74.

44. Joppke, 179.

# 7

## Conclusion

More than ten years have passed since the tumultuous events of 1989. That year indeed became a turning point for Germany, one unlike 1848 with its attempted revolution when Germany's quest for a more open, democratic society failed, or was at least delayed. In 1989 the wave of protests that swept across East Germany presaged a speedy end to forty years of efforts to delimit and develop a Communist state in the former Soviet zone of occupation.

Leipzig's demonstrators heralded the "turn," the *Wende*, with their persistent courage and with their massive numbers in the streets each Monday. As Charles Maier succinctly concludes, "the fate of the East German regime was decided on the Leipzig Ring on four successive Monday evenings between September 25 and October 16," then confirmed in Berlin, November 4 and November 9.[1] The demands articulated in Leipzig both formed and reflected the agenda for all East Germany. Leipzig's unique situation made it the center and its activists the leaders of protest in the GDR. Leipzig's tradition of protest and the more organized cooperation there among diverse activists and clergy leadership also contributed to its emergence as the national center of protest by 1988. The deficiencies of the regime revealed themselves more blatantly in Leipzig than in other cities in its neglected infrastructure, in its increasingly polluted air and water, and in the lack of concern or competence of Party and State officials. East Berlin, capital and "showcase" of the regime, also deserves recognition as a protest center but was less neglected and more alertly controlled. Its oppositionists remained less organized and perhaps more divided among themselves. Dresden demonstrators played a significant role, too, yet Modrow and the Party leaders arguably handled the situation there a bit better than in most cities. Smaller towns such as Jena and Plauen witnessed dramatic protests but could not command the national stage because of their size and location.

The regime's efforts to repress all opposition and to co-opt the churches and use them to channel and tame activists ultimately backfired. A sophisticated blend of surveillance, harassment, and discrimination toward nonconformists seemed to work well enough from the 1960s into the mid-1980s. Those who refused to join in "building socialism" or to retreat quietly to their private niches after nominally conforming were allowed a limited toleration within the shelter of the churches, the only institutions with an alternative *Weltanschauung* and semi-autonomy. Rather than compliant clergy taming the opposition, the opposition used their opportunities to meet in the churches to publicize their agenda and encourage and network with each other. The Leipzig prayer meetings constitute perhaps the most successful, but by no means the only, example. Church leaders understood, but disliked, the role of "temple police" which the state sought to foist on them.[2] They remained divided and ambivalent toward public political protests; they talked politely and soothingly to officials with "pliant firmness." At the same time they protected, if reluctantly, the activists among the clergy, sheltered the groups, and continued to defend the prayer meetings as they became more political and oppositional. An activist minority of clergy exercised much-needed leadership and conferred a certain legitimacy on the opposition. From the perspective of the "hard-core" activists, the church leadership remained too timid and accommodationist. Nonetheless, some clergy, a dozen or so in Leipzig, spoke up frankly to the authorities about existing problems and advised and supported the groups despite the risks.

The Leipzig groups and their protest activities in the 1980s are an interesting phenomenon to explore. Though overwhelmingly reformist socialists, not typical revolutionaries, and very small in numbers, they kept oppositional activity alive. Through all the ups and downs of their relationships with Church leaders, they programmed the prayer meetings and the more activist groups led in the early demonstrations. They defined the oppositional scene which others, especially those wanting to exit the country, joined.[3] Organization of a coordinating committee, the BSA, to program the prayer meetings was a key step in stabilizing the groups' rather fluid and chaotic existence and in bringing them together in a common purpose.

Some who have studied these groups would downplay their role and define them as too individualistic, too politically naive, and too marginalized within society to deserve credit for anything more than a little "mosquito" activity. Their connection with the mass demonstrations has even been called "spurious," the proof offered being the masses of nongroup members who made possible the mass demonstrations and the outcome in 1990, which was of course quite different from what the groups originally contemplated.[4] Yet this view may be too much colored by the hindsight of later events. Opp's view that the demonstrations developed "spontaneously" is accurate in a broad sense, yet his threshold model does help one evaluate correctly the contributions of the groups. They not only kept opposition alive in Leipzig, their persistent, public acts eventually created a sort of threshold of safety for the general public as they also began to attend the prayer meetings and finally to march. The groups developed the ideological platform, which proved a powerful blend of moral concern for justice, human rights, freedom, and the environment as well as peace. The general public never rejected this platform; they simply refused to believe it could be accomplished within a reformed GDR.

While the role of the groups in the evolution of the Monday prayer meetings seems undisputed, debate continues over the precise relationship between these meetings and the mass demonstrations. A proper evaluation of the importance of the prayer meetings' contribution to the *Wende* hinges on the definition of this relationship. The conclusion here, drawn from interviews and study of documentary materials, is that the prayer meetings should be considered more than an essential prerequisite and more than a wellspring for the demonstrations. They indeed were all of that, but they also provided the moral principles, legitimacy, and nonviolent method. Moreover, they offered *hope* and *encouragement* to both the Christians and the many non-Christians who attended. They provided a time and place to speak out, to make a public statement of concerns by attending.[5]

It would be misleading to count the influence of the meetings merely in numbers—the 9,000 who overflowed St. Nicholas Church and three other downtown churches in comparison to the more than 70,000 who filled downtown Leipzig on 9 October. One must also consider the thousands who stood patiently in the church square, awaiting dismissal of service as their cue to join in "We Shall Overcome" and the other songs of the exiting prayer meeting attendees. The candles, the flowers, the names of political victims under arrest posted inside the church and in the windows had a significant impact. Candles lit at St. Nicholas might be left burning on the steps of Stasi headquarters before the evening's march ended. The fact that thirty percent of the December demonstrators randomly surveyed on the streets by Rosk and Förster wanted to identify themselves as prayer meetings attendees offers statistical support to the thesis that the influence of these services was great.[6] More than half those responding to the author's survey stated that religious motives were important to them.

Those who assign the prayer meetings to a prelude status can correctly point out that Church leaders generally opposed public protests, that attendees were usually exhorted to go home quietly, and that prayer meetings and demonstrations remained in many ways two distinct phenomena. The response to those points depends on evaluation of nonquantifiable intangibles. Do churchgoers routinely refrain from doing what their minister warns against? How much impact did Christian principles have on the masses of non-Christians inside and outside St. Nicholas? Was the motivating power behind the marches primarily moral outrage and prayer-meeting-inspired? How important was hope in this context? Was it one of the great motivating forces? Results of this study would suggest a negative response to the first question and positive responses to the others, thus assigning a very significant role to the prayer meetings. The demonstrations, though distinct, drew inspiration and opportunity and method from them. The prayer meetings offered meaningful hope for change, and hope has been regarded historically as a universal and abiding motivator of enormous potential.[7]

The demonstrations in Leipzig and elsewhere overwhelmed the regime because they grew so large, remained so regular, and held so totally, tenaciously, confidently, and even good-naturedly to their constant slogan: *Kein Gewalt!* (No violence!) Hopes for change raised by Gorbachev, escalating frustrations with problems, lack of sympathetic regime responses, and disgust with propaganda divorced from reality all combined to arouse the general public. News of the mass exodus of fellow citizens to the West compelled many to come out of their niches onto the streets. Encouraging changes in other Eastern Bloc countries may also have served to motivate. Anger at being labeled rowdies and troublemakers stiffened the resolve of demonstrators to return each Monday and bring relatives and friends.

Leipzig set the example. The fusing or at least alliance of three disparate elements, "voice," "exit," and the general public, in an alliance unique to Leipzig, launched the mass demonstrations. Those wanting to exit provided the numbers and much of the boldness for the early demonstrations. The "voice" element, the groups and other prayer meeting attendees, then decided to demonstrate also, first on special occasions, then regularly beginning the first Monday in September. Separate marches of the two merged, and by 25 September the general public was participating in rapidly mounting numbers.

The vast numbers in the demonstration did not alone make 9 October the day of decision. Rather, decisions made by individuals all over town and in the surrounding area to take a major risk and come downtown in defiance of all the regime's prohibitions produced the vast numbers. The decision of the authorities not to use force against such numbers was the most crucial decision of all.[8] The risks seemed real enough to demonstrators with the ostentatious deployment of security forces to make the downtown area look like an armed camp. Rarely has the crowd intervened in German history with any lasting effect. Yet if the historical precedents were few, the magnitude of their concerns plus recent events, climaxing years of discontent, proved sufficiently motivational for each of the three elements.

As the demonstrations produced change—freedom to march, downfall of the SED, opening of the Berlin Wall—the composition and agenda of the demonstrations altered. Discontent with the old order mounted to anger with revelations of corruption and incompetency. The old church-related groups merged into the new secular organizations: New Forum, Democratic Awakening, Democracy Now, the new Social Democratic Party, and others which competed with the growing influence of West German political parties. Talk of reforming and humanizing the socialism of the GDR yielded to shouts of "Germany, one Fatherland!" and to a babble of chants for various special interests. Nonetheless, although the composition and agenda of the demonstrations changed in November and December, a close tie to the prayer meetings continued all through 1989 and into early 1990. Similar basic goals remained: dialogue with those in power; a more open society with freedom of speech, press, and assembly; a more just society without political restrictions on education, career advancement, travel, and especially without arbitrary political harassment, arrests, and detentions.[9] Shared hope remained, also hope that both the prayer meeting attendees and the demonstrators were bringing in a better day for themselves and their children. Certainly the goal of reunification emerged as it had not before. Or would it be more accurate to say that the timetable changed, from someday in a far distant future to 1990? The nonviolent philosophy also continued to prevail. Anger and frustration would find peaceful outlet in roundtable meetings with those in power, in free expressions by speakers, in demonstrations, and ultimately at the polls in March 1990, but not in violence. The schedule for protest remained Monday evenings after the prayer services. And as late as 18 December, the last Monday evening before the traditional Christmas break, 100,000 marchers carried candles, not weapons or even banners, as the demonstration became a giant outdoor prayer-memorial service extending the St. Nicholas service, making the downtown a glittering sea of candles with a time for silent meditation beginning and ending at the dictates of the city's church bells.

In the early months of 1990, with the progress of the election campaign, the demonstrations and Monday prayer meetings ceased to attract the crowds and no longer functioned as the locus of political activity. Election politics and the question of a united Germany dominated public interest. The elections showed that the general public wanted no more experiments in socialism, rather a quick unification with the Federal Republic. The weak showing of the reform groups in the elections and the mode of unification bitterly disappointed many veteran activists. The "better world" for which they had demonstrated turned out to be quite different from the reformed GDR they had anticipated. Complaints of a "revolution betrayed" or questions of whether the word *revolution* applied at all could be heard.[10]

The correct label for the process, be it revolution, reform, or some other is not, however, the question for this study, and neither is an evaluation of the outcome. Rather this study has sought to explore the relationships between the church-related opposition groups, the prayer meetings, and the demonstrations in Leipzig during the late 1980s and to determine the significance of these prayer meetings and demonstrations in the collapse of the GDR. The disintegration of a philosophical-economic system such as Communism and the dissolution of a sovereign state are such uncommon events as to provoke continuing interest and debate. The motivations and methods of the courageous individuals who participated merit the historian's close attention. Their own views of what happened, augmented by official documents, have served as important resources. In other times and places a few people, armed with a strong sense of the right moral cause, have upset well-established regimes, but never before in Germany. The moral strength nurtured in St. Nicholas Church and the daring public display of protest along the Ring Boulevard show once again the power of the determined few as well as the potency of the masses. They also confirm that the influence of Christian ideals runs deeper in Germany than church attendance might suggest. The decline of the U.S.S.R. and the breakup of its Eastern Bloc spelled doom in any case for the GDR as it had existed for forty years, but the outcome might have been quite different and quite bloody, had it not been for those exhilarating, extraordinary Monday nights in Leipzig!

## NOTES

1. Maier, 139.

2. Superintendent Magirius used this term, for example, in a meeting with General Rudolph Sabatowski when the latter complained about "misuse" of the prayer meetings. The reference is to the New Testament mention of the Jewish temple police in Jerusalem, who were subservient to the occupying Roman army. Minutes of this meeting of 20 March 1989 are reproduced in Uwe Schwabe, "Symbol der Befreiung—Die Friedensgebete in Leipzig," *Horch und Guck* 23, 2 (1998): 10–11.

3. Joppke's view, 135.

4. Ibid. See also Stokes, 138–39.

5. Ecclesiastes 3:7, Old Testament, was quoted at several prayer meetings: "A time to keep silence and a time to speak."

6. Roski and Förster's 11 December random survey of 2,000 demonstrators. Schneider, ed., 174.

7. Christianity teaches that hope stands with faith and love among the greatest virtues and values in life. I Corinthians 13:13, New Testament.

8. Konrad H. Jarausch, *The Rush to German Unity* (New York: Oxford University Press, 1994), 45.

9. Ralf Dahrendorf concludes that the open society, not capitalism, was the real winner in 1989. *Reflections on the Revolution in Europe* (New York: Random House, 1990), 40.

10. Bärbel Bohley spoke often in such terms. See, for example, Hagen Findeis, Detlef Pollack, and Manuel Schilling, eds., *Die Entzauberung des Politischen*, (Leipzig and Berlin: Evangelische Verlagsanstalt, 1994), 57.

# A Note on the Questionnaires, Interviews, and Respondents

After a visit to Leipzig in 1993, the author prepared in 1994 a questionnaire with the kind assistance of those individuals mentioned in the Preface. The questionnaire requested information on gender; education; occupation in 1989 and at present; church affiliation; and participation in the alternative groups, Monday prayer meetings, and demonstrations. Respondents were also asked about their motivations, the nature and extent of their involvement, harassment experienced, and their opinions on various aspects of these events. The questionnaire was mailed out in the spring of 1995 to 312 individuals still living in Leipzig who were known to have participated actively in the prayer meetings, demonstrations, or both. The number of questionnaires returned was 101, a return rate of 32.4 percent. This rate may be compared to the 40 percent return rate of a survey of a representative sample of 1,300 Leipzigers contacted in late 1990 by a Berlin polling institute for Professor Karl-Dieter Opp, a Leipzig University sociologist. This institute regarded the return rate as rather low, but not unusual in Leipzig and adequate for use.[1] Other important surveys have been conducted by Peter Förster and Günter Roski[2] and by Kurt Mühler and Steffan Wilsdorf.[3] These three were conducted from the perspective of sociologists and with different emphases from the author. Opp was particularly interested in the origins of the demonstrations and in finding out which if any sociological model could be helpful in explaining them. The other two focused on the composition of the crowds of demonstrators and on the shift of political opinion among the various movements and parties, especially the rise of sentiment for immediate reunification. The author's survey concerned itself with the alternative groups and prayer meetings and with their relationship to the demonstrations and other oppositional activities.

Results of the author's survey did not in general vary much from other findings about oppositionists in regard to their personal characteristics: more men than women (60.4 percent versus 39.6 percent); many more church members (66.3 percent) than in the general population; predominance of participants in their late twenties and early thirties; mostly lower-middle-class (63.6 percent), with considerable blue-collar representation (18.9 percent); few with university degrees and virtually no university students. One significant difference seems to be the greater length and intensity of the involvement of the respondents in the author's sample. For example 18 percent began to attend the prayer meetings in the early 1980s and 21 percent began between 1985 and 1988. Nearly all participated in demonstrations (99 percent), with 14 percent beginning before 1989. Nearly half had experienced direct discrimination or harassment (44 percent) and some (6 percent) had spent time in jail. A second difference would be the even larger number of church members in the author's sample and especially the percentage of members who regularly attended church services (52 percent). The number of clergy (12.9 percent) was also larger.

Responses in the author's survey to questions about whether the prayer meetings and demonstrations had accomplished what respondents hoped were quite divided. Only 25 percent expressed general satisfaction with the outcome, while nearly half (47.5 percent) expressed dissatisfaction and the remaining quarter remained ambiguous or uncertain. Only 8 percent thought that reunification as it actually occurred was the right result. Nonetheless, a large majority (70 percent) felt that the influence of the Church had been positive and significant.

It is worth noting that few of the respondents had benefited personally from the *Wende*. One indeed had become a *Bundestag* deputy and one a member of the Leipzig city council, but several had lost their jobs or had been forced to take early retirement. Others had managed to hold on to their jobs or find comparable employment, but not without prolonged uncertainty and anxiety. Respondents from the clergy had all been active in the opposition as group sponsors and participants and had maintained the normal course of their careers with apparently neither reward nor punishment from higher Church authorities for their involvement.

The author conducted follow-up interviews in Leipzig with respondents to the questionnaire in the summer of 1995. These interviews were recorded, translated, and transcribed. There were 31 interview sessions, lasting at least an hour, which took place in St. Mark's Parish Hall or in homes or offices. The atmosphere was informal, with much discussion; occasionally family members or friends also joined in, so that the total number interviewed approached 50. The author discovered (as did Opp) that respondents' memories of these events remained clear and detailed.[4] Their time and effort to remember is much appreciated.

These interviews, in addition to comparisons with other surveys, confirmed the author's belief that while this sample was not, strictly speaking, a scientific one, these respondents all came out of the mainstream of the Leipzig citizens' opposition movement and accurately represented its characteristics, ideas, and activities.

## NOTES

1. Opp, 253–68.
2. Roski and Förster in Schneider, ed., 173–76. See also Förster and Roski, *DDR Zwischen Wende und Wahl*, chapter 1.
3. Mühler and Wilsdorf in Grabner et al., eds., 159–63.
4. Opp 259.

# *Appendix*

The documents and excerpts from documents listed below have been translated from the original German into English by the author with the assistance of Professor Brian Kirby. Herr Thomas Seliger served as translator for the interviews in Leipzig. While deeply grateful for their work, the author accepts full responsibility for these translations.

## DOCUMENTS

1. Friedrich Schorlemmer's "Twenty Theses from Wittenberg," 1988
2. Michael Arnold's Memoir of the 14 March 1988 Demonstration
3. Emigrant Applicant's Letter to Pastor Christian Führer, 1988
4. Underground Leaflet Announcing a Demonstration, 15 January 1989
5. Stasi Report of 16 January 1989
6. State Secretary Kurt Löffler's Report on a Conference with Bishop Johannes Hempel, 23 January 1989
7. Karsten Boche's Memoir of His Arrest and Detention, 11 September 1989
8. Memoir of Party Militia Member Gerald Pilz, September 1989
9. Memoir of an SED Member Who Attended the 9 October Prayer Meeting
10. Appeal of the Leipzig Six, 9 October
11. Appeal of the Groups, 9 October
12. Pastor Christian Führer's Memories of 9 October

## INTERVIEWS

All interviews were conducted in June and July 1995 except the interview with Pastor Führer, which took place in July 1993.

Interview with Carola Barnschlegel

Interview with Reinhard Bohse

Interview with Konrad Fehr

Interview with Pastor Christian Führer

Interview with Pastor Rolf-Dieter Hannsmann

Interview with Marianne Ramson

Interview with Uwe Schwabe and Pastor Michael Turek

## *PASTOR FRIEDRICH SCHORLEMMER'S "TWENTY THESES FROM WITTENBERG," 1988*

At the regional Lutheran Church Synod in June 1988 Pastor Friedrich Schorlemmer presented twenty theses, which had been developed in the Wittenberg parishes. These circulated among the alternative groups and represented the boldest and most direct criticism of the regime to date from church sources.[1]

## TWENTY THESES FROM WITTENBERG FOR THE RENEWAL AND REORGANIZATION OF THE GERMAN DEMOCRATIC REPUBLIC

"The time for silence is past, and the time for speaking has come."
(Martin Luther, 1520)

With that which we concretely outline, we want to provoke a productive dialogue. For this to take place in our society, we need anxiety-free and democratic forms as well as courage. We know about the constraints on action in which we find ourselves in the meantime. We want to free ourselves from them. Just how we solve this problem will require competence and commitment.

1. Because we as Christians in the freedom and common ties of faith feel jointly responsible and therefore also complicit in that which our nation is becoming, we find it necessary, indeed required, that we overcome our fear, our mistrust, and our lack of expectancy, and instead see and seize the chances for change and gain an honesty out of which we can with critical solidarity press for a renewal of our society.

2. Because apathy, resignation, and stagnation are spreading in society and consequently the number of people who are withdrawing or not wanting to live here is increasing, we find it necessary to discuss these developments openly and to restructure the framework of society so that more citizens can experience meaningful involvement in public affairs.

3. Because the development of socialist states has shown how bureaucracy and governmental abuses, conformity and dogmatism, official arbitrariness and fear of authority lead to a societal depression and denigrate the essence of socialism, we must urgently uncover such instances and also overcome the abuses even in ourselves.

4. Because each citizen has a legitimate right of thorough information regarding all relevant life-questions, we find it necessary to change our media policies so that the complexity and contradiction of reality is reflected in order to enable individuals to form opinions and to encourage conscious action.

5. Because a continuing tipping of the balance toward successes, a looking through rose-colored glasses, or silencing of failures, abuses, and truths does not stir us to take on accumulated problems, we find it urgent to create a social climate characterized by openness, truthfulness, and critical readiness to take responsibility.

6. Because the election process to date has hindered competition, we find it necessary that each election offer distinct choices between several candidates.

7. Because a societal consciousness as well as public participation can only be expected from citizens who think of themselves as having a voice, we find it necessary that participation possibilities noticeably increase in all areas of society in order to provide a basis for official decisions, thereby making them understood.

8. Because the right to petition has not proved sufficient and official decisions have remained difficult to contest, we find it necessary to establish an independent administrative legal process.

9. Because the criminal code and the penal system are not in accordance with much of the humanistic image and ideals of a new society, we find it necessary to carry out a revision in language, content, and practice.

10. Because only a culture enlivened by a struggle for truth and for the best means of human coexistence leads to a humane and just world that is capable of surviving, we find it necessary that the Communists abdicate their power-enforced monopoly on truth and their claim in principle to societal superiority.

[Theses 11–18 attack militaristic high school courses, restrictions on travel, and lack of concern for the environment. They urge open dialogue and help for disadvantaged Third-World counties.]

19. Because we have the responsibility to leave behind to our children and grand-children a livable earth, we find it pressing that, especially in a socialist country, the conflict between ecology and the economy not have a loser.

20. Because the coming generation must be prepared for the pressing problems of the future, we find it necessary, that the rearing and educational process become more creative, closer to nature, and more unified, with a priority for the reverence of life before the domination over life becomes a practice field for "societal inventions."

We will come to see that we will gain life through this renewal. But are we personally ready to carry the burdens along the way?

## NOTE

1. The German text is published in Rein, ed., *Die Opposition*, 81–85.

# MICHAEL ARNOLD'S MEMOIR OF THE
# 14 MARCH 1988 DEMONSTRATION

Many protest actions took place before the mass demonstrations of the fall of 1989 and were often associated with the Monday prayer services. This report of the demonstration of 14 March 1988 was written shortly afterward by a participant, Michael Arnold. Note the emphasis on the importance of cooperation between the emigrant applicants and oppositionists intending to stay in the GDR.[1]

Demonstrations in the Trade Fair metropolis of the GDR. After the end of peace prayers in the St. Nicholas Church on Monday, 14 March 1988, in which roughly 900 Leipzigers participated, a majority of participants gathered in the church square and just about filled it. After twenty minutes of standing around, still discussing unanswered questions—even though they had been spoken to in the peace prayers, the questions were certainly still not sufficiently answered for the majority—one group of participants began a movement toward the center of town. More and more of the people on the square joined them, so that around 400 prayer meeting participants began to walk toward St. Thomas Church. The march which had begun so spontaneously went by a review line made up of civilian security officials, curious onlookers, interested passersby, and visitors to the Spring Trade Fair. [This was] an impressive demonstration as an expression of protest against the detention of two Leipzigers, Karin Moran and Hans-Joachim Pfeifer, out of protest against the "display-window peace"[2] on the occasion of the Spring Trade Fair and in order to bring into the public arena the problem of traveling abroad. A certain helplessness on the part of the State Security, as to how they could disband and bring an end to this march, without causing a stir and exciting possible suspicion from the Trade Fair visitors, could not be overlooked. Reaching St. Thomas Church, the demonstrators formed a circle. At the same time, they were trying to encircle a group of security officials. On a clever hunch, these immediately tried to get away, rather than be left for open ridicule. During the attempt to enclose each of them inside the circle they flew from the outstretched hands. After the circle was closed, like a chain, the prayer meeting participants began to sing the verse "Hewenu Schalom Elechem" ("We Are Bringing You Peace"). Then the group walked back to the Market Square and continued their song, and formed there too a hand-to-hand ring and walked further in a chain back to St. Nicholas Church. On the way from the Market Square to the church, a police patrol car asked the demonstrators for the first time to disband the march. Disregarding this request, the group of singing demonstrators walked back to St. Nicholas Church and did not disband until several minutes had passed.

Without a direct appeal, coming simply out of an inner agreement, we succeeded after a long while in Leipzig to grow also outside the church community and to express protest in the form of a march. People who wanted to travel abroad were not the only ones in the march, but others included representatives from the group Initiative Group for Life, among others, who support the push for human rights in the GDR. A first good sign is that the right of free choice of where to live is no longer just seen as a problem and task of the emigrant applicant, but rather the people who want to travel abroad need to show solidarity with those who do not want to leave the country, but still recognize this basic human right, and finally actively work together to support the affected applicants. A good sign also is that the notion is no longer being tolerated that people who want to find their purpose in life in another country are seen as outcasts of our country. Lastly, it also needs to be emphasized, that this time it did not come to a riot on the part of the police or the demonstrators, so that the parade made a good close to the peace prayers. This primitive right of forming a peaceful march, that on that Monday had been simply claimed as unlawful under the laws of the GDR, must remain the content of our further work.

## NOTES

1. The German text is published in Dietrich and Schwabe, eds., 142–43.
2. During the spring and fall Trade Fairs, Leipzig was "dressed up" for foreign visitors by the regime to exude an atmosphere of contentment and prosperity. Display windows were filled with items not available for purchase the rest of the year.

## EMIGRANT APPLICANT'S LETTER TO PASTOR CHRISTIAN FÜHRER, 1988

This letter, dated 23 May 1988, carries a confessional tone, probably not typical of the emigrant applicants, yet it refers to many of the conflicts that led them to apply to emigrate. Those who applied often waited years and might lose their jobs or otherwise face discrimination. Pastor Führer had organized special groups and programs to make them feel welcome at St. Nicholas.[1]

Dear Pastor Führer!
I write you this letter because I am a somewhat hesitant and timid person who lacks the courage to speak at the right time and place. I have never managed to before and still can't. This isn't the everyday sort of letter and is to serve as an explanation, to a certain extent a confession. But not to God or his servants, but to a special public, to an unusual, purposeful congregation that gathers every Monday evening in St. Nicholas Church. It is before this group that I wish to offer my confession and ask that you bring it to be read there.[2] . . . I feel sure that all of this must be spoken openly and I am also sure that I'm writing here the unspoken thoughts of many and that many in the Monday congregation will find [their own thoughts] in my words.

Allow me, then please, from here on to use "we" and "us." Those, however, who don't feel that my words relate to them can consider themselves fortunate. It is true we are not, or are only half-hearted, Christians, and in the past we have concerned ourselves very little for the Christian community, and we are not doing much more in the present. Also, we cannot claim to be convinced atheists. We found little time for problems of this sort in the past. After the "Berlin events" and the unhappy role the Church played in them,[3] we slipped into the Leipzig peace prayers, hoping that the same thing or some similar event would throw us out of this country. We are, nonetheless, cowards, petty bourgeois opportunists who in the last resort are cautious about conflict with this State. We don't want to risk anything, we just want to be nearby when things happen because of others.

And so we sit in St. Nicholas Church every Monday and put our hopes on the others, those determined to stay here, that they will go to court before the State and all society. We applaud like children every statement that seems daring and imagine ourselves conspirators. . . . We are doubtful of those who believe that they can bring change to this land which has materially and in terms of official morality gone downhill. We think only one thing: out, out, out. . . .

The "peace prayers" are supposed to assure our personal peace, peace for our last years or days in the G.D.R. . . .

But we are cowards "going along—getting along" in the past and present. We don't get involved without calculating the risk. We have made the most we could out of our lives in the GDR and want to maintain that. We went through this stupid *Jugendweihe*;[4] we always accepted leadership posts, while lacking convictions. We waved flags when it was expected, sang Red songs, collected money, made wall posters. . . . We, like everyone, concealed our true feelings and didn't stop the lies even within our family circle. We never have, however, risked trying to climb over the Wall or swim the Elbe.[5] We only secretly balled up our fists and complained softly in our closets. We never stood up against the craziness of militarization, we didn't resist the primitive consumerist urge, or enter the hopeless struggle for the environment. Socialism stopped at the front door, but any objections to it never began. And finally we share responsibility for the election results, which always begin with a 99 before the decimal point, for we never needed a pencil or voting booth.[6] We swore loyalty to a Party and disowned our relatives in the West. . . . But we have taken up golf, have two color television sets, and have been often in Hungary and Bulgaria. We have a country cottage, a job with a retirement plan and a comfortable savings account. . . . And now we sit here under the cross, renewed in our search for the optimum. Yet we have miscalculated. Doubts arise. Will we be punished for our opportunism, our hesitation? Will we be unable to get off the sinking ship in time? Is everyone plotting against us? Are we lost? What can we do? We the creators, the prime examples of individuals "getting along" in society, have come to the end. There is nothing left to make the optimum. We feel very small and come into the church. We, the grand opportunists, the grand petty bourgeois, no longer feel the need to "get along." Our opportunism is no longer the question. We simply need help. We are now ready even to consider Jesus Christ and his way of helping. We want to be comforted.

Dear Pastor Führer!

We need this Monday, even if the prayer service and Church truly don't deserve guests of this sort. We need the few pastors who, without considerations of religious logic or Church procedures, are standing by us. We want to continue to enjoy guest privileges from you and are very appreciative of you. Excuse us for having become what we are without even knowing!

[Signature blocked out]

## NOTES

1. The German text is published in Dietrich and Schwabe, eds., 168–70.

2. Pastor Führer read the last part of the letter to the congregation at the first Monday meeting after the summer break, 29 August 1988.

3. This apparently refers to the police raid on the Environmental Library at Zion Church in Berlin on 24 November 1987 and the accompanying arrests and church protests.

4. The secular coming-of-age ceremony intended to replace Church confirmation rites and inculcate loyalty to Party and State.

5. The Elbe River formed the boundary for some distance between the two Germanies.

6. Voters in the GDR elections were encouraged to vote yes by immediately dropping their ballots into the boxes; only those wishing to cast a negative vote needed to enter the voting booths and mark their ballot.

# UNDERGROUND LEAFLET ANNOUNCING A DEMONSTRATION, 15 JANUARY 1989

## APPEAL TO ALL CITIZENS OF LEIPZIG[1]

It is the 70th anniversary of the murder of two leaders of the working class—Rosa Luxemburg and Karl Liebknecht—and again thousands of workers are required to attend a rally at which the speakers annually repeat their speeches.

Both leaders of the workers stood for the all-encompassing political and economic interests of the working class, also for the unhindered right to organize and assemble, for an uncensored press, for open elections and the free exchange of opinions.

People who claim this legacy, appealing to the constitution of our country after forty years of the GDR, are regularly being criminalized.

The anniversary day of the murder of Rosa Luxemburg and Karl Liebknecht should offer an occasion to stand up for a democratization of our socialist state. This is the right time to state our opinion, bravely and openly: and the paralyzing lack of participation and the indifference! Let us together stand up

- for the right to express opinions freely

- for freedom to assemble and organize

- for freedom of the press and to protest the prohibition of the magazine *Sputnik* and critical Soviet films

In order not to disturb the official rally we call upon you, in accordance with Articles 27 and 28 of the constitution

- to assemble on 15 January at 4:00 P.M. in Market Square in front of the Old Town Hall, and following that [to join] the planned march of silence with candles to the [Luxemburg-Liebknecht] Memorial on the Brautstrasse.

> "Socialist democracy cannot begin even in the Promised Land, until the foundation of the Socialist economy has been built" (Rosa Luxemburg, from her *Collected Works*, vol. 4 (1914–1919), pp. 358–64).

Initiative for Democratic Renewal of our Society.

## NOTE

1. The German text of this leaflet is in the underground publication, *Die Mücke (The Mosquito)*, 21–22 January 1989, and is published as an appendix to the Stasi report of 16 January 1989 in Mitter and Wolle, eds., 13.

## *STASI REPORT OF 16 JANUARY 1989*

MfS, ZAIG, Nr. 25/89 Berlin, 16.1.1989[1]
Top Secret!
On 12 January about 2:00 A.M. one male person, age 26, . . . and one female person, age 19, . . . were caught in the act of distributing inflammatory leaflets in Leipzig-Gohlis and detained. . . . [2]
From the above persons 102 copies were taken and according to them they had already distributed 150 in mailboxes. . . . 9 other persons were also detained who had taken part in the provocative-demonstrative action. There were six males, ages 22–27, . . . and three females, ages 18 to 24. . . .
Investigation thus far has shown that: all eleven belong to various groups that are under the responsibility of the pastor of St. Luke's Church, Leipzig, Wonneberger. Many of them had previously in October 1988 become known [to the Stasi] for their activities against public order and safety. In connection with the so-called peace prayer meeting in Leipzig's St. Nicholas Church they had read in front of the church a protest letter to the State Secretary for Church Affairs. . . . Existing evidence indicates some 750 leaflets were distributed. Searches of apartments secured a total of 3,457 leaflets. . . .
On 15 January, after 4:00 P.M., some 150–200 persons ganged up in front of the Underground Fair Hall in the city center of Leipzig. A male person read a prepared text which urged participation in the march of silence announced by the inflammatory leaflets. Thereafter this group began moving in the direction of the New Town Hall. No signs were carried. When the participants ignored the repeated orders of the police to disband the march, the security forces detained a total of 53 persons. . . .
All detained persons were . . . released by 10:00 P.M. . . .
It is recommended that the State Secretary for Church Affairs inform the Saxon Regional Evangelical-Lutheran bishop, Hempel, in Dresden and that the representative of the chairman of the Leipzig District State Council for internal affairs inform

Superintendent Magirius in Leipzig. They should be told that this is a matter of serious, illegal acts of people in organizing a political provocation involving misuse of the 70th anniversary of the murders of Karl Liebknecht and Rosa Luxemburg. This threatens to damage seriously the relationship between Church and State and will be used by the western mass media for a renewed campaign of agitation and lies against the GDR, which is in fact already underway. They should be further informed that among the participants, part of them are involved with Church institutions and part of them are members of the church [alternative] groups.

This report is authorized only for personal information in order to avoid jeopardizing sources.

[Signed] Mielke[3]

## NOTES

1. The German text is published in Mitter and Wolle, eds., 11–14; MfS = Ministry for State Security, i.e. Stasi; ZAIG = Central Evaluation and Information Bureau of the State Security
2. See interview with Carola Barnschlegel.
3. Erich Mielke, Minister for State Security since 1958.


## STATE SECRETARY KURT LÖFFLER'S REPORT ON A CONFERENCE WITH BISHOP JOHANNES HEMPEL, 23 JANUARY 1989

Conversations between Church and State officials constituted a sort of ritual of polite exchanges of goodwill followed by complaints offered by each to the other. Party officials made policy but left to government officials the task of conversing directly with Church leaders. Kurt Löffler was the highest-ranking State official with oversight of Church affairs. Excerpts here from his detailed, eight-page report in convoluted, bureaucratic language show the regime's concern about growing oppositional activity in Leipzig and the expectation that the bishop could and would curtail it.[1]

The conversation, which had been planned for some time, took place on 23 January 1989 in the regional church office in Dresden.

. . . With a visible gesture Bishop Dr. Hempel showed thanks for the greetings and the appreciation of his work. He expressed the desire to have a new meeting with Comrade Dr. Jarowinsky sometime.[2] At the same time he emphasized that he had always stood up for a just assessment of the development of the GDR and for recognition of the achievements of the GDR socialist order which served individuals, as closely related to the Christian ideal on German soil, and that he would continue to support these things. At the same time it would be necessary in the coming weeks in view of the elections and the fortieth anniversary to address some of the questions that concerned him and the regional church of Saxony at large. . . . According to him, it was most especially necessary that information [in the public press], along with the representation of the irrefutable existing social safety and security for the citizens, also should include discussion of our own weaknesses and inadequacies, of our faults and the resulting growing demands, because the reports were without exception always "success stories." Since these reports are in contrast to many every-day facts of life, they challenge the citizens as contradictions and allow room for speculation about the relationship of the government to life. In his opinion, this openness and sovereignty of individual achievement are necessary in the face of the tasks that still need solving especially through the "initial effect" of Gorbachev, but also where no "copying of Soviet methods" is required in the GDR.

. . . Later in the course of the conversation urgent requests were expressed by me in regard to the absolutely necessary influence of the bishop and the regional Church office to prevent in the future the political misuse of Church space for activities by alternative groups and other groups,[3] activities directed against the State and social order of the GDR. At the same time I informed him about the events of 15 January 1989 in Leipzig and the conspiracy of hostile forces in the preparation of this action. Bishop Hempel had explained that no such information had been made known to him in time to have allowed a precautionary intervention. Strong consternation could be seen in him regarding the amount of activities, which have already gone on a long time and are negative and aimed at political confrontation, on the part of church groups in Leipzig and the activities they further intend. He gave assurances that— just as he had often done in recent months—he would continue to act with a sense of reason, but that at the same time, there were "no means of power" at his disposal with which to carry through his view, "even among parish pastors." He asked for understanding and effective help in open discussion with those groups, "that often look for useful causes, such as protecting the environment, for their activity or some-times only want to talk about their opinion of the soul." He said that the large and growing dissatisfaction in many of these groups was also founded on the fact that no one [in the government] was available to be a dialogue partner with them.

. . .

On the whole, the conversation proceeded in a calm and matter-of-fact atmo-sphere, without any tension or sharpness. Bishop Hempel let his relief over the con-tinuation of the meetings and the demonstrated readiness for friendly dialogue be felt. He asked once again that he be remembered to Comrade Dr. Jarowinsky and expressed thanks for the marked evidence of trust.

[Signed] Löffler

Attachment[4]

Regarding the conversation with Bishop Dr. Hempel about the *Kirchentag* in Leip-zig: . . . Already at the time of the Leipzig Trade Fair in 1988 and the International Leipzig Documentary and Short Film Weeks, among other occasions, . . . public, politically confrontational activities were carried out.[5] Are not the peace prayers (among others) political events dedicated to [combining] the exercise of faith with attacks against the socialist state . . . ? With the leaflet-action and the mob formation on 15 January 1989, the high point of the activities of enemies of the state to date has been reached.

. . .

Without any doubt whatsoever, the concentration of hostile activity in Leipzig— always to emphasize, despite the resistance of many Church officials in the city against such activities—that the construction of illegal structures whose testing through conspiratorial actions is clearly aimed at political disturbance of the planned *Kirchentag* in July. Such an action in July would lead inevitably for an indeterminate time to difficult burdens on State and Church relations, yes, and noticeably disturb the existing good relationship of trust.

At this time Pastor Wonneberger gives extensive support to the negative forces, some of which are outside the Church, also through storage of illegal writings.

The so-called peace prayers, which have been planned again by the alternative groups for Mondays since 2 January 1989, give cause for serious concern.

## NOTES

1. The German text is published in Dietrich and Schwabe, eds., 269–72.

2. Werner Jarowinsky was the Politburo member responsible for Church affairs.

3. The alternative "grassroots" groups were in some fashion tied to the Church. Sometimes nonchurch groups also met in churches.

4. Informal notes about other concerns Löffler discussed with the bishop.

5. Refers among others to the March 1988 demonstration. See Michael Arnold's report earlier in this Appendix.

## KARSTEN BOCHE'S MEMOIR OF HIS ARREST AND DETENTION, 11 SEPTEMBER 1989

Not all those detained were activist leaders; any participant might be caught up, especially on a Monday like 11 September 1989 when the authorities had determined to "crack down" after the demonstration of the previous Monday. Then it had been Fair Week, and western news media were present; now the media were no longer in Leipzig. GDR law allowed the police and Stasi to arrest and detain anyone for 24 hours without having to show cause or allowing the detainee any rights.[1]

The usual worship service took place in St. Nicholas Church on 11 September, beginning at 5:00 P.M. Very conspicuous to us all was the enormous force of police reservists, VP,[2] and Stasi which had taken up positions all around the church long before the time for the prayer service. Even more units of the BePo[3] were positioned with police vans in the side streets and among them was also a transport truck with dogs!

The Monday prayer service followed its normal schedule and ended just before 6:00 P.M. About a quarter-hour passed as the congregation poured out of the overcrowded church. During this time the several BePo units had already formed a massive cordon, hermetically sealing off the whole area around the church. Not far from the crowd, the Stasi were filming with a video camera, and in addition the VP and Stasi were repeatedly photographing us. We ourselves remained calm and relaxed, did not allow ourselves to be provoked, and divided up into small groups.

Suddenly over a loudspeaker there came an order that we leave the square immediately and break up our groups. That struck us as incomprehensible, because our standing around peacefully together had in no way been a demonstration!

At the same time we noticed units of the BePo armed with rubber nightsticks moving in around us and many of the Stasi coming toward us. Seconds later the first men of the Stasi and VP rushed into the crowd, which was slowly becoming restless, and shoved the first people into the waiting police vans in the most brutal manner. After that Stasi agents already in the midst of the crowd grabbed individuals who were protesting and shoved some of them in [groups of] fours and fives into the vans. Loudspeaker demands which followed in the next moments were drowned out with shouts of "Pfui!" and whistles. Then the BePos with arms linked moved in and pushed the crowd, which now panicked helplessly, from three sides into a narrow side street. Again and again officials came through the line and indiscriminately pulled out people as they pleased! Nearly all who were seized had their arms twisted very painfully, and girls and women were also struck and treated extremely brutally. One punk[4] was taken behind a construction truck and mistreated. Among those taken into custody at the same time were curiosity seekers not at all participating, people several hundred meters away, housewives who were out shopping.

Once I noticed how the police grabbed an elderly lady! Then, as the side street became so blocked that no escape was possible, I was picked up, too. We were taken in batches to a huge building on Dimitroff Street, which contains a police headquarters, Stasi, jail, and court all together. There our personal effects were taken from us and we waited in a training room for further developments. About a half-hour later we were called for questioning by the Kripo[5] officials. On the whole, the questioning was matter-of-factly handled. After a short time of routine note-taking, we were put into groups of eight and again loaded into vans by the BePo. Our questions about where we were going went unanswered. After a long drive into the unknown, we arrived in Leipzig-Paunsdorf and were taken to a police gymnasium where some 40 detainees were sitting on wooden benches. Gradually other small groups came in—around midnight there were 59 male and 20 female prisoners! The women and girls were segregated from us a bit later and put into an adjacent room. Conditions in the gym bordered on disrespect for human dignity. The harshest fluorescent lights burned all the 24 hours we spent in this place; also there were no windows or anything else for air. The toilets were the dirtiest possible, to which we were only allowed to go one at a time with an escort—no toilet paper, smoking strictly forbidden—all things which seemed to us absolutely malicious.

There were many guards on duty and dogs outside the exit door. The only things available for sleep or rest were some sport mats, filthy dirty, vermin-infested, and covered with dog hair. Sometime about 1:00 A.M. (with the arrival of the last transports) something to eat and a bucket of tea was brought in. Each of us received one cold bockwurst and a rather stale roll . . . Sometime early [in the morning] a couple of names were called, and those called received a receipt for their personal IDs and were allowed to go. A few hours later the next [were called] but were again loaded into a van of the BePo and driven off.

About the middle of the day on Tuesday there was again something to eat: a lukewarm bratwurst and a hard roll. . . .

During an interval of several hours more transports came, so that by 6:00 P.M. there were only about ten men left. With an escort of 20 BePos and police persons we were driven back to Dimitroff Street and put in a training room. Minutes later each one was called in by the Stasi and Kripos. We were informed that a charge under Article 217 (riotous assembly) had been placed against us. We were given the opportunity to read in the book on legal punishments what the consequences for us were.

In the statement I was required to make I told the Stasi that I refused to acknowledge that the event of the previous day was a riotous assembly! I repeated that our peaceful stopping in front of St. Nicholas Church showed no criminal intent whatever. This was all I had to say! Then I was taken back to the training room. About ten minutes later I was taken to the Stasi and police officials in the Beethoven Street jail, had to wait five minutes, then was taken to a state attorney. She informed me that a penalty fine had been assessed against me and pushed a written copy of it across the table.

I understood [from it] that because of violation of Article 217/1 I had to pay a fine in the amount of 3,000DM! Then the attorney took back the copy and told me that payment of this sum must be made within one week. If not, the fine would be converted into a jail sentence—thus [was] her response to my verbal protest.

Lastly she handed me a form which stated that I would accept the penalty and refrain from all legal actions—I naturally refused to sign. Later I learned to my dismay that most of those accused let themselves be affected by the psychological pressure and signed.

Between 6:30 and 7:30 we, then being in a state of nervous exhaustion, were released.

## NOTES

1. The German text is printed in Dietrich and Schwabe, eds., 388–90.
2. The *Volkspolizei*, the regular police.
3. Nickname for the police reservists, the *Bereitschaftspolizei*.
4. Punks were those who usually had long hair and wore very casual or sloppy clothing as a form of protest.
5. The criminal police.

## MEMOIR OF PARTY MILITIA MEMBER GERALD PILZ, SEPTEMBER 1989

The Party Militia (*Kampfgruppen*) were among the many sorts of police, security, and armed units created to protect Party and State. This paramilitary force was composed of Party members organized in their work places. As discontent with the regime mounted in 1989, the reliability of these groups became questionable, as illustrated in this memoir.[1]

I have been in the Party Militia (*Kampfgruppe*) for eleven years and recently became a group leader. Each has ten men under him. We have always taken our job seriously and continued to do so, although after 7 May, big discussions started about the election fraud. That was when we complained to the Party leadership that we wanted straightforward reporting, not gushing, nothing more, but also nothing less.

We already noticed in September that something was amiss here [in Leipzig]. On 25 September people first marched out from the [St. Nicholas] Church Square—and a larger crowd was expected on 2 October. And about 1:00 P.M. [on 2 October] the alarm was given, meaning we had to get ourselves to the assembly points and pick up our uniforms. Between 3:00 and 3:30 our commander and two others came to us and explained about the inquiry to Berlin. The SED district leadership first received the reply to do whatever they thought best. Later, however, they received the order to proceed against the demonstrators with all possible means. That included in my opinion even weapons. Our Party Militia commander refused to issue weapons, and so did the district commander of the police (VP). So we were clearly somewhat relieved. We were supposed to take up a position at the *Schwanenteich* [Swan pond, near the opera house], across from the *Delikat* store, in a row of intervals of three meters without weapons, just in uniform. If the demonstrators came, armed policemen from the police barracks would place themselves in front of us—so we would be there, but no longer in sight. (That made us somewhat suspicious.) Our task was first of all not to let the demonstrators into the inner city, so they could not disrupt the market day. Secondly, we were not to let them approach the main train station, but to push them toward the *Michhof.* We few fellows were to do all that.

We were told only punks would be coming and we should protect citizens from the rioting of these anarchistic people and groups. About 6:20 we heard rumblings from Karl-Marx Square. Then a police squad came—but they ran on by and we were standing there, eyeing the area—for whom? I saw no anarchists! Furthermore, what they shouted to me, while hardly flattering, sounded rather right. My group felt pretty much conned. We then went back to our quarters and heard that later there was a disturbance at the *Konsument*[2] and at St. Thomas Church. Indeed, there were water cannons, units armed with riot helmets and shields and with dogs. They hunted people down throughout the city, many of whom had nothing at all to do with the demonstrations; they just happened to be out on the streets.

Later we heard that the people were supposed to be provoked by our mere presence, so that there could be [police] intervention. Heinz Fröhlich, the first secretary of the city SED, was said to have urged the most loudly that we be placed there.

The next day when we read in the paper that we had defended the city against punks and rowdies, we in our unit decided: if an order to move out comes down again, we would refuse it. We would not go out again.

Gerald Pilz,
Group Leader, Party Militia

## NOTES

1. German text printed in Bohse et al., eds., 47–48.
2. A large store located on the Ring Boulevard. See map at the beginning of chapter 1.

## MEMOIR OF AN SED MEMBER WHO
## ATTENDED THE 9 OCTOBER
## PRAYER MEETING

A female Party member wrote this letter to pastor Turek in 1992. At that time she was still active in politics and held elective office in Leipzig.[1]

. . . The hurt ran deeply. The shame more deeply. Thousands had already left the GDR and sat in embassies in Prague, Warsaw, Budapest. All fans of Egon Krenz! He was exiting the plane in Frankfurt/Main when I heard him; his answer had burned a hole in me, as he told his opinion on the Tiananmen Square massacre in Peking. I had looked into the fear-ridden faces of the young soldiers, who were forced on their own people so senselessly; I had also seen the burned bodies of soldiers, which the Chinese television censored. My son was a soldier at the time. It was unimaginable, that he too would have to [sentence unfinished].

I had heard that there was no need to cry for those who left the GDR.[2] But I had seen tears flow—from mothers and fathers. I cried too, because of shame—indeed I was not alone—but that wasn't the only reason. I was also angry: where was our Party leadership and government in August?

Earlier, I had regularly gone secretly to St. Nicholas Church. I also gave two marks for Espenhain, instead of one, as an apology for not daring to sign my name![3] Because it was clear to me that the signatures were inspected.

And then in Dresden on October 4th! How could they allow the train to pass through the main train station, indeed through Dresden at all, through such a major city with these problems! Once again a policeman with a beat-up jaw! And the panic, the confusion! Did they ever actually think it was only the "embassy-fence-climbers" who were so hysterical?

So, late afternoon [on Saturday, 7 October], into the city with my mother, my husband, to St. Nicholas Church. A few booths on Grimmaische Street, a few people, depressing atmosphere. A police cordon in front of the church square directly in front of us (one of the police with a dog). Later, my husband pointed out to me that the police had been wearing riot gear instead of their usual uniforms. He was first and went alone. My mother and I came to the police cordon by way of Ritter Street; as we went through the cordon, the policeman standing the closest to us pressed the dog's head into his knee—we had made it. It was eerie, but no one had done anything to us. Not one of the policemen said anything to us, nothing.

In front of the church square, piercing whistling and a policeman with a loudspeaker demanded that the square be cleared immediately. Each word of his instructions was made unintelligible by all the whistling, and every time the policeman caught his breath, the pause was filled by the unison chanting: "We are staying here, we are the people," and maybe other things. We went once around the church, once again down St. Nicholas Street, on Grimmaische Street, crossed through another police cordon with dogs, their backs to us, blocking off the entire St. Nicholas Street. Police cordons were everywhere.

[On Monday, 9 October, early morning at her job] . . . Several coworkers were obviously already aware of what was happening. Colleague Y and I were sent to Colleague X. There it was revealed to us that today the hard-core [demonstrators] would be seized. Therefore, the church should be filled at the appropriate time in order that they would be able to grab the ones left outside if all went according to plan. In any event, we should leave the area as soon as humanly possible after the prayer meeting, since that would be the favorable moment for the hard core to begin a demonstration. We were told that we would probably be among those demonstrators who would be loaded onto trucks and taken into custody. We were to have nothing on us except IDs. There was a possibility that we wouldn't be free until early Tuesday although our names were to be distributed to the police. We were to leave our bags at the university and under no circumstances should we wear our Party insignia. My sarcasm was limitless. If my "Party and government" wanted a Chinese solution, I wanted to have at least the chance to be among the victims. My coworkers, my mother, and my husband all thought I was crazy. At noon the orientation of the Party secretary was completely different. Then there was talk of our being ready to enter into a dialogue in the church and to be ready for discussion as things progressed. If things developed dramatically, however, we would need to be ready to be taken into custody. We needed to reckon with that possibility. Then a central orientation at City Hall. I learned later that there must have been 1,000 from the university, 500 from the national level of the Party, and at least half were women. Apparently the directions were given in different rooms. Some had rejected the plan, not wanting to be against the Church and misused as part of some sinister action. . . .

There were massive protests from not a few students and also from one or two younger scientists. . . . They didn't want to allow themselves to be stand-ins for some group of people behind the scenes. A general readiness to cooperate didn't come until a professor who is well respected by the students guaranteed the dialogue option. . . . I have to say also that I almost hoped for and believed that the dialogue option was possible. On the whole, though, I was very uncertain. But cowardice was never a question. If the worst were to occur, then I wanted to know it for sure, without a doubt, to be personally involved. Too many times I have experienced second hand deceitful interpretations, and I had had enough. By 1:30 P.M. there were maybe 700 people in the nave; the prayer service was to begin at 5:00 P.M. The church filled up, red-faced church workers ran around, letting the incoming crowds into the balconies. The church was closed once all the spaces were filled. The doors were beaten against constantly from the outside; admission much in demand. What otherwise happened could only be speculated or feared by those on the inside. The prayers for peace began, individuals went forward, reported their fears that came after reading this or that announcement in the LVZ[4] in recent days; they mentioned that they felt these articles to be death threats against themselves. If some wanted to defend socialism, if necessary even with weapons in hand against the punks, gangs, and the like, then they were the punks that were meant. That, which we (members of the SED—at least myself, in any case) threw around as clichés, which for my part were never directed at these people, was taken seriously, examined in a literal sense.

With the experiences of October 2d, because the demonstrations had always ended with police force at the *Konsument*, there was a massive police presence at the train station. There had been the violence in Dresden on October 4th, and the 8th in Berlin. At the time on the inside of the church I recovered a trait, for which I am very thankful, where I can place myself in someone else's shoes in my attempt to gain a better self-control. I will never forget that. The prayers for peace were supposed to end around 5:45 or 6:00 P.M. However, another representative from Dresden came forward and reported how yesterday it was possible for them to enter into dialogue with the authorities, thereby avoiding violence, which was not the case in Berlin. In Leipzig there had probably been only water cannons on October 8th—not nearly as bad as things had been in Berlin. Time passed and passed. Then Bishop Hempel was announced, who was already at the Church of St. Thomas, and if he was able to make it through he also wanted to come here. In the meantime, things [outside] became louder and louder and more threatening. Those waiting [outside] for the end of the prayer service engaged in their whistling duel with the police. The noise swelled threateningly and was eerily magnified inside the church. I had an almost insane fear since it was conceivable that outside the fighting had already begun. Several had started beating loudly on the door again as well. The thought came to me that we had become captives inside—maybe that was even planned—since one couldn't tell us apart from the others, and 50 percent of us were women. I realized that on the way to the church. Then the bishop came and the appeal of the Leipzig Six was read aloud, then the call to nonviolence and the request not to break through any police cordons, to watch out for each other peacefully going home, not to provoke or be provoked.

As we left the church (which took a while, since normally there were not so many people in the church), we had to make our way through an extremely narrow corridor. The ones that formed this corridor asked, "Hey, what's going on here? Why are they all leaving, why aren't they waiting?" We stood there for a while, but then left. I was still a little afraid. My mother was waiting. It was the first demonstration that—still without me—went peacefully around the entire Ring. Later I read in the Stasi report about how the demonstration broke up peacefully at the main train station. That was incorrect. Reports of success still had to be sent to Berlin then, or they expected it, who knows?

## NOTES

1. Letter used by permission of Paster Turek.
2. A remark made by Honecker.
3. Envirnomentalist groups had collected signatures on petitions and raised money for this suburb of Leipzig experiencing pollution problems from coal production. The campaign appealed for "One Mark for Espenhain." For the appeal, see ABL, H1.
4. The principal Leipzig newspaper, the *Leipzige Volkszeitung*.

# APPEAL OF THE LEIPZIG SIX, 9 OCTOBER

This appeal, drafted at a hastily called meeting in the home of Kurt Masur, world-famous music conductor, was read during the evening prayer services on Monday, 9 October, and later broadcast. Zimmerman was a theologian, Lange a well-known performer in the political cabarets. The other three were local party officials who took the unheard-of step of signing this appeal without the consent of their superiors.[1]

Leipzig citizens Professor Kurt Masur, Pastor Dr. Peter Zimmerman, cabarettist Bernd-Lutz Lange, and secretaries of the SED District Dr. Kurt Meyer, Jochen Pommert, and Dr. Roland Wötzel direct the following appeal to all Leipzigers:

"Our common concern and responsibility have drawn us together today. We are dismayed by developments in our city and seek a solution. We all need a free exchange of opinions about the further direction of Socialism in our country. Therefore the above-named promise today to all citizens to devote our entire energy and authority to the end that this dialogue will be conducted not only in the Leipzig District, but also with our [national] government.

"We urgently ask you for levelheadedness, so that peaceful dialogue will be possible."

**NOTE**

1. The German text is published in Ekkehard Kuhn, *Der Tag der Entscheidung: Leipzig, 9. October 1989* Berlin: Verlag Ulstein, 1992), 122–23.

# APPEAL OF THE GROUPS, 9 OCTOBER

In addition to the well-known "Appeal of the Leipzig Six," other appeals were issued. The appeal of these three groups also appeared on 9 October. It not only urges nonviolence in general terms but lists specifically actions in past demonstrations around the country that had on occasion provoked police action. It is worth noting that the slogan "We are one people" as used here means the citizens of the GDR are a united people. Only later did the meaning shift to refer to reunification of all Germans.[1]

In recent weeks there have been many demonstrations in the various cities of the GDR which have led to violence. Pavement stones have been thrown, windshields broken, cars burned, with [use of] rubber nightsticks and water cannons. An unknown number have been injured and there is talk of some killed. Last Monday in Leipzig also ended with violence.

We are fearful, fearful for ourselves, fearful for our friends, for the people around us and for those who stand in uniform opposing us. We are fearful for the future of our country. Violence and ever again violence! Violence solves no problems. Violence is inhuman. Violence cannot be the signal for a new and better society.

We urge everyone:

- Restrain yourselves from any violence!
- Break through no police cordons, keep your distance from all barricades!
- Don't attack anybody or damage any vehicle!
- Don't take any clothing or equipment item of the [police or military] units.[2]
- Don't throw any objects or use violent slogans!
- Support each other and prevent provocations!
- Stick to peaceful, creative forms of protest!

To the [police and military] units we appeal:

- Restrain yourselves from the use of force!
- Don't respond to peaceableness with force!

We are one people!
Violence among us will leave bloody wounds that will never heal!
Party and government must above all be held responsible for the existing, grave situation. However, *today* it is up to us to prevent any further escalation of violence, because our own future depends on this!

Workgroup for Justice
Workgroup for Human Rights
Workgroup for Environmental Protection

## NOTES

1. The German text is published in Rein, ed., *Die Protestantische Revolution* 265.
2. Demonstrators had sometimes grabbed police caps and tossed them about.

## *PASTOR CHRISTIAN FÜHRER'S MEMORIES OF 9 OCTOBER*

This is an excerpt from a memorandum and from an interview in the St. Nicholas Church concerning the events of 9 October 1989.[1]

The events preceding this Monday were frightening: anonymous telephone threats ("If you hold another Peace Prayer in this church, your church will stand in flames"), unveiled threats in the press of which the article in LVZ[2] of October 6, 1989 was the most shocking ("Subversion Must No Longer Be Tolerated;" ". . . in order to stop definitely and effectively these counterrevolutionary actions. If it must be, with weapon in hand!"). How seriously these threats were to be taken was shown by the events of October 7. As always on state holidays (May 1 and October 7) our church was not open. From our apartment[3] we became witnesses of the most violent police action that we have ever personally experienced against a defenseless, nonviolent crowd of people who nonetheless, astonishingly, showed no fear. The attack on defenseless people who already were in custody frightened us all the more since we had never before experienced such conduct by an organ of the state. On Sunday there was (for the Twentieth Sunday after Trinity) an amazingly high attendance at worship. Victims reported to us afterwards about the severity of the action, about injuries, whereby a count of the injured could not be determined.

There was a meeting in the middle of the day [on Monday] at which it was decided that some 1,000 to 1,500 party members would be called together at the New Town Hall and told to go to the "sit-in" in the church. That is what happened, so that by 2:00 P.M. the main part of the church was filled with people. That was a unique situation for us. The sexton came for me and I went over about 2:30. The peace prayer service would not begin until 5:00. They sat with stone faces behind their *Neues Deutschland* [newspapers], many of them at a peace prayer service for the first time in their lives. They had indeed been told that here was where the counterrevolution was being prepared, here was where criminals and political rowdies ganged up. So they sat there with these ideas and I thought one needed to lighten up the situation with a bit of humor. It couldn't go on like this until 5:00. I just had to tell them that I knew who they were. So I made an attempt and said: "The St. Nicholas Church is open for everyone, that is literally true without limitation, and you are heartily welcome in our church. It is just unusual that you are already here at half past 2:00. The working proletariat can only come after 4:00, so we begin our peace prayer service at 5:00. But there is no problem, we welcome you: however, you will understand that we have kept the balcony closed [until later], so that a few out of the working population and a few Christians can get into the church."

That was understood as a signal, and so the time passed quietly and without incidents. Then the peace prayer service took place in an entirely special, intense, and suspenseful situation, which I would describe as an *Andacht*.[4] Of course, I had to make several appeals out the windows, because by 3:30 the church simply could not hold any more people. We had in fact asked people who came this day to go to other churches, our intention being to get as many people as possible off the streets, thus to avoid police intervention. We wanted to bring them into the safety of the churches and above all things to be able to communicate with them. They certainly couldn't hear our appeals for nonviolence if they were outside. And what happened was that some 9,000 people were brought into the downtown churches by 5:00.

When the service ended, the crowd in the St. Nicholas Church Square was so dense that I was afraid that there would not be space for the 2,000 people [as they left]. But the exodus progressed calmly. There was only the demand that next Monday the peace prayer service be broadcast outside on the square with loudspeakers. And the miracle continued: nonviolence did not remain a helpless word in the church, but was taken along to the street. When provocative shouts like "Stasi Out!" were raised, a mighty, billowing chant arose, "No Violence!" "No Violence!", so that the other shouts were silenced. A stream of 70,000 people began [moving] through the center of the city. It was moving [to see] just how nonviolently the stream of people progressed. Commandos and police were engaged in discussions and entered into discussions. It became clear that these 70,000 people were no rowdies or criminals, nor counterrevolutionaries. The dominant chants: "No Violence!", "Gorbi," "We are the People," "Join Together," "Allow New Forum," "Introduce Reforms with Us or You will Go to the Rest Home" also could be heard for a short time. Only those who experienced this demonstration of nonviolence can understand what it meant.

The most miraculous part for us was that this peace prayer service could occur in an atmosphere of an *Andacht* and that the next day party members [were] here to thank me for the service. They had experienced a prayer service for the first time; no one could ever erase it from their minds and it was in obvious, stark contrast to what party propaganda had said about our peace prayer services. Thus these party members, perhaps 600, became part of the peace process themselves and were so impressed that they not only did not disturb the prayer service, they even joined in the reverent atmosphere of the prayer service. That is an incredible event. We could never have reached so many party members through any written effort or by any other means all at once, and something in writing would not have been accomplished this; one simply had to have been there and have experienced it.

## NOTES

1. Paragraphs 1, 3 and 4 come from a "memorandum of record" written by Pastor Führer on 11 October, translated by Dean W. Bard and presented at an International Ecumenical Seminar in Strasbourg, France, in 1990. The German text of the interview is printed in Kuhn 120–121. Both are used by kind permission of Pastor Führer.

2. The LVZ (*Leipzige Volkszeitung*) was the main newspaper.

3. The Führer family lived upstairs in the St. Nicholas parish hall; just across St. Nicholas Square from the church.

4. An inspirational or very solemn prayer service, such as for example was held to pray for those imprisoned.

## *INTERVIEW WITH CAROLA BARNSCHLEGEL*

Q: Could you tell something about your life story that would help explain your involvement in the peace prayer meetings and the demonstrations?

A: I began going to the peace prayer meetings in 1988 and I met people there like Uwe Schwabe and others, and I had friends who were wanting to leave the GDR who encouraged me to go—that's how it began. I was a part of the IGL [Initiative Group for Life].

Q: Could you talk about this IGL, please?

A: It was composed of all different sorts of people from different backgrounds who wanted to make the public aware of the situation in the GDR in Leipzig, but not just in a strict and dry political way.

Q: Did the group pursue particular causes, such as environment, or something like that?

A: We were not particularly concerned with environmental matters because there was an environment group that specialized in that. But we organized various events, like the street musician's festival.[1]

Q: Were you involved with other alternative groups or opposition groups—that is, before '88?

A: No, '88 was when I met these people and became active. Before that I didn't do much.

Q: Can you describe the group? Tell some more about it—how many members it had, how often it met?

A: The number of people coming to the meetings depended, varied. It depended on where we met and what we discussed. We met in various homes and apartments. Sometimes we met at Uwe Schwabe's apartment. For instance, for the observing of the elections, we met at St. Mark's parish hall.[2]

Q: I'm interested in the motivation of yourself and the others. It is quite unusual to have so many people doing so many things. I would like to know more about their motivation.

A: Are you speaking of the people who were going to the peace prayer meetings or to the demonstrations?

Q: Both, please. Of course, I know that the motives were varied.

A: Yes, indeed, they were varied. One motivation was to show in public that one was concerned with the situation here. People were used to discussing political matters in the pubs, but that didn't lead to anything. So, for me, it was a better forum to go to the church, even though we knew we could be arrested afterward. There were several forms of repression that could happen to us. Part of the group were non-Christians; that included me. Of course, others believed that their prayers would help.

Q: So, for you it was more the political side?

A: Yes.

Q: And you were arrested, were you not?

A: Yes.

Q: Can you talk a little bit about that and explain why that happened.

A: The first time I was arrested was in January 1989, when I helped organize a counterdemonstration to the traditional parade in honor of Rosa Luxemburg and Karl Liebknecht. This parade just honored the political system. It didn't have anything to do with the aims of Rosa Luxemburg, and I was distributing some fliers. The police caught us doing this and we still had 102 leaflets in our box. So that was the first time, but it was only for three days, and then I was released. This was at the time of the Vienna Conference to follow up on the Helsinki Agreement, and the second time I was arrested was in September of that year, and I think the police were looking for us intentionally. It didn't just happen to be us. Because it was the Fair Monday in September, and all those who had carried a placard at that time were the ones arrested.

Q: What sort of words were on these placards?

A: There were many different ones. For example, "Freedom to travel," "Freedom of the press," and various political slogans like "Perestroika."

Q: You knew of course that this was dangerous. Where did you get the courage to do this?

A: I didn't really care what happened to me. The situation just demanded it. Three or four months in prison could have happened, but it didn't really matter to me. I had to go to the demonstrations.

Q: Although there were many events, could you mention one that was perhaps the spark that particularly caused you to want to do this?

A: Well, in March '89 most of my friends left the GDR and I wanted to stay here. I felt like I had to do something here or I would go mad.

Q: And were you involved with any of the other groups?

A: Well, we all knew each other and as things got better organized, each group did its own work. For example, the environmental group collected facts and information about environmental issues.

Q: I am also interested in the role played by the Church, by the Church leadership, and by church people in these events. What is your general, overall evaluation of that?

A: Well, I can't be very objective here. There was a rather big difference between the Church leadership and the groups. It was okay that the church provided a place for us to meet, but I can't agree with some of the Church leaders.

Q: So on the ninth of October you were in jail, so you were not present at the big demonstration. Is that correct?

A: Yes.

Q: Can you describe the differences you noted in things between the time before you went to jail and then after you came out of jail?

A: [One difference was] the numbers that were coming because earlier on there had been only a few hundred. But even when I was in jail I could hear the demonstrations going on. When we asked the guards, they were just smiling rather timidly, and they gave us more freedom inside the prison at that time. When we walked free then, we were really shocked.

Q: How about the conditions in the prison? How were you treated there?

A: You had to undergo more questioning there the second time. There was a change. In the beginning there was more questioning than there was later on and we had a problem with the lawyer. He fell ill. There was another one, and then the first one came back.

Q: Do you mean the government attorney or your own lawyer?

A: Our own lawyer. And some of the guards behaved very badly. Not that they beat us up, but we felt that they felt very insecure, that they didn't know exactly what to do. So one could sense it [the change].

Q: And the state security police—the Stasi—were they there?

A: The prison where I was, was the Stasi prison.

Q: Concerning the relationship between the peace prayer meetings and demonstrations, we know, of course, that people came out of the one and joined in the other, and that in the early days this seemed to be important, but what about later on, in the time of the big demonstrations, did there continue to be a strong relationship or not?

A: I think the change only took place after the appearance of the flags and the call for unification.[3] From then on, there was quite a difference, and even a contradiction between the prayer meetings and the demonstrations.

Q: Concerning the slogan "One Fatherland," the call for reunification, when did you first notice that and why do you think that became important?

A: I didn't like this new tendency at all. I wanted a reformed GDR, a Gorbachev-type reform, and I can't agree with the system we have now.

Q: Could you explain a little bit more in what way you might have been watched or harassed by the authorities?

A: After a while I got used to it and I knew which one [of the Stasi] was responsible for me, and when I went to the Pleisse pilgrimage I spoke to him, greeted him on the way, and then I took another streetcar home, but I wasn't happy with all these official warnings I kept getting. And my mother had problems at school because of my commitment, and I think that should have been my business and should have had nothing to do with her. And of course, I didn't like the police coming and searching my house, my apartment.

Q: And it still isn't quite clear to me why, in the beginning, you were so brave, and you took such an active part.

A: I considered it necessary to commit to this in order to prove to myself that I did something about this situation.

Q: Many people have said that to me, but yet they were fearful about the consequences for their family or about their work position, so they sort of held back.

A: As far as family, I was only eighteen, so I didn't have any family of my own to worry about. I was ready to leave the job I had anyway, and then I worked for the Church and the Church agreed with my commitment.

Q: What sort of work did you do for the Church?

A: I worked in an old people's home.

## NOTES

1. A major activist event of the summer of 1989. See Lieberwirth.
2. St. Mark's was Pastor Turek's parish.
3. After the opening of the Berlin Wall on 9 November.

## *INTERVIEW WITH REINHARD BOHSE*

Q: Would you please tell me something about your own life history that would help to explain your interest and participation in the peace prayers and the demonstrations?

A: I was born in a small village near Meissen. Meissen is a historic old town situated between Leipzig and Dresden. My parents were teachers. . . . My father was a member of the SED and very involved in what was going on in the GDR. At the state level, he carried through a number of his programs very successfully. My mother was a Christian, raised as a Christian, and my childhood in this village was very happy. There was a kind of an ideal world in this little village, and I was brought up very idealistically on socialism. And my grandparents, my mother's parents, were Christian, and they showed me that there was another *Weltanschauung.* After I graduated from high school in 1967, I went to the army. And I still held onto my socialist ideals, although I had begun to have some small reservations already. And while I was in the army, Dubček came to power in Czechoslovakia and the armies of the Warsaw Pact nations intervened.

Q: Did you go yourself?

A: No, I spent five months crawling around in forests all over the GDR under orders that if we didn't obey we could be shot. But thank goodness I didn't have to go.

Q: So the army was on a war footing?

A: Yes, it was like a war situation. And I must add that I myself sympathized with the Prague Spring, yet I was in the army that was standing against these ideas. And so I experienced life in this so-called socialist army. And I found it brutal and cruel, even fascistlike. And the ideal did not at all fit with the reality. In the GDR there was sort of a '68 generation who distanced themselves from any political involvement. And I didn't exercise my political activity anymore at all. I didn't join the party. I stayed away from the functions of the Free German Youth. I was a part of the '68 generation, but I didn't enter into any oppositional movements in the '70s. Then they wanted me to join the special reserves, the *Kampfgruppen* [Party militia]. And that was just not acceptable to me. Which meant that there was no future in my career. I looked for alternatives, but I found none. . . . I started meetings on Mondays, not every Monday, but one Monday a month, to have discussions. And this Monday tradition came to include friends also, at least by 1976; I can remember that exactly because that was the year that Biermann was expelled. So people knew that if they came to Bohse's place, they could find out what the latest news was and talk about events such as this. Although we had a very small apartment at that time, 20 to 25 people would gather there to express their opinions. So, it's quite interesting that Mondays have a very long tradition of political discussion in my family. And in the Stasi files of myself and others, there is little mention of these discussions. They do refer to them, but they say nothing about the content of them. I had only the usual problems of GDR citizens. For example, I wanted to work abroad, but they wouldn't even accept my application for that. And my wife had many, many problems at school, her school where she taught, because she said what she thought. We had hardly any contact with any church or the St. Nicholas Church and the peace prayer meetings until 1989. My wife was once asked to speak at a church where educational matters were under discussion.

Then in the spring of '89 we realized that this is it, the time had come. And in our discussions it was determined that it was time to build organizations, that it was necessary for a democratization. I had many relatives in West Germany, and I had been permitted to travel there since '87. So I had gotten an idea of what life could be like. It was already obvious to me in '87 that this system in the GDR was going to have to be brought to an end and would end. The only question was when and in what manner.

Q: Why in 1987 did it become so clear?

A: I saw what life was like in the west. I experienced what democracy was, how politics worked there. How politics worked for people in the street, how they could participate in politics. And that's when I saw that this system here was at an end. The world situation had changed since 1968. Now it was led by a reformist group. Back in '68 it was led by a Stalinist regime. My wife and I were in West Germany in the Summer of '89. And then my whole family went to Hungary, where we experienced firsthand the people from the GDR fleeing via Hungary, although we ourselves never wanted to leave. And in September '89, I began going to the peace prayer meetings. Of course, they were already popular. And people wanting to leave the country had been attending them. But I heard that they were discussing many political matters and how to renew the country, so I began going. Not on the Fair Monday, the first Monday, but the one after that.[1] And regularly thereafter. And after the prayer meetings, some of us would meet in my apartment and watch western television, see what it was saying and discuss most recent events, what was going on.

Q: Could you perhaps tell a little more about the 9th of October and what the feeling was then?

A: I knew there could be consequences of being in an illegal group when I joined the New Forum, and I took over the publishing for them. That was my profession. And I was among the older, more experienced ones in the group. Most of them were young. I knew that there could be consequences, even shooting, but I also knew, on the other hand, that my children couldn't endure this system if they had to grow up in it. But participating just seemed the natural thing to do to us. People knew on the 9th of October that it would be the decisive day. They saw the police and the military forces being directed into the city center. And as we left for the demonstrations, our neighbor came out, who is a medical doctor. And he said, "Oh, you're not going there, are you? Extra beds have been put out in the hospitals and extra supplies of blood have been prepared." But we came on into the city rather early, about 3 o'clock in the afternoon, and the city was already crowded. We did not go into the church, we watched everything very closely. We just kept walking around and observing, and we went by the St. Thomas Church. And on the west side of it, we saw a Red Cross flag and a station set up where people could be brought who might need help. We didn't go to the peace prayer meetings. And the streets were, of course, crowded with military personnel.

Q: And there were peace prayer meetings going on in the St. Thomas Church and the other downtown churches?

A: Yes, there were peace prayer meetings going on at all these churches. And I very conscientiously tried to observe everything. There was so much to see. And my wife was with me and she had brought a bunch of flowers. We wanted these flowers to be a kind of peace symbol and planned to give them to someone in the army. And in one place we saw a group of police and they were hitting their sticks against their shields and it made a sound that seemed like shots. And my wife wanted to give her flowers to some soldiers sitting on a military vehicle, but the soldiers didn't want to take them. So she just tossed her bouquet over into the truck. And when it fell into the truck, the dogs who were in there, which we could not see, began to bark and howl and shake the whole truck. That was frightening. And people continued to gather slowly, as was what usually happened on Monday nights there around the St. Nicholas Church. Then the prayer meeting was over and people began to come out; I saw one young man who was about 17 come running out, and he kept on running and he said, "I have to get home. They're going to shoot this time." And as the demonstration began I remember there was a kind of silence punctuated by the chanting of the slogan, "We're staying here, we're staying here." And of course there was smog in the air, it was thick with it! There was a great tension in the air, and it was a very unusual, tense situation. And as we walked on toward the Augustus [Karl-Marx] Square I remember I kept looking around from side to side for possible places where I could run to hide in case the shooting began. Then I remember as we crossed the great square, the Augustus Square, and turned then on the street down toward the train station on the Ring. The atmosphere seemed a little freer, and there were other chants. "Gorby, Gorby" as well as "We're staying here" and some people began to sing the Communist Internationale. And as we came in front of the central station, we began to feel almost free, even though there were a lot of military forces there. And it was only later I learned that originally the plan had been for them to intervene there in front of the train station. Originally the plan had been to march only to the big footbridge just past the train station and not to go on around the Ring in front of the state security building. And I remember we got out of the demonstration march at the footbridge and we met a friend there and we hugged him and we had tears in our eyes, real tears. Then we came back to the apartment here and met with some others and we were very happy about the turnout. And we had already decided that the next Monday we would do it again.

## NOTE

1. Fair Monday was 4 September.

## *INTERVIEW WITH KONRAD FEHR*

Q: Could you please tell me something about your life story that would help me understand your involvement in peace prayer meetings and demonstrations here in Leipzig?

A: I was no activist in the demonstrations here [earlier]. I joined in later. I took a critical stance during my university studies at University of Jena, 1963 to 1968. Then when I was called to military service I refused to go, and I did agree to become a *Bausoldat* in the alternative service even though their work had to do with military installations. But I refused to take up any weapons.

Q: Were you able to obtain your university degree?

A: Yes, because my refusal came after I had finished my studies and had gotten my degree. Although this refusal was legal, I was regarded as a black sheep from then on.

Q: That made for difficulties in securing jobs and promotions?

A: Yes. My time in the alternate service program was a very significant one for me because of the many people I met there and the discussions that we had concerning peace, problems, and other sorts of things. After my time in the service, I came here to Leipzig and got a job with a big publishing company as a reader, but I was not involved in politics. I was not anti-GDR. I never went to elections, although that wasn't any big step. I might have attended some peace prayer meeting before they became so important, but I don't really remember. I do remember the Leipzig Fair days in the fall of '89, it must have been early in September, seeing a small group that were demonstrating and the police using violence against them. I saw that on television and then I remember hearing the speech of a Leipzig priest about the importance of the peace prayer meetings. That inspired me to begin going. That was in late September or early October—I don't remember exactly, but from then on I was going.

Q: I'm interested in the influence of the Church and religion on these demonstrations. You are Catholic, are you not? Could you please tell me what you think about the Church influence from the Catholic Church leadership and others? What is your feeling about this?

A: I don't know a lot about the Church leadership. I do know there was a priest here in the Leipzig area. I don't recall his name. He was active in the Pax Christi.[1] I remember he was the one whose speech inspired me to become involved. Most of the pastors and prayer meetings were Protestant, but he was one from the Catholic side.

Q: And you knew other Catholics who were involved?

A: Yes, of course, but I couldn't name them for you.

Q: Do you remember the first demonstration in which you, yourself, participated?

A: Yes. I was very frightened. I had a wife, a two-year-old child, and a second child just born in June—two small children. I felt I should be cautious and careful. So when I began to go to the prayer meetings I went to the demonstrations connected with them, but I only went a little ways at first, just as far as the train station. I was afraid of the violence, and the violence that might take place particularly as the demonstrators went by the Stasi headquarters at the Round Corner.

Q: Do you think the economic factors were very, very significant in all this?

A: Oh, it wasn't that important, although there was lack of consumer goods of various kinds in the shops. For some people, the state of the environment and the pollution played a role in their opposition. This was also important for me.

Q: We often say in English that it takes a spark to start a fire. I wonder if you could say what, in this situation, was the spark that started all this. The spark that would explain why this happened at this particular time.

A: I don't know really how much I might have been [later] influenced by the media or by histories written about this period, but I think that the opening of the boundaries of Hungary was a decisive thing.

## NOTE

1. Pax Christi is an international Catholic peace organization founded in 1945 to foster reconciliation between the French and the Germans. It grew to have chapters in many countries, but remained focused on strictly religious activities and did not take positions on political questions. The Leipzig chapter did not participate in the peace prayer meetings in Leipzig.

## INTERVIEW WITH PASTOR CHRISTIAN FÜHRER

Q: Why and how did you as a Christian minister take a lead in such dangerous activities?

A: Let's go back to 1918. A separation was forced on the church, and even more later by the GDR. The church didn't itself choose to separate, yet I should say God forced it on us for our own good. The state was atheistic. Many left, but those who stayed [in the church] really believed Jesus' words: "You are the salt of the earth, but if the salt has lost its saltiness . . ." Remember the prophet Nathan, who came to David to tell him of his sin concerning Bathsheba? It should have been the high priest; that was his job. But State and "Church" were too closely and comfortably connected. We were freed from all that and could really become the conscience of society.

Q: When and why did the Monday peace prayer meetings begin?

A: When I came here in 1980 we had twice a year the peace *Dekaden* [10-day periods of special prayers]. The armaments thing [placing intermediate missiles in Western Europe] became a big issue in 1982, and we made the peace prayer meetings a weekly event on Mondays.

In 1986 I put out the sign in front of the church: "Open for all," meaning non-Christians as well as Christians. That really irritated the state authorities. They wanted to keep the churches inside their buildings. They thought the only good church was a closed church, or a museum-church. Our prayer meetings grew and grew in numbers. After a while those attending were 90 percent non-Christian! The authorities later said they were ready for riots, violence, almost anything but prayer meetings and candles! The Bible says, "Not by might, nor by power, but by my spirit, says the Lord." I thought the nonviolent approach was our only chance.

Q: Like Martin Luther King, Jr., in the U.S.A.?

A: Exactly, and like Gandhi. It is to our shame as Christians that though we have read the words for 2,000 years we had to learn it again from a Hindu!

I organized some special groups such as the group for would-be emigrants from the people who had careers, but had somehow gotten crosswise with the government and wanted to leave the country. We invited 50, and 800 showed up! People—

including the youth—saw that the church was acting as a conscience. It was the one place where honest opinions and criticisms could be heard. I always said what I thought was right—I didn't try to cover up.

Q: Did the police or Stasi directly try to hinder you or your work?

A: The police always respected the sanctity of the church itself. When people in flight came to us here [the parish hall, a combination office and residence building across from St. Nicholas Church], we had a special door to help them get away if the police came. The Stasi were always coming to the prayer meetings. I just welcomed them and told them I was pleased they could have an opportunity to come to church!

Q: Did some of the other clergy question your activities?

A: Oh, yes. Some thought this was a false way, that it would be better to keep quiet. The church has just been reading these Bible verses for so long. Who would have imagined how this would come into reality and we would live through it all! "If you have the faith of a grain of mustard seed!"

Q: Have you seen your Stasi file?

A: Well, they were very interested in me and even had a code name: "Eagle." After the turn [*Wende*] I was asked if it could be made public, and I said I didn't mind, but I would like to read it first.[1]

## NOTE

1. A special office has been given custody of these massive files and will make available to an individual his or her file upon request. Since there are millions of files, individuals must expect to wait a year or so.

## *INTERVIEW WITH PASTOR ROLF-DIETER HANNSMANN*

Q: Would you please discuss events in your own life which led you to become a participant in the peace prayer meetings and the demonstrations in Leipzig?

A: I was born in 1939, so I was six years old when the war was over. The earliest picture in my mind is of the air raids on Leipzig. The red sky, the burning houses. My father was in the war. At the end he was imprisoned by the British after the war. He didn't come home until 1949. My parents were divorced. Of course, as a child I didn't experience all of the problems of the war fully, but nonetheless these experiences form the basis of my pacifism today. I went to school and I wanted to go on to high school, but at first I wasn't allowed to because my mother was a small capitalist—because she had a little shop. Then after the changes in 1953. I was allowed to go on to a high school. I learned some technical things in order to take over my mother's shop. Later I studied engineering. I didn't follow my mother's wishes in all of this, but I was very committed to the Church and to work with the church young people. After working hours I organized church youth groups and I decided to study theology and get a theological education. During that time both parts of Germany began to create armies again. During the time of my theological studies, according to the new law I was called for military service, but I refused to go on the grounds that I was a Christian. I did not intend to take up weapons. I wrote that in a letter to the authorities.

Q: Did you then become a *Bausoldat* in the alternative to military service?

A: That law came a year later. We have no way of knowing how many people refused to take up arms, but at that time there was no legal alternative—that came a year later. So they had to think about what to do with me, and since I was a student nothing was done at the time. Then, when my studies were over, I was put into a government technical staff position. During this time I was influenced by Mahatma Gandhi and Martin Luther King, Jr., and what they had accomplished using nonviolence. And, of course. I was inspired by Jesus too. So, that's why I became committed to peace matters. And so I became a pastor and was given a parish. In 1982 I began to come to the peace prayer meetings in St. Michael's Church.

Q: That was at the very beginning of the regular Monday meetings, wasn't it?

A: Yes, yes. I came and brought some of the young people from my parish. I was trying to influence them in the direction of peace movements. And I tried to influence them to refuse military service.

Q: Was it a small group attending the prayer meetings in those early days?

A: Yes, it was small. The number varied. Another human reason for my position was that German soldiers would have been fighting German soldiers and that in itself was a contradiction. There was another man who had influence on me, and that was Albert Schweitzer.

Q: As you attended the peace prayer meeting, were you with a special group or involved in a special group?

A: It was young people, mainly from our parish. Each November we had the peace decade [10-day prayer period]. We held that in our own small parish each November as did all parishes.

Q: Let me ask about the motivation of the other people who came. As the numbers began to increase and increase, what is your opinion about the motivations of the others?

A: Well, one part of it was the peace movement in western Germany, led by Martin Niemöller and others, and the marches they had and the protests against the missiles there. Then there were more and more people wanting to leave the GDR because the GDR wasn't fulfilling its obligations under the Helsinki treaty concerning human rights. The largest number attending the peace prayer meetings were those people wanting to leave the country, and they found in the church a sort of shelter and a place where they could state their protests.

Q: Could you say something about the demonstrations? In addition to the peace prayer meetings there began to be demonstrations.

A: I didn't participate, but I have two daughters and they regularly participated. The police arrested people who were taking part and so that's why I did not encourage the people in my congregation to march. We held our own peace prayers in my parish and with prayers for those who were imprisoned.

Q: Concerning the nonviolence. This is a marvel and with few examples in modern history, this nonviolence.

A: Yes. And I must say the spirit of nonviolence came from the church out into the streets. Then in '89, another important thing is that the Russians would not use their tanks against the people.

Q: How was it that the people seemed to be so confident that the Russians would not use their tanks? Or were they really that sure in the fall of '89? Did it have to do with what Gorbachev had said?

A: People had studied Gorbachev's speeches and felt quite sure that the Russians wouldn't intervene, but the question was "what would our own army do?" What would people like the *Kampfgruppen* [the Party militia] do? They weren't sure but that there might be a second Peking, or what Honecker or Krenz might do.

Q: Is there anything else you could say that could help me, as a foreigner, understand why people came out for these demonstrations? They must have been fearful, they knew about the Stasi and all of that. On the 7th of October there were arrests and yet they kept coming out.

A: Well, for one thing, they had lost their fear. Some were in prison, some had fled. Those who were here intended to stay here, and that gave them courage. One could think that the most courageous people were the ones who had left, and that those who remained were the ones with less courage. That was not correct. Many of those who left had a kind of courage based on doubt and a willingness to make a new start. While things here seemed to be getting worse, less freedom . . .

Q: . . . and those who remained had a different sort of courage?

A: Yes, a different sort of courage. They had a certain kind of hope. They had a hope that the State could open up, that it could reform itself. On the other hand, people were well informed about the west from television, and I think that deep in their hearts people wanted Germany reunited, one fatherland.

## INTERVIEW WITH MARIANNE RAMSON

Ramson was a member of the St. Nicholas Church parish council during 1988 and 1989, when it was dealing with conflicts between higher Church authorities, the groups, and state officials. She also belonged to the Leipzig chapter of Women for Peace.

Q: Would you please tell me something about your own life story that would relate to reasons for your own involvement in the Leipzig demonstrations?

A: I grew up in a Christian home, with a Christian family. During my school days I was involved with the Christian youth groups. I somewhat lost my contact with the Church, and I came here to Leipzig to work and I began to have some political involvement. I had problems at my work because I was supposed to report any matters or contacts that I had with the west. My work was in geology, and when the trade fairs came I had some contacts with people in the west and I had visitors from there. My job situation and problems reached the point where the factory wanted to fire me, but they couldn't then because I was pregnant. Then, after my pregnancy, I left that job. I wasn't fired, I left on my own. My first contact with St. Nicholas Church was through their kindergarten, as I sent my child there. They were very interested in helping the parents to make contact with each other. So that's how my first contacts there came about. And a third thing, I was invited to join the group Women for Peace, and I did join them and it was connected with the St. Nicholas Church. Through this women's group I became more and more involved in political matters.

Q: May I ask you some more about this women's group? Just what was the purpose of this group? Were the members all church people?

A: No. It was a mixed group. It was begun as a Christian group, but after a while there were many members who had nothing to do with the church. It was a Christian group, and we did arrange programs for peace prayer meetings. We were personally friends and we discussed women's interests and problems with children and so on, but no women's problems with men, no. We wanted to make society aware of women's problems.

Q: You began attending the peace prayer meetings rather early, not in 1989, but back in the mid-80s?

A: Yes.

Q: And can you describe what the peace prayer meetings were like then?

A: It was always political. And the themes for the peace prayer meetings that my group organized had to do with women and their problems. Of course, there were many other themes. There were those who wanted permission to emigrate from the country.

Q: In these early peace prayer meetings, did the women meet separately for a time for the men? Did you have your own peace prayer meetings?

A: We were responsible for the program sometimes, and sometimes our meetings were more emotional. But it was in the church; it was for everyone, both men and women. And then I remember one of the trade fairs, I believe it was the Spring Fair in 1989. And the western television people were here in the St. Nicholas Square by the church. And in one corner a group waved to the TV and chanted, "We want to leave, we want to leave," and then in the other corner, the television turned to a group who were chanting, "We are staying here, we are staying here."

Q: Then came the great demonstrations and masses of people in the streets?

A: Yes, and there were some other events before that. I was at the Pleisse pilgrimage and the street music festival. Those were smaller events, not exactly demonstrations. Then when the really big demonstrations began in the fall, my husband and I took turns going to them because of our small children, and I was expecting again.

Q: Could you tell us something more about this Pleisse pilgrimage?

A: Yes, there was already a small demonstration in 1988 about the pollution, especially the Pleisse River. And in '88 the police just observed it; they did not intervene.

Q: This was done without any official permission?

A: That's correct. And then in 1989, there was the second Pleisse Pilgrimage, and the Stasi knew about it. A couple of days before, I was asked to come to the police station and to promise not to take part in it. But I refused to sign the pledge, and then I was asked about the street musicians' festival, and I denied being there or knowing anything about it.

Q: Although, in fact, you had been there?

A: Yes.

Q: And that was at the Stasi headquarters?

A: No, no, it was at police headquarters, but the Stasi were the ones organizing it. And on the very day of the Pleisse pilgrimage, there was a car waiting in front of our house. And as our family left to go to it, a man approached us and said, "Oh, well, you know what can happen if you take part in this." And I said to him, "Don't you feel ashamed to yourself, supporting this system, and we're going to do what we want to do and what we think is right." So we went on to the meeting point.

Q: That took some courage to speak like that, did it not?

A: Oh, not really.

Q: And what did he have to say back to you?

A: Oh, nothing. He didn't say anything. There were really two of them, and older man and a younger man, and the younger man had to do the dirty work. The children thought it was all very exciting.

Q: Did you then go and participate in the observation of the elections?

A: Yes, I went to the elections, and I observed everything. And I was in a special location. A special voting place where one could vote a day in advance if one wanted to. And afterward, I had a conversation with the person in charge of this voting location, and there were two or three members of the Stasi there, and later I found a notice in my Stasi file about that.

Q: Could you explain to me how these elections were conducted, how people voted?

A: Well, they gave you a ballot and usually you voted in public, you voted yes and left it open. And some people would go in the booth and vote no, and some people would vote no in public. And some would just leave the ballot blank. But as soon as one folded the ballot, one was under suspicion.

Q: To return to one of my main interests, the role of the Church and church people in the demonstrations, what is your opinion? We know that the church buildings were a place, about the only place, where groups could meet. But what about later? What is your evaluation?

A: I think the Church had a real problem at that time. On the one hand, they wanted to do something for the people, but on the other hand, in no way did they want to come to a confrontation with the State. And I can't really reproach them, the way they handled it. They did the best they could.

Q: Concerning the change of opinion from the slogan, "We are the people" to the slogan, "We are one people," why do you think that took place? Did it have to do with the opening of the Wall?

A: Yes, I assume it had to do with the coming down of the Wall. Only after that people really knew what they wanted, namely a reunified country. The demonstrations before were almost unreal, almost like a dream.

Q: What about your own feelings? Did you own feelings change in this way? Did you become interested in unification or did you vote for reform within a separate state?

A: I belong to the generation that was brought up in the divided Germany. I never knew Germany as one, so I hoped for reforms within the GDR. But when people demanded reunification I knew it was an illusion [to oppose it], that it was impossible to stop this trend, so I just accepted it. I might also add that while peace and non-violence are good, I wonder if maybe a little violence might have been helpful. A little violence that might have helped take over the Stasi headquarters sooner and prevented the destruction of the records there.

## *INTERVIEW WITH PASTOR MICHAEL TUREK AND UWE SCHWABE*

Q: Could you both discuss some events out of your own lives that have to do with your involvement in the peace prayer meetings and the demonstrations?

Turek: For me there has to be a separation in the motivations between the prayer meetings and the demonstrations. The motivations for me for the demonstrations were, for one, that it was a form of political expression. It was an important form for me and in the course of my life I have tried various forms and activities. The first public forms began about 1965 as I tried different sorts of things to do when I was still a student. I remember that as a high school student and onward, in different circles we tried different ways of making our protests. We used plays and programs. Then in '68 I was in the army and was a participant in the preparations for the invasion of Czechoslovakia and I felt very helpless that there was so little one could do. The mask, you might say, fell off the regime for me and socialism as a social idea became for me very questionable. But I learned to live and get along with these people who were running the German Democratic Republic. Then, as the demonstrations began to develop, I saw it as a form of expressing my own political feelings and a good form. Now the peace prayers, that is another story. The peace prayers were a religious act, a religious form of expression, and to show my interest in peace and justice. These prayers were not just a time to put everything over onto God, but a time to think and inform myself, to meditate on the sources of injustice and to take some responsibility for myself, that I would accept responsibility for my own part of it. I had no idea about praying that I should simply pray "Lord, there are things wrong in the world. You must do something about it," as if I had nothing to do with it myself. So, for me it was one way of working for peace. So that, in brief, has to do with my motivations. My motivations were different between the prayer meetings and the demonstrations, but you might say they complemented each other.

Schwabe: I came from a Christian family and a political family. However, I myself grew up very unpolitical. I grew up in a very average, normal way. I belonged to the Young Pioneers. I first began to think more about politics when I went in the army. I was in the army for three years. That was in the time when everyone had to serve for three years, that was the duty, the requirement. I wanted to go to sea, that was my dream, my wish, to go sea. To serve in the navy, one had to sign up for four years, and had to be politically acceptable. I wanted to travel, I wanted to see other parts of the world. But I began to notice during my army years how the political system functioned in order to make one acceptable; then there was the system of spies and informers. The system where one person was supposed to inform on another, and there were so many little ins and outs to it. Those who had been there a longer time were supposed to spy on the newcomers. So I came out of the army, and then I was wondering what to do, how to express my own opinions. I had the good fortune while I was in the army to get acquainted with a young man who had connections in the Christian community. He belonged to the youth congregation of the St. Nicholas Church in Leipzig. At the meetings of this group, one could talk about the meaningless things that were going on and the problems and feel a certain freedom and I learned about the problems in environment and I became a member of the environmental group. Pastor Führer was the pastor there. That was in '82 or maybe '83. I noticed that the group felt that it was up to us to do some things, to make some things happen. But I began to see that this was very complex and there were many other problems and they were interrelated and they were political. So then two or three of us left that group and formed our own group, because we felt that defense of the environment could not be separated from the other interests like the desire to promote peace.[1] It was all very complex, one couldn't be concerned just about the environment. There was disarmament too, for example, and human rights. Concerning my motivation to take part in the peace prayers, it seemed to offer a real opportunity to inform people, to articulate political positions. We felt that it was part of the task of the Church to articulate these things. It was their job. It was part of the liberation theology that we learned from Martin Luther King, Jr. So it seemed a very legitimate means, this nonviolent approach, which came out of the peace prayer meetings. The Church leadership weren't so much in favor of this, so the demonstrations had to come away from the church because the leadership didn't want us to express all our political ideas there. So we looked for another way, and the other way was to stand outside the church and inform people. So we kept our appeals and our activities strictly separate from the peace prayer meetings, as for example the Pleisse pilgrimage in '88 in June. So both ways were used to try to inform people and move them, the peace prayer meetings and the demonstrations. These demonstrations were legitimate means, in my opinion, during the time of the GDR, because the regime had so much angst about these kind of demonstrations. Now there are other ways, but then about the only way one could publicly express one's ideas was to go out on the streets in a demonstration.

Q: What is your opinion about the motivations of the other people who took part in the demonstrations? No doubt there were many motivations, but what do you think were the strongest that they had?

Schwabe: This is a difficult question. There are various answers. Some say it was for bananas! (jokingly)

Turek: I think the motivations changed over time. My own feeling is that people were looking for some form, some way, to make a protest. A form with a minimum amount of risk. It was an outlet, an escape. Some people found their escape in just forgetting or ignoring, some in hobbies, and others sought forms of protest. It was a form of rejection of society as it was. People lived in two worlds: the protest world and where they were. There was great potential for protest as things developed more and more. People discovered in the demonstrations a way of putting forward their demands, what they wanted, and there was the feeling of camaraderie, of unity, that came with the demonstrations. Just to be a part of such a big unified thing became a motive in itself. It really astonished me. The State and the State security apparatus had sought to isolate people. These demonstrations became a way of reacting to this fear and this isolation that one felt in one's life. The demonstrations became the high point in their whole lives.

Schwabe: Yes, and joining the demonstrations was a part of people's search, their search for a way to articulate their situation. So people used this form of demonstrations in the fall of '89, but there is a long prehistory to the demonstrations in Leipzig back into the '80s and especially from early '88, and then other people heard about it and saw it on television. Then Leipzig, a central location with a rather enclosed sort of central city and with the peace prayer meetings already being held every Monday, was a good place for the demonstrations.

## NOTE

1. The new group was the Initiative Group for Life (IGL), organized in 1987.

# Selected Bibliography

## ARCHIVES AND SPECIAL LIBRARIES CONSULTED

Das Archiv Bürgerbewegung e.V. Archiv des zivilen Ungehorsams in der DDR sowie
verschiedener bundesdeutscher Bürgerinitiativen in Leipzig (ABL).
Deutsche Bücherei, Leipzig.
Regional Kunde Bibliothek in Stadtsbibliothek Leipzig.

## UNPUBLISHED DISSERTATIONS, THESES, PAPERS, AND MEMOIRS

Elvers, Wolfgang, and Hagen Findeis. "Was ist aus den alternativen Gruppen geworden?" Praktikumarbeit, Religionsoziologisches Institut of the Theological Faculty, University of Leipzig, 1990.
Feldhaus, Friedhelm. "Politisch-alternativen Gruppen im sozialen Raum der DDR—
am Beispiel politischer Dokumente und Erklärungen Leipziger Oppositionsbewegungen." Dissertation, University of Hannover, 1993.
Führer, Katharina. "Vom Friedensgebet zur Montagsdemonstration: Zur Geschichte
der Friedensgebete in der Leipziger Nikolaikirche vom November 1980 bis
zum 9. Oktober 1989. Diplomarbeit, University of Berlin, 1995.
Haufe, Gerda, ed. "Die Bürgerbewegungung in der DDR und in der ostdeutschen
Bundesländern." Berlin: Unpublished manuscript, 1998.
Kettler, Anja. "Von der Friedensbewegung zur Oppositionsbewegung—Die Arbeitsgruppe Friedensdienst und die Initiativgruppe Leben in Leipzig in der achtzigen Jahren." Diplomarbeit, University of Münster, 1999.
Lutz, Annabelle. "Widerstand und Loyalität—Ein Vergleich zwischen Ostdeutsch-
land und der Tschechoslowakei." Dissertation, University of Potsdam, 1997.

Müller, Peter. "Die alternativen Gruppen in der DDR: Ideale und Realitäten. Eine Reminiszenz." Leipzig: Unpublished manuscript, Feb. 1990.

Raschka, Johannes. "Für Delikte ist kein Platz in der Kriminalitätsstatistik—Zur Zahl der politischen Häftlinge wahrend der Amtzeit Honeckers." Dresden: Technische Universtität Dresden, Hannah-Arendt-Institut für Totalitarismusforschung, Berichte und Studien Nr. 11, 1997.

Schmidt, Christian. "Hausarbeit: Aufstieg und Niedergang der Oppositionspresse in der DDR." Seminar paper, University of Leipzig, 1998.

Schwabe, Uwe. "Friedensgebete in Leipzig." Unpublished paper, 1995.

———. "Wir waren doch das Volk? Oder? Warum schon wieder eine Chronik?" Unpublished paper, 1996.

Weissgerber, Gunter. "1989/90: Die SED zwischen Massenausreise, Leipziger Montagsdemonstrationen, Mauerfall und deutscher Einheit: Aus der Sicht eines Demonstranten." Unpublished memoir, with appendix, a collection of newspaper articles and speeches at Monday demonstrations by the author and others. No date.

Winter, Christian. "Die Auseinandersetzungen um die Universitätskirche. Vorgeschichte und Umstände der Zerstörung." Dissertation, Theological Faculty, University of Leipzig, 1993.


## PUBLISHED WORKS

Ahbe, Thomas, Michael Hoffman, and Wolker Stiehler. *Wir bleiben hier: Erinnerungen an den Herbst '89.* Leipzig: Gustav Kiepenheuer, 1999.

Ash, Timothy Garton. *The Magic Lantern: The Revolution of '89 Witnessed in Warsaw, Budapest, Berlin and Prague.* New York: Random House, 1990.

Asmus, Ronald D. "Is There a Peace Movement in the GDR?" *Orbis,* Summer 1983, 301–41.

Bahrmann, Hannes, and Christoph Links. *Chronik der Wende: Die DDR zwischen 7. Oktober und 18. Dezember 1989.* Berlin: Christoph Links Verlag, 1994.

Baring, Arnulf. *Der 17. June 1953.* Bonn: Deutscher Bundes-Verlag, 1957.

Bark, Dennis L., and David R. Gress. *A History of West Germany.* 2 vols. Oxford, Eng., and Cambridge, Mass.: Blackwell, 1993.

Barnett, Victoria. "New Questions for the 'Church in Socialism.' " *Christian Century* 109 (15 April 1992), 400–402.

Besier, Gerhard. *Der SED Staat und die Kirche: Der Weg in die Anpassung.* Munich: C. Bertelsmann, 1993.

Besier, Gerhard, and Stephan Wolf, eds. *Pfarrer, Christen und Katholiken: Das Ministerium für Staatssicherheit der ehemaligen DDR und die Kirchen,* 2d, ed. Neukirchen/Vluyn: Neukirchener, 1991.

Bickardt, Stefan, ed. *Recht ströme wie Wasser: Christen in der DDR für Absage an Praxis und Princip der Abgrenzung.* Berlin: Wichern Verlag, 1988.

Blanke, Thomas, and Rainer Erd, eds. *DDR—Ein Staat vergeht.* Frankfurt/Main: Fischer Taschenbuch Verlag, 1990.

Bohley, Bärbel, et al., eds. *40 Jahre DDR: Und die Bürger melden sich zu Wort.* Frankfurt/Main: Carl Hauser Verlag, 1989.

Bohse, Reinhard, et al., eds. *Jetzt oder nie—Demokratie!: Leipziger Herbst 1989.* Leipzig: Forum Verlag, 1989.

Bryson, Phillip J. *The End of the East German Economy: From Honecker to Reunification.* New York: St. Martin's Press 1991.

Bürgerkomitee Leipzig, eds. *Stasi Intern: Macht und Banalität,* 2d ed. Leipzig: Forum Verlag, 1992.

Burgess, John T. *The East German Church and the End of Communism.* New York: Oxford University Press, 1997.

Büscher, Wolfgang, Peter Wensierski, and Klaus Wolschner, eds. *Friedensbewegungen in der DDR: Texte 1978–1982.* Hattingen: Scandica Verlag, 1982.

Conway, John S. "The 'Stasi' and the Churches: Between Coercion and Compromise in East German Protestantism, 1949–1989." *Journal of Church and State* 36 (Autumn 1994), 725–45.

Dahrendorf, Ralf. *Reflections on the Revolution in Europe.* New York: Random House, 1990.

Dennis, Mike. *Social and Economic Modernization in Eastern Germany from Honecker to Kohl.* New York: St. Martin's Press, 1993.

*DDR Handbuch.* 3d ed. 2 vols. Cologne: Verlag Wissenschaft and Politik, 1984.

Dietrich, Christian. "Fallstudie Leipzig: Die politisch-alternative Gruppen in Leipzig vor der Revolution," in *Material der Enquete-Kommission: Aufarbeitung von Geschichte und Folgen der SED-Diktatur in Deutschland,* vol. 2, *Widerstand, Opposition, Revolution.* Berlin: the Bundestag, 1995.

Dietrich, Christian, and Uwe Schwabe, eds. *Freunde und Feinde; Dokumente zu den Friedensgebeten in Leipzig zwischen 1981 und dem 9. Oktober 1989.* Leipzig: Evangelische Verlagsanstalt, 1994.

"Doktorarbeiten in Auftrag der Stasi." *Deutschland Archiv* 12 (December 1993), 1439–59.

Drawert, Kurt. "Haus ohne Menschen." *Der Spiegel,* 5 July 1993, 149–51.

Ehring, Klaus, and Martin Dallwitz. *Schwerter zu Pflugscharen: Friedensbewegungen in der DDR.* Reinbeck: Rowohlt, 1982.

Falcke, Heino. "The Place of the Two Kingdoms Doctrine in the Life of the Evangelical Churches in the GDR." *Lutheran World* 24 (1977), 23–31.

Findeis, Hagen, Detlef Pollack, and Manuel Schilling, eds. *Die Entzauberung des Politischen: Was ist aus den politisch alternativen Gruppen der DDR geworden.* Leipzig and Berlin: Evangelische Verlagsanstalt, 1994.

Fischbach, Günter ed. *DDR Almanach '90.* Stuttgart: Bonn Aktuell, 1990.

Fisher, Marc. *After the Wall: Germany, the Germans and the Burdens of History.* New York: Simon & Schuster, 1995.

*Forschungszentrum Aktuell—Mitteilungen des Forschungszentrum zu den Verbrechen des Stalinismus.* Nrs. 1, 2, 3. Dresden, 1992.

Förster, Peter, and Günter Roski. *DDR zwischen Wende und Wahl: Meinungsforscher analysieren den Umbruch.* Berlin: LinksDruck Verlag, 1990.

Frick, Karl Wilhelm. *Opposition und Widerstand in der DDR: Eine politische Report.* Köln: Verlag Wissenschaft und Politik, 1984.

Friedrich, Carl F., and Zbigniew Brezezinski. *Totalitarian Dictatorship and Autocracy.* Cambridge, Mass: Harvard University Press, 1965.

Friedrich, Walter. "Mentalitätswandlungen der Jugend in der DDR." *Aus Politik und Zeitgeschichte* 16–17 (13 April 1990): 25–37.

Friedrich, Walter, and Hartmut Griese, eds. *Jugend und Jugendforschung in der DDR.* Opladen: Leske & Budrich, 1991.

Frindte, Wolfgang, and Horst Schwarz. "Der Mythos von der Kontrolle—Der gesellschaftliche Umbruch in der DDR aus sozialpsychologischer Sicht." *Psychologie und Geschichte* 2, 4 (April 1991): 189–201.

Fullbrook, Mary. *Anatomy of a Dictatorship: Inside the GDR.* New York: Oxford University Press, 1995.

Gauck, Joachim. *Die Stasi Akten: Das unheimliche Erbe der DDR.* Reinbeck: Rowohlt, 1991.

Gedmin, Jeffrey. *The Hidden Hand: Gorbachev and the Collapse of East Germany.* Washington: American Enterprise Institute Press, 1992.

Gillis, John R. "Political Decay and the European Revolutions, 1789–1848." *World Politics* 22, 3 (April 1970): 344–370.

Glässner, Gert-Joachim, and Ian Wallace, eds. *The German Revolution of 1989: Causes and Consequences.* Oxford: Berg, 1992.

Gleye, Paul. *Behind the Wall: An American in East Germany, 1988–89.* Carbondale: Southern Illinois University Press, 1991.

Goeckel, Robert. *The Lutheran Church and the East German State: Political Conflict and Change under Ulbricht and Honecker.* Ithaca, N.Y.: Cornell University Press, 1990.

Goertz, Joachim, ed. *Die solidarische Kirche in der DDR: Erfahrungen, Erinnerungen, Erkentnisse.* Berlin: BasisDruck, 1999.

Grabner, Wolf-Jürgen, Christiane Heinze, and Detlef Pollack, eds. *Leipzig in Oktober: Kirchen und alternativen Gruppen im Umbruch der DDR: Analyzen zur Wende.* Berlin: Wichern Verlag, 1990.

Hahn, Annegret, Gisela Pucher, Henning Schaller, and Lothar Scharsich, eds. *4 November '89: Der Protest, die Menschen, die Reden.* Berlin: Propyläen Verlag, 1990.

Hahn, Udo, and Johannes Hempel. *Annehmen und Freibleiben: Landesbischof i. R. Johannes Hempel im Gespräch.* Hannover: Lutherisches Verlagshaus, 1996.

Hanisch, Günter, Gottfried Hänisch, Friedrich Magirius, and Johannes Richter, eds. *Dona Nobis Pacem: Fürbitten und Friedensgebete, Herbst '89 in Leipzig.* Berlin: Evangelische Verlagsanstalt, 1990.

Heitzer, Hans. *GDR: An Historical Outline.* Dresden; Verlag ZeitimBild, 1981.

Henkys, Reinhard, ed. *Bund der Evangelischen Kirchen in der DDR: Dokumente zu seiner Entstehung.* Wittenberg and Berlin: Eckart Verlag, 1970.

———. *Die evangelischen Kirchen in der DDR: Beiträge zu einer Bestandaufnahme.* Munich: Kaiser, 1982.

Henrich, Rolf. *Der Vormundschaftliche Staat.* Hamburg: Rowohlt, 1989.

Heydemann, Günther, and Lothar Kettenacker, eds. *Kirchen in der Diktatur: Drittes Reich und SED-Staat.* Göttingen: Vandenhoek & Ruprecht, 1993.

Heym, Stefan, and Werner Heiduczek, eds. *Die sanfte Revolution: Prosa, Lyrik, Protokolle, Erlebnisberichte, Reden.* Leipzig and Weimar: Gustav Kiepenheuer Verlag, 1990.

Hocquél, Wolfgang. *Leipzig: Baumeister und Bauten von der Romanik bis zur Gegenwart.* Berlin-Leipzig: Tourist Verlag, 1990.

Hugler, Klaus. *Missbrauchtes Vertrauen: Christliche Jugendarbeit unter den Augen der Stasi.* Neukirchen/Vluyn: Aussaat Verlag, 1994.

Israel, Jürgen. *Zur Freiheit berufen: Die Kirche in der DDR als Schutzraum der Opposition 1981–1989.* Berlin: Aufbau Verlag, 1991.

Jarausch, Konrad. *The Rush to German Unity.* New York: Oxford University Press, 1994.

Joppke, Christian. *East German Dissidents and the Revolution of 1989: Social Movement in a Leninist Regime.* London: Macmillan, 1995.

Kaelble, Hartmut, Jürgen Kocka, and Hartmut Zwahr, eds. *Sozialgeschichte der DDR.* Stuttgart: Klett-Cotta, 1994.

Kaufmann, Christoph, Doris Mundus, and Kurt Nowak, eds. *Sorget nicht, was ihr reden werdet: Kirche und Staat in Leipzig im Spiegel kirchlicher Gesprächsprotokolle, 1977–1989.* Leipzig: Evangelische Verlagsanstalt, 1993.

Keithly, David M. *The Collapse of East German Communism: The Year the Wall Came Down.* Westport, Conn.: Praeger, 1992.

Klaus, Michael. "Samisdat-Literatur in der DDR und der Einfluss der Staatssicherheit." *Deutschland Archiv* 11 (November 1993): 1255–66.

Krenz, Egon. *Wenn Mauern fallen: Die friedliche Revolution: Vorgeschichte-Ablauf-Auswirkungen.* Vienna: Paul Neff Verlag, 1990.

Krisch, Henry. *The German Democratic Republic: The Search for Identity.* Boulder, Colo.: Westview, 1985.

Kuhn, Ekkehard. *Der Tag der Entscheidung: Leipzig; 9. Oktober 1989.* Berlin: Verlag Ulstein, 1992.

Kuhrt, Eberhard, H. F. Buck, and Gunter Holzweissig eds. *Am Ende des realen Sozialismus: Beiträge zu einer Bestandsaufnahme der DDR—Wirklichkeit in der 80er Jahren.* 3 vols. Opladen: Leske and Budrich 1996–1998.

Kuran, Timmer. "Now or Never: The Element of Surprise in the East European Revolutions of 1989." *World Politics* 44/1: 7–48.

Kuttler, Thomas, and Jean Curt Röder. *Die Wende in Plauen: Ein Dokumentation.* Plauen: Vogtländischer Heimatverlag Neupert, 1991.

Latk, Klaus-Reiner. *Stasi-Kirche.* Uhldingen: Stephanus-Edition, 1992.

Lemke, Christiane, and Gary Marks, eds. *The Crisis of Socialism in Europe.* Durham, N.C.: Duke University Press, 1992.

Lieberwirth, Steffen. *"Wer eynen Spielmann zu Tode schlägt . . .": Ein mittelalterliches Zeitdokument anno 1989.* Leipzig: Edition Peters, Militzke Verlag, 1990.

Lindner, Bernd. *Die democratische Revolution in der DDR 1989/90.* Bonn: Bundeszentrale für politische Bildung, 1998.

———, ed. *Zum Herbst '89: Demokratische Bewegung in der DDR.* Leipzig: Forum Verlag, 1994.

Lindner, Bernd, and Ralph Grüneberger, eds. *Demonteure: Biographien des Leipziger Herbst.* Bielefeld: Aisthesis Verlag, 1992.

Loest, Ernst. *Der Zorn des Schafes: Aus meinen Tagewerk.* Künzelsau and Leipzig: Linden-Verlag, 1990.

Luxemburg, Rosa. *The Russian Revolution and Leninism or Marxism?* Ann Arbor: University of Michigan Press, 1961.

Maier, Charles S. *Across the Wall: Revolution and Reunification of Germany.* Princeton: Princeton University Press, 1994.

———. *Dissolution: The Crisis of Communism and the End of East Germany.* Princeton: Princeton University Press, 1997.

Marcuse, Peter. *Missing Marx: A Personal and Political Journal of a Year in East Germany, 1989–1990.* New York: Monthly Review Press, 1991.

Maser, Peter. *Glauben im Sozialismus.* Berlin: Verlag Gebrüder Holzapfel, 1989.

———. *Kirchen und Religionsgemeinschaften in der DDR, 1949–1989.* Konstanz: Christliche Verlagsanstalt, 1992.

Materne, Ulrich, and Günter Balders, eds. *Erlebt in der DDR: Berichte aus dem Bund Evangelisch-Freikirchlicher Gemeinden.* Wuppertal and Kassel: Oncken Verlag, 1995.

Mau, Rudolf. *Eingebunden in den Realsozialismus? Die evangelische Kirche als Problem der SED.* Göttingen: Vandenhoek & Rupprecht, 1994.

Mittag, Günter. *Um jeden Preis: Im Spannungsfeld zweier Systeme.* Berlin: Aufbau Verlag, 1991.

Mitter, Armin, and Stefan Wolle, eds. *Ich liebe euch doch alle! Befehle und Lageberichte des MfS, Januar–November 1989.* 2d ed. Berlin: BasisDruck, 1990.

Modrow, Hans. *Aufbruch und Ende.* Hamburg: Konkret Literatur Verlag, 1991.

Müller, Manfred. *Protestanten: Begegnungen mit Zeitgenossen.* Halle/Leipzig: Mitteldeutscher Verlag, 1990.

Neubert, Ehrhart. *Geschichte der Opposition in der DDR 1949–1989.* Berlin: Christoph Links Verlag, 1997.

———. *Gesellschaftliche Kommunikation im sozialen Wandel: Auf dem Weg zu einer politische Ökologie.* Berlin: Edition Context, 1989.

Oldenburg, Fred S. "The October Revolution in the GDR—System, History and Causes." *Eastern European Economics* 29/2 (Fall 1990): 55–77.

Opp, Karl-Dieter, Peter Voss, and Christiane Gern. *Origins of a Spontaneous Revolution: East Germany, 1989.* Ann Arbor: University of Michigan Press, 1995.

Pechmann, Roland, and Jürgen Vogel, eds. *Abgesang der Stasi: Das Jahr 1989 in Presseartikeln und Stasi Dokumenten.* Braunschweig: Steinweig-Verlag, 1991.

Pfaff, Steven. "Collective Identity and Informal Groups in Revolutionary Mobilization: East Germany in 1989." *Social Forces* 75/1 (September 1996): 91–118.

Philipsen, Dirk. *We Were the People: Voices from Germany's Revolutionary Autumn of 1989.* Durham, N.C., and London: Duke University Press, 1993.

Pierard, Richard V. "The Church and the Revolution in East Germany." *Covenant Quarterly* 48 (November 1990): 43–52.

———. "Civil Religiosity in a Marxist-Leninist Country: The Example of East Germany." *Christian Scholar's Review* 22 (December 1992): 116–30.

Pollack, Detlef, ed. *Die Legitimität der Freiheit: Politisch-alternative Gruppen in der DDR unter dem Dach der Kirche.* Frankfurt/Main: Peter Lang, 1990.

Przybylski, Peter. *Tatort Politburo,* vol 2, *Honecker, Mittag and Schalck-Golodkowski.* Berlin: Rowohlt, 1992.

Rauhut, Michael. "Wir mussen etwas Besseres bieten: Rock Musik und Politik in der DDR." *Deutschland Archiv* 4 (July/August 1997): 572–87.

Rein, Gerhard, ed. *Die Opposition in der DDR: Entwürfe für einen anderen Sozialismus.* Berlin: Wichern Verlag, 1989.

———, ed. *Die Protestantische Revolution, 1987–1990: Ein deutsches Lesebuch.* Berlin: Wichern Verlag, 1990.

Riecker, Ariane, Annete Schwarz and Dirk Schneider, eds. *Stasi Intim: Gespräche mit ehemaligen MfS-angehörigen.* Leipzig: Forum Verlag, 1990.

Rüddenklau, Wolfgang, ed. *Störenfried: DDR Opposition 1986–1989, mit Texten aus dem "Umweltblättern."* Berlin: BasisDruck Verlag, 1992.

Rudé, George. *The Crowd in History: A Study of Popular Disturbances in France and England, 1730–1848.* New York: Riley, 1964.

Sandford, John. *The Sword and the Ploughshare: Autonomous Peace Initiatives in East Germany.* London: Merlin Press, 1983.

Schabowski, Günter. *Das Politburo: Ende eines Mythos.* Hamburg: Rowohlt, 1990.

Schneider, Wolfgang, ed. *Leipziger Demontagebuch.* Leipzig and Weimar: Gustav Kiepenheuer Verlag, 1992.

Schönherr, Albrecht . . . *aber die Zeit war nicht verloren.* Berlin: Aufbau, 1993.

Schorlemmer, Friedrich. *Bis alle Mauern fallen: Texte aus einem verschwundenen Land.* Berlin: Verlag der Nation, 1990.

Schüddekopf, Charles, ed. *Wir sind das Volk: Flugschriften, Aufrufe und Texte einer deutschen Revolution.* Reinbeck: Rowohlt, 1990.

Schwabe, Uwe. "Symbol der Befreiung—Die Friedensgebete in Leipzig." *Horch und Guck* 23/2 (1998): 1–22.

Scott, James. *Domination and the Arts of Resistence: Hidden Transcripts.* New Haven: Yale University Press, 1990.

Siegele-Wenschkewitz, Leonore, ed. *Die evangelischen Kirchen und der SED Staat— Ein Thema kirchlicher Zeitgeschichte.* Frankfurt/Main: Haag & Herchen, 1993.

Sievers, Hans-Jürgen. *Stundenbuch einer deutschen Revolution*: Göttingen: Vandenhoek & Ruprecht, 1990.

Sodaro, Michael J. *Moscow, Germany and the West from Khruschchev to Gorbachev.* Ithaca, N.Y.: Cornell University Press, 1990.

Stokes, Gale. *The Walls Came Tumbling Down: The Collapse of Communism in Eastern Europe.* New York: Oxford University Press, 1993.

Stolpe, Manfred. *Den Menschen Hoffnung geben: Reden, Aufsätze, Interviews aus Zwölfe Jahren.* Berlin: Wichern Verlag, 1991.

———. *Schwieriger Aufbruch.* Munich: Siedler, 1992.

Swoboda, Jörg, ed. *Die Revolution der Kerzen.* Wuppental and Kassel: Oncken verlag, 1990. [Abridged English edition edited by Richard V. Pierard. *The Revolution of the Candles.* Macon, Ga.: Mercer University Press, 1996.]

*Die Tagezeitung: DDR-Journal zur November Revolution, August bis Dezember 1989.* 2d expanded ed. Bertin: TAZ, 1990.

Tetzner, Reinert. *Leipziger Ring: Aufzeichnungen eines Montagsdemonstranten, Oktober 1989 bis 1. Mai 1990.* Frankfurt/Main: Luchterhand Literatur Verlag, 1990.

Turner, Henry A., Jr. *Germany from Partition to Reunification.* New Haven, Conn.: Yale University Press, 1992.

Wallach, H. G., and Ronald Francisco. *Uniting Germany: The Past, Politics, Prospects.* Westport, Conn.: Greenwood Press, 1992.

Weber, Christian. *Alltag einer friedlichen Revolution: Notizen aus der DDR.* Stuttgart: Quell Verlag, 1990.

Wolf, Christa. *Reden im Herbst.* Berlin: Aufbau Verlag, 1990.

Wolfe, Nancy Travis. *Policing a Socialist Society: The German Democratic Republic.* Westport, Conn.: Greenwood Press, 1992.

Wood, Roger. *Opposition in the GDR under Honecker, 1971–1985.* New York: St. Martin's Press, 1986.

Zander, Helmut. *Die Christen und die Friedensbewegungen in beiden deutschen Staaten.* Berlin: Duncker & Humblot, 1989.

Zwahr, Hartmut. *Ende einer Selbstzerstörung: Leipzig und die Revolution in der DDR,* 2d ed. Göttingen: Vandenhoek & Ruprecht, 1993.

# Index

**About the Author**

WAYNE C. BARTEE is Professor of History at Southwest Missouri State University in Springfield, Missouri.

LaVergne, TN USA
28 April 2010
180869LV00002B/25/P